Ordinary People Extraordinary Lives Series

Contents

About the Authors	ii – iii
Foreword by Lord Triesman of Tottenham	iv – v
Introduction	vi – vii
Susy's Life in Education	2
Early Years	3
Teacher Training and My First Teaching Post	12
Motherhood and Educational Choices for our Children	20
Primary Teaching at Last	30
Headship	36
Good to Outstanding – the Challenges Ahead	44
Other Projects	50
Jean's Life in Education	64
The Early Years	65
The Teaching Years	85
Studies in Indiscipline	129
Jean's Postscript	136
Michael's Life in Education	142
A Wartime Child	143
The Immediate Post-war Years	155
Growing Up	159
Hackney Downs School	167
Northern Polytechnic London	175
Setting Academic Values	185
A New Life in Sheffield	192
Coventry Polytechnic	203
Coventry University	221
Further Reading	259

About the Authors

Susy Stone
Susy Stone is Headteacher of Akiva School, one of three progressive Jewish schools in United Kingdom, and previously Headteacher of Bell Lane Primary School in North West London. A graduate of French from London University, she completed her PGCE at Goldsmiths College. She has an Advanced Diploma in Special Needs and a Masters in Education from the Open University. In the Jewish community Susy has served as a local correspondent for the Jewish Chronicle newspaper, as a teacher then a parent governor at Jews Free School (JFS), and as Chair of the New North London Synagogue, where she also ran the religion school.

Jean Lawrence
Jean Lawrence attended Central Foundation School, a grammar school in the East End of London, University College, London, and the University of London Institute of Education. She was Head of two schools, a secondary modern and a London comprehensive, the latter a 'sink' school, which led to a career characterised by innovative research into disruptive behaviour in schools and teacher coping strategies for more than twenty years, from 1967. She was among the very first to point to the importance of this field in the British Isles and Western Europe. She has a PhD in Mediaeval Romance Languages, and a Masters Degree in the Psychology of Education, and has held a Social Science Research Council Fellowship. She has trained post-graduate teachers at University of London Goldsmiths College, has published widely, and is now retired.

Michael Goldstein
Michael Goldstein is a product of the Polytechnic system and has long been committed to vocational higher education and social inclusion. After an earlier scientific and science education career, his interests developed in the role of higher education in economic and social development, particularly in support of local areas and regions. He managed the establishment of

Coventry Polytechnic as an independent Higher Education Corporation outside the control of the Local Education Authority, and the subsequent transition to Coventry University. He led the growth of the institution from about 7,000 to 17,000 students; major physical development and substantial academic growth in terms of volume and innovation. Since retiring in 2004, he undertakes a number of consultancy assignments and several roles with public and public/private bodies, locally and nationally. He was awarded the CBE for services to Higher Education in 1997.

Foreword

In recent years there has been a good deal of research into the rate at which the children of immigrant families progress into higher education. And much of it has focused on why some communities do far worse than others.

Of course, we all want to understand the outstanding performance of, for example, Indian and Chinese communities at present. It might hold clues to the cultural mix that creates aspiration, motivation and application. If those attributes are grasped could they be spread among ethnic communities where higher education is still rare, where the opportunities that flow from it have infrequently appeared?

When I read these volumes of research, I am often surprised that so little has been undertaken on the minority communities that arrived in Britain three or four generations back. Perhaps their successes in assimilation and education have made them almost invisible amongst others who have trod the same path? In particular I have wondered why so little has been written about this subject within the corpus of work about Jewish immigration in the latter part of Queen Victoria's reign through the turn of the century.

A few immigrant families arrived with a professional among them, but most of the European Jews had barely seen anywhere beyond their village or ghetto before their journey west. They were, when they arrived, citizens of concentrated, teeming slums just as later immigrants were. Few spoke English and few had links beyond their community.

Yet within two generations those families were transformed. The grandchildren had pushed their way into the professions and business, into politics and trades unions. Finally, they even pushed their way into golf clubs. In short, they too faced professional and cultural discrimination but showed that nothing finally halts aspiration.

It is for these reasons that this book is overdue. Susy Stone, Jean Lawrence and Mike Goldstein tell the story through the experience of one family. Each has made an incredible mark on education because each draws so heavily and successfully on their own education: niece, aunt and nephew.

Susy has headed a multicultural Primary School, facing all the cultural tensions and synergies that remain vital to our cities – a benchmark of whether they can succeed.

Jean in schools and universities headed secondary modern and comprehensive schools, and specialised in the management of disruptive behaviours. This is a mission that has continued in schools over the years.

Michael led and managed a major Polytechnic and University at the heart of the regeneration of country and region. As one of the architects of widening participation he was engaged in a project that is now central to the Labour Government.

Between them they explore the range of issues that should concern us all. They are well placed to do so. But over and above that, by example as much as analysis, they show a path that goes from immigration and the streets of Bethnal Green – exactly my own family path – to seizing educational opportunity, and in turn giving so much more back as educational leaders. It can be done; and they did it.

Lord David Triesman.

Lord David Triesman, of Tottenham was until 2010 the first independent Chairman of the English Football Association. Prior to this he was the Parliamentary Under-Secretary of State for the Department of Innovation, Universities and Skills. His first governmental appointment was as Under-Secretary in the Foreign and Commonwealth Office. His earlier career was as a lecturer and then a full-time union official at the National Association of Teachers in Further and Higher Education. He was General Secretary of the Association of University Teachers, and then General Secretary of the Labour Party before becoming a Life Peer in 2004.

Introduction

As three members of the same Polish-Jewish immigrant family, we set out to write a book about the three sectors of education, to one of which we each contributed throughout our careers: Susy in Primary Education; Jean in Secondary, and Michael in Tertiary (mainly Higher). In the main, we would write about our careers and particular interests within them, and our aspirations, successes and failures, but set in the context of our beginnings, as children of working-class immigrants. Spending our early years in or very close to the East End of London with its large Jewish population, we attended humble primary schools and gravitated to fine secondary schools, colleges and universities, where we learnt, taught, researched and managed.

We were inspired by the pleasures to be had by writing as a family. Jean's sister, Esther, had edited a family book in 1998, written by eight brothers and sisters of the original eleven siblings. No fewer than nine of them and their families had become teachers, and had made solid contributions to education, as the descendants of immigrants. This is worth remembering today, as Europe exchanges its large numbers of immigrants and some people wince at what they perceive Britain is becoming. Anti-semitism and racism are perceived as rising here in Britain; perhaps we could show another side of immigration.

There are many differences between the three lives described in this book, but running through all three is a strong feeling for the socially and educationally disadvantaged, those with disabilities, the under-achieving; and a wish to help them, be they children or young people, to be fulfilled through rich experience and to achieve happiness through self-esteem throughout their lives; and at the same time to enrich the lives of their families and communities. Working towards this has given all three of us fulfilment too, and the great joy of spending a life with the young, and with older enquiring minds.

The story of our lives is both historical and contemporaneous, and also looks to future directions we think are worth following in the complex search for an education system of which to be proud.

INTRODUCTION

This is an interesting book in that it unites not just three members of the same family, but all three sectors of education, which are so often, because of the complexity of each, kept separate. It must be of benefit for teachers to know about sectors other than their own, and for the public to see education as a vast and unified profession, with big 'over-arching' themes linking the sectors together. There are several in this book: there is the relation between schools and colleges in the community; there is the effect of the new world of migration of populations, bringing ethnic mixing on a vast scale to the twenty-first century, and there is the fight against under-achievement and disadvantage of all kinds. There is the job the education profession does in all its sectors, with parents and families of course; the passing on of the changing culture through teaching in the best ways known to the profession, and the searching for new and better ways of doing the job. All the sectors want to develop potential; want to create fulfilled, contented people, valuable citizens, thriving communities. We are all in this world of education and development together, and we need to understand it through books like this. Of course, the sectors meet at conferences, in journals, teacher unions, and in books on specialized topics. But there is room for more joining of hands across the profession; after all we do take the child, with the parents and the community, from infancy to adulthood. And, believe us, we do strive to meet our responsibilities. We hope that this book might also remind readers that teachers are a precious resource, deserve more respect and recognition, both material and psychological, and every possible support from government and the public.

Susy's life in education

To my beloved father, Mick Goldstein, who opened my eyes and my heart to the value of living life to the full; to my mother Sylvia, my teacher and friend, and to my wonderful 'boys', Maurice, Danny and Gab who daily fill my life with joy and pride.

Early Years

Educational experts frequently assert that a key, perhaps *the* key to success in education is the vital triangle of child, home and school. I am a successful leader of a 'good' primary school (Ofsted 2006, 2008) and a lifelong learner. I am, I think I can safely say, a success of the education system, and one for whom, I believe, the triangle theory holds true.

My parents were cousins. Sylvia was born Sarah in Poland and brought to England as a baby, the youngest of five siblings. Michael was born Meir in London, one of eleven siblings, later to be ubiquitously and very affectionately known as Mick, Uncle Mick or Sergeant Mick. They were raised respectively in the Jewish immigrant communities of Hackney and Bethnal Green, my mother in a flat above her father's engineering workshop, my father in the house below his father's tailoring business.

My mother was an enthusiastic and able student with a deep love of literature, who wrote her own poetry. When she won a scholarship to high school her primary school had a day off to celebrate. In a cruel twist of fate, because she was still a Polish citizen she was precluded from taking up the place. She went instead to Shoreditch Central School, where she learnt shorthand and typing, leaving at fifteen to become a secretary. She would have loved to have been a teacher.

Daddy also left school at fifteen. He dearly wanted to become an architect, but his father, a tailor, held it more important to have *parnosseh*, a livelihood, so it was hairdressing, not architecture that he studied at the Regent Polytechnic. His lack of opportunity was compounded by the war. Having served in the Royal Artillery and risen to the rank of sergeant major in the Jewish Brigade, he was demobbed in 1946. Eager to marry his beloved Sylvia, he found work with a cousin in retail fashion, the trade in which he would remain until he was sixty-five.

These were indeed cruel circumstances for two intelligent young people both with real potential to shine in the careers of their dreams. They never complained, and I think that my sister Naomi and I only benefited from their determination that we would have what they had been denied. This determination, despite limited resources, and their love for each other and for us are the bedrock of our successes.

Jean has been know to refer to my parents as 'intellectuals manqué'. While Naomi and I might have chosen Enid Blyton or E. Nesbit at the library, our bedtime tales included great works of literature like David Copperfield, or poems such as *The Foresaken Merman* and *The Lady of Shallot*. There were 78 rpm records of the *1812 Overture*, *Für Elise*, and the *Flight of the Bumblebee*. The radio was always on the Third Programme for music or the Home Service for serials and light entertainment. We were taken to the English National Opera at the London Coliseum and to the ballet. I have a Proust-like memory of the smell of cloves in the striped sweets we sucked as we watched *Les Patineurs*.

I remember clearly the childhood illnesses during which our darling mother, who had been an auxiliary nurse during the war, would feed us grilled plaice with mashed potato and cauliflower, washed down with Lucozade. I was prone to bronchitis and daddy used to sing to me 'Wheezyanna, Wheezyanna, down where the watermelons grow, and they all got pips in'.

In the summers he taught us to swim. A talented artist, he gave us an eye for colour and form and an acute awareness of the beauty of the world around us.

Our rented house in Ferntower Road, Highbury was just around the corner from the local synagogue which we attended with our father each *Shabbat*. I still have the cards with stickers for each of the weekly Torah portions, chronicling our good attendance. Growing up in Bethnal Green, my father had reaped great benefit from leisure time spent at the Cambridge and Bethnal Green Boys' Club. Eager to pass on such benefits to a new generation, he founded and ran the Highbury and Dalston Jewish Youth Club. Our involvement with the synagogue inculcated a deep appreciation of the value of community, which continues to motivate me and for which I will always be thankful.

Grandma, my mother's mother (as distinct from Booba, our father's mother), could not read or write English, a situation my sister and I were keen to remedy. I remember clearly the day we went to see Cecil B. de Mille's new epic *The Ten Commandments*. Grandma was immaculate as ever in a grey coat and grey gloves. 'You look lovely grandma', I remarked. 'Vell', she replied, 'me (we are) goin' to da Vest End!' We drove down Oxford Street. 'Look', she remarked, 'C & A'. 'Oh, grandma', I cried, 'you can read!'

My first school was Newington Green Primary. From the very first day I simply loved school. I made my first best friend, another Jewish girl called

Naomi Tucker. Once when I talked too much I was slapped on the back of the leg by a teacher called, ironically, Mrs Legg, and made to sit under her desk.

On the walls were numbers to ten, each with the relevant amount of big black dots. To this day I see them in my mind's eye when I add complements to ten, and I am a keen advocate of visual support for learners in my school. I whizzed through the 'Through the Rainbow' reading scheme ('Bang, bang, bang went the pots as they rolled down the hill…') I am also a great advocate of phonics teaching.

One Christmas I was chosen to be an angel in the nativity play. Knowing that I was Jewish the teacher asked permission of my mother who, after some deliberation, said yes. The day of the play dawned bright and crisp and I awoke with the measles. The decision about my participation had evidently been overridden by a higher authority!

One day during that first year at school the dreadful words 'notice to quit' entered my vocabulary and we found ourselves thirty-eight stairs up in a flat above the 'Jax'[1] shop in Muswell Hill, where mummy would work as manageress while daddy travelled as a supervisor for Great Universal Stores, and where they were to live for some fifty years.

Of my years in Muswell Hill I have nothing but happy memories. Within days of moving we were in the heart of a warm and welcoming Jewish community, where we acquired a plethora of honorary uncles and aunts.

I remember as if it was yesterday my first day at Muswell Hill Primary, standing in the playground with Naomi, wearing matching red button-through cardigans and green flared skirts with a white wavy line around the bottom, all lovingly hand-made by our wonderful mum. All the other children were dressed in pink and brown, the uniform I would wear with pride until age eleven. That moment was replayed frequently in my mind when children arrived mid-year at high mobility Bell Lane Primary. 'Are you Jewish?' a tentative voice asked, and so began my friendship with Carol-Ann, who was to become my best friend until she married and moved away to Manchester.

Muswell Hill Primary, a temporary pre-fabricated corrugated iron building from the wartime, was affectionately known as 'The Tin Pot'. There was pungent red carbolic soap in the washrooms and the toilets were outside.

---

1 The 'Jax' stores were women's clothing retail outlets, part of the Morrison's group of companies which in turn was part of Great Universal Stores, the company owned by Sir Isaac Wolfson, for which my father worked.

I was always so happy there. It had six classes, five of them off the hall, just like Bell Lane, and one up the road in a building called 'The Club'.

I spent one day with Miss Elliot, a short round lady with beige short socks and sandals, in class one. I wrote on an A4 sized chalkboard, 'Our bulbs are now in a dark place' (though I had not planted one) and drew a plant pot with a flower growing tall and proud. I used green chalk to colour the stem and leaves, and pink for the flower. The following day, in a move we might now call 'personalised learning', I was transferred to Miss Harris in class two, where we learnt about the black children who lived in the far-flung reaches of 'Our Commonwealth'.

After school we spent our pocket money at Mr James's, where sherbert-filled 'Flying Saucers' were four for a penny, 'Fruit Salads' and 'Black Jacks' eight for a penny. On fine summer Thursdays (her afternoon off) mummy would collect us to spend blissful twilight hours with a picnic at 'The Grove' by Alexandra Palace or in Highgate Woods.

Carol-Ann and I were always in trouble for giggling in class. When she came to play, Naomi often had to banish one of us to the walk-in pantry to overcome our silliness.

There was a nativity play at Muswell Hill Primary too, but I do not think I ever appeared in it. Modern day health and safety authorities would have been horrified at the use of potassium permanganate on young limbs to make the actors, all white British, look more authentically Middle Eastern! I had to laugh at this watching the wonderful multicultural school community at Bell Lane perform the nativity story. I did star as Father Christmas, the narrator in the Christmas mummers' play about George and the Dragon. I still remember some of the lines and the pride I took in the role and I am delighted that dedicated staff in the schools I have led are enthusiastic about staging productions.

On Friday afternoons we sewed coloured rows of stitches on fabric called binka while Miss Frowde, our caring grey-haired Headmistress read to us from a compilation of fairy stories like the volume I still have which I won in a Cadbury's essay competition in 1963.

Birthdays were celebrated in assembly with a painted cake made of clay, with holes for the candles. Celebrants were given 'Dolly Mixture' sweets wrapped in coloured tissue paper (it wouldn't happen in my 'Healthy School'!). Paul Levrant, another Jewish child, got told off for not singing hymns. Paul's father was a jeweller and he told my mum that he was going to buy me a watch for my birthday. We planned to marry one day.

One incident from my primary school days taught me one of my most valuable lessons in life. Valerie was a diminutive girl in my class. One day as I walked past her flats her mum came out and told me that Valerie had said that I was bullying her and I was to leave her alone. I was devastated – I had done nothing, and I can feel to this day the hurt at the injustice of that moment. Even now, many years after the event I do not understand what motivated the accusation. One day a few months later Valerie died. She had undergone an unsuccessful operation for a hole in her heart. The whole school stood on the painted lines in the playground to watch her funeral procession go by.

That evening I bought a posy of red and purple anemones and wrote a card to her parents, which I left on their doorstep on my way to school the following morning. Her mother visited mine in the shop to say thank you and would always thereafter wave and talk to me kindly when I saw her in the street. Since that day I have never hesitated to open the channels of communication to people in trouble.

The impact of my rapid promotion to class two was the benefit of two years with the splendid John Walters in class six. For the 1950s Mr Walters, a smiling chubby Welshman, was a remarkable primary school teacher. In the same school, skeletal Mr B taught Class 4 in 'The Club'. He sat children in rows according to ability. He taught didactically and presided over writing activities undertaken in silence, punctuated only with, 'Finished, sir', as the hierarchy completed the task at their anticipated pace. Next door to Mr Walters, Mrs R used a ruler to exact punishment for giggling or for less than satisfactory handwriting.

In John Walters' class pupils were grouped, six to a table, by ability and the work was differentiated. There was 'class made rain' in science – ice cubes in a tin tray over a boiling kettle. In history we wrote 'I was there' stories. We were treated to stirring renditions of 'How Horatius kept the Bridge', and in his pursuit of excellence we perfected choral recitations of T. S. Eliot cat poems for the Hornsey schools' festival at the Town Hall. I remember a teacher from another school approaching Mr Walters at the end of a show to exclaim, 'Well you've done it again, you Welsh wizard'.

It was John Walters, who sadly died far too young, who inspired me to become a primary school teacher. He taught not just poetry and highest and lowest common denominators, but also values. I remember one day being hauled to the front of the class for saying, 'Shut up' to a classmate. 'Who's that saying "Shut up" in my class?' he bellowed; I never did it again and no child has ever got away with saying it in a class of mine. My other inspiration was my Auntie Jean. The youngest of my father's siblings, she was the only one of the eleven to go to university. For as long as I can remember I wanted to be a Headteacher just like her.

Mr Walters' (top left) Class 6, Muswell Hill Primary School. Author seated first girls' row, third right.

The tests for secondary school transfer were not announced in advance and when the day arrived I was uncharacteristically absent with a cold. I hurried back, armed with one of my father's handkerchiefs, and took the tests in Miss Frowde's office. They included, I recall, items like providing the female equivalent of 'lad'. I sometimes think of them when I query the appropriateness of some of the testing material we are required to present to the diversity of pupils in primary schools now. But I passed and at the age of eleven, to my parents' immense pride I followed my sister to the Henrietta Barnett Grammar School for Girls in Hampstead Garden Suburb.

Given the choice of Henrietta or Camden Girls' our parents had taken Miss Frowde's advice to 'send them out of the smoke'. Usually we travelled to school on the highly unpredictable 102 bus, but some mornings we got a lift. This was a great delight for our artistic and sensitive father, who would spend the journey in raptures over the autumn colours or the spring blossoms that adorned our route.

Henrietta Barnett School is set in an area of considerable affluence and my arrival at the school brought for the first time, an awareness of my parents' limited financial situation. My classmates mostly lived in large private houses in the Suburb and Golders Green and it took me a long time to summon up the courage to invite them to our rented flat above a shop in Muswell Hill. I began to notice that their winter boots were leather, while mine were plastic.

My favourite subjects were the arts and my dislikes were physics and PE, especially hockey, because I never understood it. I became a regular on the uncomfortable benches in the 'gods' at the Old Vic, where I was enthralled by Maggie Smith and Robert Stevens, Ian Holm, Charles Dance, and the legendary Laurence Olivier. In English lessons eccentric Mrs Berkeley regularly asked, 'Have I told you about my theory that Iago was impotent?'

I rejoiced at my A grade for an essay on 'The Sea in Under Milk Wood', one of my favourite texts. Shakespeare, Tacitus, Gide, I revelled in all of them.

In 1967 Israel was attacked by her neighbours. My strong Jewish identity and my best friend Carol-Ann had led me to Jewish Youth Study Groups, a youth movement where we socialised and learnt about Judaism and Israel. Because of its location our school was very popular with the surrounding upwardly mobile Jewish population and at that time over 50% of the intake was Jewish. We followed avidly the politics of the Middle East and a rash of transistor radios appeared in school as we listened nervously to the unfolding events of the Six Day War. As Moshe Dayan emerged as the hero of the conflict we pinned his picture to the classroom wall. Nancy Silver, then our form tutor, was a pacifist and hauled us back to the classroom in our break time to tell us that she was, 'Not going to see a group of fifteen year-old girls whipped into war hysteria'. I took my first sortie into political debate as I confronted her as to what she would do if someone was threatening to push her and her loved ones into the Mediterranean Sea.

The Middle East was the backdrop too, for heated arguments as Naomi asserted her identity. She and mum used to disagree fiercely about Israel as Naomi sought to express her appreciation of the complexity of the situation.

Her strong political convictions would lead her to play an active part in the radical student movements of the 1960s. She became Chair at Birmingham University of the South African Student Fund, which raised money to bring black student victims of apartheid to study in England. She joined the Ban the Bomb movement and the Aldermaston marches. She also had an Ibo boyfriend from Biafra.

I was fifteen when Naomi went away to Birmingham. I was bereft. I felt that the symmetry of our family was destroyed, from a comfortable two and two we had become two and one. The change became permanent when she left soon after university to study criminology in Israel, which has been her home ever since. While friends from Zionist youth movements 'made aliyah', only to return disillusioned, I believe that Naomi's more realistic understanding of the complexity of Israel, voiced in the arguments at home, underpinned her ability to settle there.

During Naomi's years at university I also became more acutely aware of the financial constraints on my parents. I watched their troubled expressions when the requests for more money inevitably came towards the end of term.

In the sixth form at Henrietta I studied English, French and Latin. The Latin was a mistake. Though I loved the literature I was not competent enough in the grammar and did badly in the A level. This spoiled my chances of taking up a place for French with European Studies at Sussex. Taking into account the financial burden on my parents, most of my other choices were in London, so that I could live at home and I rather bizarrely ended up studying French at Bedford College in Regent's Park. Originally a ladies' college, Bedford was a 'twin set and pearls' kind of place, where the professor took out reams of yellowing notes, changed his distance glasses for reading glasses and ploughed on, oblivious to his impact, or lack of it on the student body. From my perspective the course was dry and dusty, far too heavy on ancient texts, and it was only in the final year, when I was able to take options in modern literature, particularly absurdist drama, that I enjoyed aspects of my studies. Emerging with a lower second degree, disappointed in myself at failing to match Naomi's upper second, I vowed that my days of studying were at an end.

I asserted at the beginning of this section that I am a success of the education system. This is a good point at which to pause to consider the extent to which my primary, secondary and university education contributed to that success.

I was an able pupil. In primary school John Walters, in particular, tapped into my potential. By the time I left his class I knew that I was able. He challenged me and I responded. I knew that I was doing hard work of which I was capable, that I was artistic and a competent performer. In the context of the child, home, school theory his encouragement, support and praise mirrored that of my parents and I strove to please him as I strove to please them. I deeply regret that he did not live long enough for me to show him and thank him for his part in making me the person I am now.

I was privileged to go to Henrietta Barnett. It was a good school, a reputation that is certainly confirmed by external evaluation of the school today. Yet when I consider the influences that have made me the learner and leader that I am, I am not sure that Henrietta played a particularly significant part. I was a B/C student. The most able girls were groomed for Oxbridge and there was scant tolerance of underperformers. I do not think that I was particularly nurtured. I cannot identify a teacher or teachers who had the John Walters effect. I do not recall being told, 'This is your attainment level, this is where we think you can be, and these are the steps you need to take to get there.' This is why I am passionate about and excited by the curricular target setting agenda (not to be confused with the school performance target agenda, on which I have a very different view!) I took from the school opportunities that were on offer to achieve around the expected level, but I know that I was capable of more. Perhaps they could have released my potential if they had really got to know me. It is, interestingly, a criticism of the two good secondary schools that my own children attended.

As for leadership skills, one year I directed my class's production for the drama competition, and in the sixth form I became a prefect. It was a privilege bestowed by staff and peers. We had our own room, sold (and ate!) tuck and did duties around the school. I do not remember any training other than being told by the head that we had to be: 'Like Caesar's wife, above suspicion.'

As for my university education, I made the wrong choice. My parents, the usual source of support and advice were not able to help. My form tutor, a French teacher, fleetingly recommended Bedford College as 'good for French'. I do not think she knew me well enough to be able to judge if it was good for me. It was also one of the few French courses that did not require a year in France, which suited me fine. At university I gained knowledge, and I got my average degree by reproducing that knowledge adequately in exams.

Teacher Training and My First Teaching Post

Earlier I mentioned the importance of community, and in particular the Jewish community, which has made a massive contribution to the person I am today.

That contribution started in my youth and it will be helpful to preface this section with an explanation of youth activity within the Jewish community, which merits close attention from politicians seeking to improve outcomes for young people.

As well as synagogue groups the community has a plethora of youth movements across the religious spectrum, many embracing different facets of the Zionist ideology, e.g. socialist, religious. I include the Association of Jewish Sixth Formers and the highly impressive Union of Jewish Students, which as well as providing vital practical, social and Jewish educational facilities on campus, does sophisticated political campaigning and interfaith dialogue. Jewish community organisations deserve every respect for their support of all these endeavours.

Youngsters can begin their involvement in youth activities from the age of about seven or eight. With some adult support, but increasingly as they grow older taking responsibility with their peers, they organise and run their groups. As a *madrich* or *madricha* (male/female leader) adolescents lead younger children. Summer camps are the annual highlight, and in the Zionist movements these build towards the highly anticipated Israel tour at the end of the GCSE year. Then there is leadership training, including gap year programmes here and in Israel, which can lead to paid employment as a *mazkir* or *mazkira* (director), or as a camps organiser or other officer for the group.

The community has developed fabulous youth leadership courses, far superior now to when I was involved. At Bell Lane I had an impressive young teacher who is a product of the system. When we interviewed her alongside six others she was head and shoulders above them in her understanding of successfully planning, implementing and evaluating activities for young people. My own sons, who are products of the system, already have leadership skills that it has taken me many years to develop. Of course, affiliation to the youth movements has suffered in the age of PS3s and 24 hour push-button entertainment, but they continue to turn out impressive numbers of fine, confident, and competent young people, many of them promising leaders.

Given my father's enthusiasm for youth activity, it was natural that when we moved to Muswell Hill, we should join the synagogue youth club. In time I became a club manager, planning and running activities for younger groups.

With my background in synagogue youth clubs and Jewish Youth Study Groups, where I chaired the North West London group, it was not surprising that having made few friends on my university course, I sought companionship in the Bedford College Jewish Society, which was tiny. I inevitably became chair, which brought me into contact with the Inter-University Jewish Federation (IUJF), now Union of Jewish Students (UJS). The contrast with the disappointment I felt about the academic aspects of my university experience could not have been greater.

I threw myself into activities at the newly built Hillel House student centre in Euston. I became an activist on the Universities' Committee for Soviet Jewry, campaigning against the treatment of refuseniks, frequently organising and participating in demonstrations outside the Russian Embassy. I became London Region chair of IUJF and honed my leadership, speaking and debating skills. Convinced that I was a lousy student, I became a confident leader and an able public speaker. This confidence has encouraged me to take significant leadership roles professionally and communally ever since.

I attended and spoke at conferences in Britain, Europe and Israel. At the annual IUJF conference in Glasgow in 1971 I became friendly with an activist from the Glasgow Jewish Society called Maurice Stone. Some five years later, reader, I married him.

As I said, I left college never wanting to study again. Also, having lived on £4 a week, stretching my student grant by working weekends and holidays, I was eager to start earning. The Director of the Hillel House student centre in 1970 was Rabbi Cyril Harris, later to become Chief Rabbi of South Africa. Cyril and I worked closely together during my time in IUJF and he suggested that I should apply for the post of Student Director. I still have my letter of appointment, on an annual salary of £2000.

It was a fabulous job, in which I could continue to enjoy the aspects of student life that I loved and get paid! It is an interesting comment on the nature and nurture debate that the first paid jobs taken respectively by my sons Danny and Gab were as Campaigns Organiser of the Union of Jewish Students and as President of the Loughborough University Students' Union.

In my first year at Hillel I was one of two student directors. David Landy and I organised a full programme of educational and social activities. I laugh now when I drop a graphic or two into a desktop publication to remember the long hours we spent with Letraset, scissors and glue spray, cutting and pasting the termly programme!

Though I still lived at home I frequently spent *Shabbat* and Festivals at Hillel. On *Yom Kippur* eve of 1973 it was in Cyril's sermon from the pulpit of Dean Street synagogue (now the Soho theatre) that I heard that once again tanks from Arab countries were massing on the borders of Israel. Hillel served as a centre for volunteers. Our Israeli dance teacher was called back for military service and Maurice, who has a passion for Israeli dance, began to organise the highly successful classes that would form the foundation of the Israeli Dance Institute that he runs so inspirationally today. Our romance blossomed as we travelled together on the tube each morning, me to Hillel and he to Coopers and Lybrand in the City, where he was articled.

In my second year at Hillel David left and aged 22 I was promoted to Assistant Director. I learnt to manage office staff and developed a wide set of skills that I use extensively still to run my school.

After two years and with some money in the bank the desire to study returned. The decision to teach was a simple one. Maybe it is in the genes, if that is the case there is certainly a teaching gene in the Goldstein family.

Having made such a poor undergraduate choice I researched carefully, consulted Jean and selected the one year PGCE course at Goldsmiths College. I rented a cheap flat in Lewisham with a Jewish friend from Muswell Hill who was also studying teaching in south London. The entrance looked like a poster from the charity Shelter, but we made it as homely as we could. Anyway, I headed home every weekend to be with Maurice, who was living in East Finchley.

The course at Goldsmiths was in the vanguard of primary practice at that time. Following the *Bullock Report* of 1975 we were taught to provide a rich and stimulating learning environment which would inspire children to speak, read and write freely. We learnt to work with a range of natural materials that would promote 'discovery learning'. Starting from the fleece, we wove wool and dyed it with vegetable dyes, we carded and spun. We even had our very own anthrax scare! We soaked corn stalks to make corn dollies and did calligraphy with italic pens. Our fabric-draped displays of natural materials and objects paid homage to Henry Pluckrose, the guru of the primary classroom environment. Oblivious to the impact on the rainforests we triple mounted children's work.

A debate was just beginning to emerge as to whether creativity was being promoted at the expense of basic skills. The Goldsmiths course combined both, but it was at this time that misunderstanding and poor teaching in the application of the approaches we learnt at Goldsmith led to some very poor practice. I remember when I first arrived at Bell Lane there was a teacher doing a week long topic on the theme of eggs. It was ill-conceived and poorly planned and very little learning happened.

It was in response to such practice that the education system became much more directive and formulaic with the introduction of the National Curriculum, followed closely by the Literacy and Numeracy Strategies with their rigid three-part lessons.

I welcome the Excellence and Enjoyment and Personalised Learning agendas. I believe that we are beginning to redress the balance to arrive at a model of primary education that may finally see the realisation of the vision of my PGCE course, but with the rigour needed to make it really effective. It has been a long time coming.

I was hugely relieved to be fascinated by the lectures and tutorials at Goldsmiths and hurried back to the flat to type up my notes every evening on the portable typewriter I requested as a leaving present from Hillel. There was real relevance in learning the theory, then having time in school to apply it, and I have loved and succeeded in action research throughout my life in teaching.

My personal tutor was Rhona Hisom, a teacher on secondment from a school in Hertfordshire. I enjoyed her tutorials and valued her constructive criticism and practical suggestions when she visited me on teaching practice in Gravesend, Plumstead, and Abbey Wood. I am, as a result, a strong supporter of school based training and eager to welcome students to my school.

But it was the children who did it for me. I loved my teaching practices. I could do this! I tried ideas from our lectures and workshops and drew heavily on my own primary school experience. With one group I did a Literacy project using the five senses. We scrutinised daffodils and wrote stories in response to the sound of footsteps. In another school I got the children to drop coloured ink in water as a stimulus to write poetry, with some impressive outcomes. I taught about the Victorians and the children wrote 'I was there' stories.

Then there were the individuals. Michael was a scrawny blond boy with matted hair. He organised a small gang to steal the Headteacher's handbag from her office, appointing himself as the lookout man. Being so close to the Kent border I encountered Traveller children who left suddenly to harvest the strawberry crop. Moses was a tight little ball of insecurity, barely able to hold a pencil. My teaching practice journal chronicles a growing awareness of the need to make individual provision for such children, which would lay the foundations for my lifelong passion for special needs teaching.

The year flew by and I began to apply for jobs. It has always amazed me how poorly those who plan teacher training match supply and demand, and when I left Goldsmiths there was a glut of graduates from primary PGCE courses. I sent dozens of applications. Those who bothered to reply regretted. I have kept a letter from Brent Council rejecting me from the probationary pool due to over-demand, which I pull out to show in times of shortage.

There was no job for me and I was devastated. I needed to earn and so with the help of a family member I found myself managing a branch of an employment agency in Holloway. We received bonuses for placements, an approach I found particularly distasteful when staff tried to place people inappropriately just for the money. More distasteful was the racism I was shocked to encounter. Every month we had to sign the Race Relations Act, but this did not prevent the attitude of an individual in another part of the company when I phoned up to see if they had any vacancies for someone I could not place. Hearing that the request was from Holloway she replied, 'I suppose she's a coon?' It is to my eternal shame that I did not challenge or report this at the time. I would certainly do so now.

I continued to search for a teaching post and towards the end of 1976 spotted a job in what was then called the 'remedial' department at JFS

Comprehensive.[2] I had not really considered teaching in the Jewish sector. Firstly, I wanted my first job to be in the kind of school in which I had trained. Second, all Jewish schools at that time were orthodox and I knew that there would be expectations about my level of religious observance. However, the special needs aspect of the job appealed to me so I applied. I didn't get it, but within days I received a call from the Head to say that he noted that I was a French graduate and there was a vacancy they were having difficulty filling in the French department. It was secondary French and it was in a Jewish school, but it was a job in teaching and I jumped at the chance.

On 2 January 1977 Maurice and I were married and on my return from honeymoon I started at JFS. As for religious credentials I had been told at interview, 'The governors of the school expect Jewish teachers to be orthodox. Are you orthodox?' Now this is a strange question in the Anglo-Jewish community with its myriad shades of belief and practice. What does orthodox mean? Is it the same as orthoprax? Is it enough to observe *Shabbat* and *kashrut* or does it require close observance of all 613 commandments? My family had for many years been members of the United Synagogue, the mainstream orthodox movement, under whose auspices I was about to be married. So I asked no questions and answered yes. When I began work I realised that many Jewish teachers at the school were a lot less observant than me.

My first year was hard. I inherited a timetable designed to encourage the person before me to leave. I taught a very needy bottom set in the second year (Y8). Teaching them to tell the time in French I discovered a child who could not yet tell the time in English! The winter timetable for Friday was designed to enable the school to finish early for *Shabbat*. There were two long lessons in the morning, early lunch, then three very short sessions and home. One of the afternoon sessions was with a challenging first-year (Y7) class in a commerce room. The lesson was punctuated with the occasional ping of a typewriter bell as the children fiddled under the desks. I felt I was in a goldfish bowl because the Head of Commerce had a free period in her glass-fronted office at the back of the room. Some Fridays twenty-five minutes was barely enough to get the class in the room, settled and out again!

---

2 JFS (Jews' Free School) is Europe's largest and most successful Jewish secondary school. It was established in 1732 as the Talmud Torah of the Great Synagogue of London serving orphans in the community. In 1822 the school relocated to Bell Lane in the heart of the East End of London, where throughout the nineteenth century, it absorbed thousands of immigrant children. At one time JFS had 4000 children on roll and was the largest school in the world. See http://www.jfs.brent.sch.uk/jfs-history.aspx

But with the support of some exceptional colleagues I passed my probationary year and went on to spend four very happy years at the school. Daphne Hassett was my head of department. She lived close to me and became a firm friend during our journeys home together in her beloved green Citroen deux chevaux, as it struggled in top gear up Highgate West Hill. Daphne ran a highly organised and effective department and I felt very well supported.

Though the teaching was very text book and worksheet based I drew on my primary training, spending many evenings with sugar paper, felt tips and tacky back plastic drawing and labelling visual aids to teach the vocabulary for fruit, furniture or parts of the body. I recall these times affectionately as I watch my teachers browse a resource bank and click a button to call up a labelled image on the Smartboard! What a conundrum that with this level of technological support and ten percent dedicated planning time they have even less time to breathe than we had then.

Starting in January, I had not been allocated a tutor group and I looked forward to having one from September. The primary teacher in me craved a class of my own and I requested one of the eight first forms, or Y7 as they would be known now. 1SW was a joy. They were smart and funny. I loved them and I think most of them loved me. I ran a tight ship, expecting

Author with form group at JFS.

immaculate uniform (still an obsession!), boys always wearing their *kippot* (skullcaps) and homework diaries in every week, well presented and signed. We frequently won the first year house point competition and enjoyed a wonderful residential week together at a somewhat decrepit centre called Gaynes Park, whose uneven floors and loose light switches would certainly not have survived scrutiny under today's obligatory risk assessment regime!

My second year timetable was better and I was becoming more confident and competent. In addition to the CSE (now obsolete Certificate of Secondary Education) I had taught successfully in the first year I was trusted with an O level/GCE class and had the joy of revisiting favourite French novelists and poets with my bright group of sixth formers.

I took an active part in the Jewish life of the school, leading assemblies and helping to organise events for the Jewish festivals. A highlight was the Israeli dance session I organised in the front playground for Israel Independence Day, with an audience of commuters in the buses and cars on the busy Camden Road. Security at Jewish schools has become so tight that I blanch at the thought of trying to organise a similar event now.

At the end of my second year I made a successful application for promotion to a pastoral role as Deputy Head of House. The pastoral system was organised around four houses, Angel, Brodetsky, Weizmann and Zangwill, named after Anglo-Jewish luminaries. I became Deputy of my house, Weizmann. With my enthusiasm for special needs I relished a pastoral role and I loved working closely with the smart young people who served as house officers. The head of house was John Partridge, a highly intelligent historian and brilliantly kind and skilful disciplinarian from whom I learnt so much.

Across the four houses there was a range of styles of behaviour management. One Head of House would shriek down the corridor after a miscreant who ran off when caught in the act. John, however, would make a careful mental note and ensure that the matter was effectively dealt with at their next encounter, skilfully orchestrated by him shortly afterwards. It is an approach that has served me well. You can imagine my delight when I discovered many years later that John was to be my son Danny's History teacher at JFS. Danny loved his lessons and of course did well in the subject.

One day towards the end of my fourth year at JFS I was called into the Head's office and offered a more senior newly created pastoral post. It was, by chance, the same day that I had chosen to tell him that I was leaving because I was pregnant. Despite the financial incentives I did not plan to return. I wanted to be a full time mum and I still craved a post in primary education.

I hate goodbyes and leaving the school was a real wrench. To be a Jewish teacher in a Jewish school was like being in a second home. Despite my concerns about my level of religious practice no one had ever questioned me. I had wonderful colleagues across the religious spectrum in all departments. I also had wonderful non-Jewish colleagues. How I admired their commitment to the school and their respect for my religion, which for many went as far as learning all the Hebrew words of the school song and lengthy afternoon prayers broadcast daily over the tannoy system (a practice I am delighted to say has been abandoned!)

I had stayed with 1SW and they were now 3SW. If leaving the school was difficult, saying goodbye to them was impossible. They had made a collection for a farewell gift and I can still see each face as they rose one by one to bring me a tiny t-shirt, bib or pair of socks to contribute to the collection of baby clothes their money had bought. I cried buckets through their goodbyes and through the farewell assembly, unable to join in the beautiful hymn Hariu, the school song, which always makes me cry anyway when it is traditionally sung at weddings.

I will leave until later further thoughts on Jewish education, for this was not to be the last of my association with JFS. Ten years later it was the school of choice for our firstborn and I was proud to serve the school again as parent governor for two four-year terms of office.

Motherhood and Educational Choices for our Children

Danny was born in November 1980 and Gaby shortly after midnight on 1 January 1983 (and no, he wasn't the first of the year so I did not get any free nappies!) I spent seven years at home with my children, a decision that I have never regretted. My two little boys were absolute joys, and as fine young men in their twenties remain so.

Though I could happily write a book about each, for the purpose of this volume I will describe and comment on their schooling, the decisions we made, and the impact of those decisions on the people they are today.

When Danny was two years old we registered him for the nursery at the local primary school, which he would later attend. It was a natural choice. Any of the local primaries might have suited. This one had an added attraction in serving a housing provision for overseas students, and I wanted my children to experience multicultural schooling.

An able child, Danny enjoyed primary school and did well. I trod carefully as a teaching parent, not wanting to seem too pushy. I went out of my way to write complimentary letters after specific events, so that any queries or criticism would be balanced. I also helped by running workshops for *Chanukah* and providing resources for teaching about Judaism, and in time was taken on briefly as an individual support assistant for a special needs pupil.

Danny only struggled with spelling and I was concerned one parents' evening in Y4 when I was shown a story he had written, nine pages long, with no indication of any support for the many inaccuracies. The teacher confirmed her approach to teaching writing – 'It's more important to just let them write'. I had begun to take an interest in dyslexia, and this concerned me.

In Y5 there was an incident in which Danny was quite badly hurt by a child with challenging behaviour. Maurice spoke to the Head about it. Other incidents followed, including the pupil breaking another's arm, and he was ultimately excluded. He managed to convince some of the other boys that it was Danny's fault and the bullying began. I can see him now, standing alone in the playground, head bowed, back slightly curved, his left arm tight across his waist clasping his right elbow, as he chewed the fingers of his right hand. He was unhappy and fast losing confidence.

By this time I was already teaching at Bell Lane Primary and we urged him to transfer, but he did not want to leave. I asked the mothers for a meeting together with the boys. They declined. It was not their problem. We saw the Head on more than one occasion, but he too did not consider that there was a problem. Eventually Danny gave in. My Head reported the conversation he had with Danny's previous Head. 'Have you met the father?' he asked Leighton, 'he's very aggressive'. Not an adjective I would readily apply to my mild-mannered husband.

So in Y6 Danny joined Bell Lane and I rejoiced in watching him uncoil during a fabulous year with my great colleague, Tom Walters, brother of the actress Julie. Tom was Danny's John Walters (must be something in the name!) He tapped into his potential and Danny shone; 1991 was an election year and in a portent of his future political involvement Danny triumphed as the Labour candidate in Tom's mock election. Tom corrected his spellings and despite the difficulties highlighted in the report we had commissioned from the Dyslexia Institute, the fog cleared and Danny began to understand the rationale to spell accurately. I truly believe that there are approaches that do a gross disservice to bright pupils struggling with spelling.

So what are my views on bullying? Frankly, it is a difficult one. It is a fact that bullying exists, and in Danny's case I have absolutely no doubt, and I had the evidence that he was being systematically bullied. On the other hand, there have been several occasions on which parents have come to me asserting that their child is being bullied and investigation has shown that either the real problem is something quite different, or that there is a problem in their relationship with another child which is not bullying and can be quite quickly and easily solved. Sometimes, too there are two individuals or groups involved, both giving as good as they get! I do, however, believe that schools must have a clear and dynamic policy on bullying, with plenty of opportunities throughout the curriculum for pupils to explore the issues. Any accusation of bullying must be taken seriously, investigated thoroughly and if proven, dealt with swiftly and decisively.

Danny, JFS.

For secondary transfer we had open minds. We visited local schools and JFS, which Danny liked. He was by this time an active member of our synagogue youth movement and enjoying his Judaism. We live, anyway, in a kind of secondary school black hole in Barnet and when the secondary school allocation arrived there was no place in any of his schools of choice in the authority. So JFS it was, and we were happy, as we felt that it was a school where he could continue to rebuild his confidence and fulfil his potential.

Danny's years at JFS were happy and fulfilling. He became a School Council representative and won achievement certificates. He was becoming a very able guitarist and his band, Bluejuice, won the Battle of the Bands. He performed in *Guys and Dolls*. Like me, he was generally a B/C student, but looking at his achievements now I think his potential was greater. He does too, freely acknowledge that he should have chosen different A level subjects and worked harder. I often wonder how well-equipped we really are at sixteen to make such choices.

The only discordant note relates to his time in the sixth form, and specifically to Jewish Studies. As I hope I have shown, I love JFS and have great admiration of the school and Danny's recently retired inspirational Head, Dame Ruth Robins. As such, I have always shied away from any public criticism, but since the issues I am about to raise have been much in the public arena, I will mention them here.

Shortly after Danny was born we joined, and subsequently became very active in the New North London Synagogue in Finchley. The synagogue is part of the Masorti movement, following the teachings of Rabbi Dr Louis Jacobs. A minister in the United Synagogue, Rabbi Jacobs was effectively excommunicated in 1964, several years after he had written his seminal non-fundamentalist work *We Have Reason to Believe*.[3] To put it far too simplistically, on the Anglo-Jewish spectrum membership of the NNLS puts us broadly to the left of the mainstream body, the United Synagogue.

By the time he entered the sixth form Danny was a proud member and leader of Noam, the Masorti youth movement. Not just following family tradition; he had thought it out for himself and was comfortable with, and well able to articulate his belief and practice.

---

3 Jacobs, L, *We Have Reason to Believe*, (Vallentine Mitchell), 1995. First published in 1957 Jacobs' attempt to synthesise orthodox Jewish teachings with that of modern biblical criticism provoked a storm of controversy within Anglo-Jewry later known as the 'Jacobs Affair'.

JFS is constituted under the auspices of the United Synagogue and accepts pupils who are Jewish according to the Office of the Chief Rabbi (I will expand on this in a later section). [4] The resulting student body covers a wide spectrum of practice and belief, but is broadly from Reform to what I term mainstream orthodox. The more observant in the community send their children to more orthodox schools like Hasmonean, Pardes House and Beis Yaacov.

It is a challenge for the school to provide an inclusive twenty-first century Jewish Studies curriculum, and one which JFS has traditionally met with admirable syllabi linking Jewish Studies and PSHCE (personal, social, health and citizenship education).

The challenge, however, is compounded by the fact that teaching staff in the department are generally at least as orthodox as the most observant pupils and often considerably more so. Success in Jewish Studies is measured by pupils becoming more observant, for example coming to school early for shacharit (morning service) and rather than taking a gap year or going straight to university, attending *Yeshiva* or Seminary. In recent years the department has moved considerably to the right with residential trips to Gateshead *Yeshiva* and heavy involvement by Aish Hatorah, an organisation with massive financial backing for quite aggressive campaigning e.g. free trips to Israel to encourage youngsters to change their lifestyle.

Danny had already had one or two run-ins with a JS (Jewish Studies) teacher who refuted Darwinian theory by suggesting that dinosaurs came from another planet, and claimed that Jews who drive on Shabbat are only half Jews. In the compulsory sixth form lessons he was presented with Aish Hatorah texts and encountered intolerance of Masorti Judaism as an authentic expression of his faith. Directly at odds with members of staff he voted with his feet and most uncharacteristically began to skip lessons. Maurice and he had meetings with the Jewish Studies staff (because I was by now a governor, I decided to let Maurice handle it). Danny even met one-to-one with the Head. Nothing changed. but no further action was taken about his absences.

It was, as I said, an unfortunately discordant note in an otherwise positive experience and in my overall and continuing admiration for the school.

---

4 This book was completed just after admissions criteria for JFS had been defined as racist by the Court of Appeal, following an unsuccessful legal challenge. At the time of publication the House of Lords has agreed to consider the Court of Appeal ruling.

I regret that the department was not able to include Danny as the proud Jew he is, eager to learn more about his heritage in an atmosphere of mutual respect. When Danny returned from his gap year in Israel his guitar case bore a sticker in Hebrew proudly proclaiming: 'There is more than one way to be a Jew'. As I watch my community becoming increasingly polarised I believe it is a slogan we would all do well to adopt.

Like his mother, Danny had one poor A-level result which prevented him taking up his first choice at Birmingham. Like his mother he made a wrong choice, taking Applied Biology at University. In contrast to JFS he found much of the teaching uninspiring and like his mother again emerged with a lower second. Like his mother (and I'm sure there's a Doctoral thesis in this!) he threw himself into Jewish Society and UJS instead. We were unspeakably proud when he led a successful campaign to stop David Irving, the Holocaust denier from addressing the Nottingham Students' Union. This, and his activism generally led to two very successful years after graduation as Campaigns Organiser of the Union of Jewish Students, which in turn led to two amazing years as Political Aide to the Jewish Lord, Greville Janner QC, during which he travelled the globe, meeting political giants like Nelson Mandela and Desmond Tutu.

Following a successful period as Senior Parliamentary Officer for the RSPB, Danny has returned to the Jewish communal arena as the Director of the All-Party Parliamentary Committee on Antisemitism

So what do I think about faith education? JFS undoubtedly taught Danny more about his faith, its culture and language. It supplemented what he was learning from home and his informal Jewish education at Noam, removing the need for Sunday morning and weekday evening faith classes, which are notoriously problematic. It provided a warm supportive learning environment broadly in harmony with his family values. Although his social life in his teens was exclusively in a Jewish milieu, he now socialises and works very comfortably in the wider multi-cultural society and has been active in interfaith work.

Essentially though, I think a good school is a good school. I believe that what governments have tapped into in their vaunting of faith schools is the notion of community. Being part of a supportive harmonious community, ideally in harmony with home, seems to provide the ideal environment for educational success, and when the feeling of community is lacking, or breaks down, problems can arise. I am also not at all convinced that faith schools are somehow unique in being able to create the kind of value-based community that supports effective education and produces fine citizens.

Danny, bless him, is a hard act to follow but our youngest, Gaby (who prefers Gab) is by no means eclipsed by his brother. He attended a different nursery at the local Reform synagogue, though I honestly cannot remember what prompted the change. Gab was clearly very smart and an avid learner. Towards the end of his time at nursery he began pleading to leave when I left him. This was the beginning of a scenario to be repeated throughout his educational career with a change in behaviour signifying the need for change.

Gab, University College, Hampstead.

Like Danny, Gab started at the local primary. By the end of Y2 we were beginning to get complaints about his behaviour. He was excellent at spelling and we discovered that he was completing his work with ease then spending the rest of the lesson, under the direction of the teacher, providing spellings for the other children. Unable to resolve the situation, we looked around for a place in another local primary, but they were all full and we took the ideologically difficult decision to try him for a place at University College, an independent boys' school in Hampstead, which we had looked at for Danny. Without even an hour of the customary tutoring Gab obtained a place.

At his state primary he was writing about a half a page in Literacy tasks. Within weeks of starting at UCS, and with impressive enthusiasm and drive he filled an exercise book with his project on medieval realms. His first year teacher, Tobiah Thomas, was his John Walters. He learnt French and Latin and succeeded in everything, thriving on his successes and on the rewards and incentives provided by school and home. His experience has greatly informed my practice in ensuring that able pupils are quickly identified and that appropriate provision is duly provided.

The wonderful facilities at UCS gave him a plethora of opportunities. There were three terms of sport on the huge playing fields; rugby, cricket and football. Gab is a great all-rounder and he participated enthusiastically, not always first team player but a valuable and valued squad member. He ran cross country, an experience that has led him to success as a marathon runner. Inter-school competitions included Saturday games. When we raised this with the sports staff, despite the large number of Jewish boys at the school, they merely pointed out that the leagues had been in place for about a hundred years.

Neither Maurice nor I are particularly interested in football and neither is Danny, so we are not quite sure how Gab became an ardent fan. When he met my relative John Smith, one of the country's leading sport agents, his professional ambition was sealed and he has worked steadily towards it from that moment.

Gab obtained an impressive set of GCSE results, but after eight years he had had enough of UCS. He chose to transfer to our local sixth form college, choosing PE and Business Studies in support of his career ambitions and Geography because an inspiring teacher had fired his enthusiasm for the subject.

'Twas ever thus! We heaved a sigh of relief because the ever-increasing fees were cleaning out our financial reserves.

So was his private education value for money? Where independent schools definitely score is in the quality of physical resources they are able to offer. As well as being good at sport Gab is an able craftsman, who made full use of the excellent Design and Technology facilities to produce some impressive outcomes. I think of them often when I watch my staff struggling to deliver the Design and Technology curriculum in our all-purpose classrooms. He produced fine works of art in the well appointed art studios. He certainly received a broad education.

In terms of the quality of teaching he had some very fine teachers at UCS, and independent schools are able to offer enhanced salaries to attract them. However, he also had some fairly mediocre teaching, which did not represent value for the money we paid.

He never really found a strong friendship group there, possibly because we are not natural independent school clientele. There were attitudes expressed which were out of kilter with our family values; attitudes about material possessions or women. I will never forget the day he came home with a reading list with no female authors. When I raised this with his English teacher he challenged me to name some worthy of inclusion!

Knowing what Gab has since achieved I am not sure that the school fully exploited his potential. Perhaps if he had stayed on it would have been different, or maybe it was because he was just one high flier amongst many.

After two years at sixth form college, Gab predictably emerged with straight As. He had made a good circle of close friends, none of them by the way Jewish. He has always been very comfortable with himself as a Jew in the wider community and comfortable in his relationships with a range of others.

He had developed his love of performance, kindled in the fabulous performing arts facilities at UCS, and took the lead in *Anything Goes*. We were called in by the Head towards the end of his time at the college for complaints about Gab's behaviour in Business Studies. The college had been a very positive experience and a correct choice, but it was clearly time for him to move on.

Like his brother, Gab spent his gap year in Israel. Danny's time there had been during the post-Oslo halcyon days when peace seemed a real possibility. There was still the occasional incident but generally it was a good time to be in Israel. By the time Gab went the second Intifada was in full flow. One Saturday night he called us from a restaurant on Ben Yehuda, the main shopping street in Jerusalem to say there had been an explosion. They had been locked in the restaurant and were able to see blood-stained people running past the door. During the conversation we heard over the telephone a massive second bomb. I gave fulsome thanks to God for saving our beautiful son, and to the leadership course organisers for their excellent post-traumatic support.

I wept yet again for more victims of this desperate situation.

On his return Gab headed off to Loughborough, a degree in Sport Science with Management at Britain's leading university for sport the natural choice. From the moment he arrived, unpacked and rushed out to make friends he simply loved it and absolutely thrived. He had found his ideal educational community.

Currently Loughborough tops the annual poll for best student experience and is sixth in the *Times Good University Guide*. Gab took full advantage, throwing himself wholeheartedly into 'The Loughborough Experience' of parties, socials, highly successful rag events and lots of fun and banter. A born leader with an irrepressible sense of fun, it was not long before he was standing for election as Chair of Social Activities. On the night of the hustings he donned his costume and sang a rather risqué Ali G song, substituting the name of the female warden of his hall. The next morning I received a phone call at school from a very distraught Gab to say that he had been told that he had to leave the hall or face a charge of sexual harassment under the university's disciplinary system. The months that followed were ghastly and he ended up out of his beloved hall with a £200 fine and the equivalent of being bound over to keep the peace.

I do not deny that in singing the song Gab clearly crossed a boundary. He acknowledged this and without prompting apologised immediately. So I have to question the motivation of the warden and university authorities in taking the action they did. I fear for the mental health of any student with less strength of character and family support facing the full force of such a punitive approach, which, incidentally, cost the university thousands of pounds.

Bell Lane has become a lead school for Restorative Justice. This is a system of conflict resolution which seeks to identify the harm done, and to whom and through mediation find a way forward that meets the needs of all involved. It is non-punitive, seeking lasting resolution rather than apportioning blame. It would have been perfect in this situation.

By the way, Gab was elected Social Chair, and then in his final year there was a very different phone call when he rang to joyously screech the news that he had been elected President of the Student's Union. Within a month he was hobnobbing at garden parties with members of the disciplinary panel.

He served his presidential year with distinction, gaining the love and respect of his executive and also becoming Star Fundraiser, and subsequently National Student Fundraiser of the Year, with the highest individual collection of the highest rag total in the country. He also managed (just) to beat Danny and I and equal his father's upper second. After Loughborough he began to live the dream as a Junior Sports Agent in a company run by Olympic gold medallist Linford Christie.

I am sometimes asked whether I think that Gab is underselling himself. A bright boy like him, could he not have gained a first at Oxbridge, gone into Law or Medicine? (It's a very Jewish question!) I have been blessed with a career that I love, yes it is hard, yes there are stresses, but I get such a buzz and a sense of fulfilment from my work. That is what I want for all 'my' children.

Also, both boys' education has, as good education should, laid the foundation for lifelong learning and I have a suspicion that there will be more studying to support their aspirations.

As for the choice of career, I have learnt much about 'futures thinking'. When we educate a cohort of youngsters we actually have little idea about the kind of world we are educating them for, especially nowadays when progress is so rapid. So, we need to be open to and excited about the types of services and professions we value. I think he has made a great choice.

Primary Teaching at Last

During the seven years with my children I both studied and worked. My interest in special needs education was growing and I decided to register with the Open University for an Advanced Diploma in Special Needs.

What a wonderful institution the university is. There was no summer school for this course and I could fit evening tutorials around Maurice's dance classes.

As for the reading and essay writing, we have a family saying that derives from my booba's advice to my mother to always put aside time to spend with her husband. A busy young mum, she asked when she should do this? 'In between', replied booba in her broken English. So that is when my studies were done.

I learnt about policy and practice, about inclusion, differentiation, dyslexia and other specific difficulties. I began to put into context some of the children I had encountered. Studying behaviour, I read with pride Steed, Young and Lawrence, understanding Jean's groundbreaking contribution to behaviour management. I delighted in being able to interview her for an essay.

I joined the council of the synagogue, then the smaller more strategic management committee and in time proudly became the community's first female co-chair. To this point I had had no formal leadership training and though experience supported me to do a competent job, I know that I could do a much better job now.

Just overlapping with my four years as chair I became Head of the *Cheder*, the synagogue religion school, where I had been teaching each Sunday morning. I have already alluded to the challenges of part-time Jewish education. It is probably one of the prime motivators for the compulsion of the Jewish community to open more and more Jewish day schools. It has become more challenging as more children from committed families go to Jewish schools and a higher percentage of children spend weekends between two parents. Personally, I have greater faith in the informal Jewish education sector to support Jewish continuity alongside the day schools. However, the almost 200 strong *Cheder* already had a good reputation locally, which I managed to retain and I enjoyed the role.

One day I received a call from a friend from student days, Jenni Frazer, currently Assistant Editor at the *Jewish Chronicle*, asking me if I would be interested in becoming local correspondent for our area. I had always enjoyed writing and at Hillel had been involved in the production of a magazine called *Mosaic*, edited by Joshua Rozenberg, now a prominent journalist.[5] I was delighted with this opportunity. My articles were published frequently and I even had a back page scoop when members of the local community hosted striking miners in 1984. I was also fortunate that my patch was Finchley, the constituency of the then Prime Minister, Margaret Thatcher.

---

5 Currently legal editor at the *Daily Telegraph*.

I thoroughly enjoyed my work for the paper, and even toyed with pursuing the journalistic path, but the pull of the primary classroom was greater.

I seized the opportunity of a few hours a week as a support assistant to a pupil at the boys' school. Hearing about this, one of the other mums, also a teacher said, 'Do you realise you could do similar work and be paid as a teacher?' Gab was by then attending school full time, so I contacted the head of service and was allocated to support pupils in three schools. Eleven years after Goldsmiths – a primary job at last!

Of the three schools my favourite was Bell Lane. It is quite hard to integrate as a part-time peripatetic support teacher. I remember one Christmas when I bought boxes of chocolates for each school. I sat in one staff room at break and no one spoke to me. I took the chocolates home.

People say that there is something special about Bell Lane, even when the children are not there. When we celebrated our centenary, the gathered alumni all spoke of it as a happy school and in 1996 the eyes of the Ofsted inspector sparkled with tears as she praised the atmosphere. The report opened with the statement: 'Bell Lane is the happiest and most welcoming of schools'.

At Bell Lane I had two pupils. One was a child with a difficult home background who lived with grandma. He was making good progress but still needed some extra help with Literacy. The other was a very angry and disturbed boy. He used to sit on the floor and rock and it was very difficult to get him to focus. On one occasion he was playing with the Legotechnic when he suddenly grabbed one of the wires and put it around another child's neck.

I started working at Bell Lane in November 1987 and in January 1989 the part-time remedial teacher was retiring. The Head was Leighton Thomas, a gregarious Welshman. Bell Lane was his second headship and he was in the process of doing what I came to admire as one of his greatest strengths: building and developing a strong team. He invited me to join the permanent staff. I was thrilled. It was part-time, it was Special Needs and it was close enough to home to be able to organise around the boys. Driving down the same road, I sometimes recall the thrill I felt driving the first morning to my permanent post.

At this point I should tell you, the reader, more about the school. Bell Lane is two form entry with a Nursery. It is a large school surrounded by smaller schools, primarily Catholic and Jewish. If you look at a socio-economic map of Barnet the severest deprivation is marked in red and the most affluent areas in white, with shades of yellow between. Bell Lane, nestled between the estates, is a small pocket of red surrounded mostly by pale yellow and white. Around it is some of the finest housing in the borough. Bell Lane children do not live there, and I was delighted when Barnet changed its logo from a detached house with a leaf in the middle.

Given the context, the school is characterised by high pupil mobility. Pupils come and go throughout the year. Last time we counted, pupils came from nine wards. Statistical reports indicate consistently high or very high levels of pupils on free school meals, refugees, asylum seekers and pupils with special needs. Around 70% do not speak English as their first language. As political crises and economic difficulties arise around the world, so the refugees come to Bell Lane. In my time we welcomed, among others, Asian Ugandans, Rwandans, Kurds, Iranians, Iraqis, Kosovans and Somalians. In 07/08 the largest immigrant group was Polish. For local benchmarking purposes the school is in family six of six, i.e. the most deprived, where in 07/08 it ranked ninth out of fourteen. In the first half term of 2008 the school took in 51 casual admissions across all years. It is, in short, a school in challenging circumstances.

In my work with individuals and groups I began to apply my learning about Special Needs as a whole school issue. Clearly there was little point in my working, for example on a child's handwriting if s/he spent the rest of the week in a class where there was no clear policy on letter formation.

When I supported in class I began to notice other pupils with similar difficulties who might benefit from help and began to advise teachers on how to adapt their planning or content to meet the needs.

In 1991 Leighton invited me to extend my role to full time SENCO, Special Needs Co-ordinator. This was a fairly new breed, a product of the Warnock Report. [6] My job was to co-ordinate provision for the SEN pupils and work with external professionals and agencies to support them. It was my

---

6 The present definition of special educational needs is based on the findings of the *Warnock Report* (DES, 1978). The Report has had lasting significance because it emphasized that special educational need is of crucial importance for all teachers and educationists, not just those in special schools. As such it emphasised that many children in mainstream schools experience difficulties (approximately 20% at some time in their school life) and consequently it is inappropriate to think of them as distinct and separate from those in special school or to educate them in separate institutions. The implications of the *Warnock Report* for ordinary schools and classroom teachers were immense. Clearly with one in five pupils likely to experience difficulties then special education would have to become an integral part of classroom teaching and the responsibility of all teachers.

dream job. My boys were of an appropriate age now and I was eager to have greater influence to raise awareness and improve practice across the school. I didn't want to be called in to take a child away and fix them. I firmly believe in the principle of every teacher a teacher of Special Needs.

Leighton was fantastically supportive. We instigated weekly SEN meetings to discuss strategy and raise children of concern. In any week we might include the school nurse, SEN governor, a psychologist, class teachers and support staff. He supported my request to dedicate some of my timetable to creating whole school spelling and handwriting programmes and released my colleague Colleen Wright, a highly talented teacher of literacy, to work alongside me on the spelling project.

We began to develop a good reputation in the authority. SENCOs from other schools visited and I was invited to address groups about our systems and policies. I attended conferences and exhibitions and began to see the impact of these outings. Our second Ofsted in 2000 praised our provision for SEN, and behaviour at the school, another aspect of my role was deemed 'good and often exemplary'.

A word about behaviour. I pay homage here to Jean for her highly significant role in highlighting the link between behaviour and context. If Special Needs is a whole school issue then behaviour is a whole school issue writ large. Policy needs to be clear. Everyone has to be involved in creating a code of conduct, clear about rewards and sanctions and absolutely consistent in application. I mentioned earlier Bell Lane's recent successful adoption of restorative approaches. To achieve success we had to commit time and resources, providing intensive training for over twenty members of teaching and support staff across the school and we constantly revisited and evaluated policy to ensure consistency.

I would have been quite content to continue in the SENCO role but in 1996 the Deputy Head resigned to take up her own headship and Leighton suggested that I should apply for the post. I enjoyed the strategic aspects of my work and with Gab at UCS the additional money would certainly be appreciated. I applied and was appointed.

It is worth noting that until this point I had not actually been a class teacher in a primary setting. Leighton rightly suggested that 'street cred' among the staff demanded that I have my own class, so in September 2000 I took up my new role as Deputy/SENCO, also teaching a vertically grouped Y5/6 class. Ofsted came in November. Once again Bell Lane was a good school.

We had a great team of very stable staff. They knew the school and the children well and were committed and well organised. I mention this because of something else that was happening. I write these words a few short months after Leighton died aged 67. During my years as deputy he was withdrawing more and more from the day to day running of the school, spending most of the day behind his desk, or talking to the office staff. He frequently commented, 'There's so much coming at you', and that the financial systems weren't providing him with up to date information. He never did classroom observation and delegated more and more to me. He was quick to temper and when we took on a member of staff who proved to be particularly difficult, he didn't seem to have the stamina to manage the situation decisively.

The staff became exasperated as he operated increasingly adrift. A particular example was a link project with schools in Holland and East Germany. It was a great project, and all credit was due to Leighton for successfully bidding for it and co-ordinating the early stages. However, his detachment from the day to day curriculum meant that staff were unclear about aims, objectives and expected outcomes. I recall particularly the exhibition to which the great and the good of the local community were invited. It coincided with the Rugby World Cup and while we climbed ladders and struggled with backing paper Leighton sat in his office watching the rugby on the television he had hired for the duration of the tournament.

During his last couple of years at the school Leighton was diagnosed with diabetes. Looking back I think his undiagnosed illness was having an impact on his ability to do the job. He travelled on the tube about an hour's journey from home each day. He arrived tired. One week he came into school by mistake on Sunday. Also, I think headteachers at that time were not well supported. I have been fortunate to have the benefits of the National College for School Leadership with its supportive development structure for heads. I have also had the benefit of being part of the Excellence Cluster, able to network with heads running schools similar to mine. It provides vital support. Leighton felt that our school was at such an extreme end of the spectrum that there was no one out there to help because no one could really understand, and so he had become increasingly insular and deskilled.

Our wonderful team worked impressively and effectively round the situation. The impact on me was considerable. I uncharacteristically lost a lot of weight. On one of my regular visits to the doctor to check my blood pressure, prone to be high, I was given a twenty-four hour heart monitor because despite the weight loss, it was unusually high.

I began to look for headships. I went for an interview in another authority and by the time they asked me the question, 'If we offered you the job, would you accept?' I had decided that I would not. The other two were in local schools. The feedback was good. In the first interview I lost out to an experienced head seeking a second post, in the second I was told I was the runner up.

While the Ofsted team had praised Leighton's strong leadership the lead inspector opened a discussion with him about retirement. In time he informed me that he intended to retire in July 2000 then he brought it forward to January. I did not really want to leave Bell Lane, so I gladly accepted the role of Acting Head, applied for the substantive role and beat two other candidates, both seeking a second headship, to become Head in February 2001.

Headship

I felt very well prepared to lead Bell Lane. Given the situation leading up to my appointment I had been actively involved in all aspects of running the school. I had also discovered that my Special Needs Diploma could count towards a Masters degree and so, during my time as deputy I took modules in mentoring and educational management to complete the qualification. I really enjoyed the course and got consistently high grades; quite an achievement for someone who had written herself off as a student aged eighteen.

My post as deputy was taken by Sarah Sands, a talented Literacy, EAL and Early Years specialist, with whom I had worked at the school for about ten years. It was a good partnership and Sarah was very supportive. To the local authority we were a 'light touch' school. We had had two successful Ofsted inspections and were deemed 'good and improving'. We did not appear high up the league tables because of our profile, but progress data shows that pupils do well, particularly the stable cohort. Outcomes usually guarantee valued targeted support from advisers for maths, literacy or both.

We were largely left to get on with it and in retrospect I think we were in a vulnerable situation. Despite my familiarity with the school I now know that as a new head I needed more support; a critical friend, a mentor. I was given the name of a mentor colleague but without a structure to support the process the relationship never got off the ground, and neither of us pursued it. This was just before Ofsted identified weaknesses in the local authority, prompting significant restructuring. The support for heads is now considerably improved.

Three things happened very shortly after I was appointed. Firstly, I attended a meeting inviting local schools to bid for lottery funding for sports facilities. It was a wonderful opportunity for our pupils, many of whom do not have gardens, and whose families need support to provide a healthy lifestyle. Through my work in Israeli dance I was acutely aware of the shortage of decent sports facilities locally and the community aspect of the project, with its potential for increasing our income from lettings held great appeal.

I put forward a proposal for a sports hall to replace our dilapidated second hall (known ironically as 'the new hall', being newer than the 'old hall'!) I was invited, with the support of sport consultants, to pursue the bid. It was a lengthy two-part process which, in the event, diverted a huge amount of my time and energy over a three year period.

Second, at my first residential conference for local heads a group of us were called together and informed of a new government initiative called 'Excellence in Clusters'. This was an extension of 'Excellence in Cities', through which the Labour Government was providing enhanced funding for areas identified under their social inclusion agenda. They had become aware that within broadly affluent and high achieving authorities like Barnet there exist scattered pockets of deprivation where children are at higher risk of failing in the education system. The idea was to bring schools like mine together as a network and provide three funding streams; learning mentors, gifted and talented provision, and a tailored strand through which we could take a chosen focus to improve teaching and learning.

The cluster has been highly successful in Barnet, and the school community has benefited greatly from it. Looking back, though, I recognise that I was not experienced enough to manage a substantial new funding stream, particularly the tailored element, which I allowed to take us off in development areas that were not relevant for our needs at that time. It is said that the Head should be like an umbrella, sheltering the school from initiative overload. I do it much better now. I also rashly took on the role of Co-Chair of the cluster, alongside a secondary colleague. I was used to chairing and excited by the opportunities offered by the network. At that point in time, though, it was not a good move.

The third change taking place was a turnover of staff. It was in fact the beginning of a period of considerable staff mobility at the school which was to last for the next five years. As I mentioned earlier, we had had a wonderfully stable staff team. Generally people like to work at Bell Lane and stay with us. However, we had a couple of retirements, several colleagues moved away to Devon, India, Italy and four colleagues went simultaneously on maternity leave, three of them senior leaders. It was a time of shortage, when the *Times Educational Supplement* made an entry in the *Guinness Book of Records* with so many vacancies in April 2002 that it ran to 950 pages. My concern about not getting staff led to some inappropriate appointments. I am much more circumspect now in waiting to get the right people.

It was in the summer of 2003 that I realised that things were not right. The barometer for Bell Lane is the achievement of the stable cohort who, as I noted previously, traditionally achieve at or above expected levels. Too many of them had underachieved. I called my Link Inspector. Surprised at the concern in my voice, she told me to be my normal calm, intelligent self and not to panic. Easier said than done for I recall very clearly a weekend break in Oxford with Maurice during the half term that October when I sat on the edge of the bed trying hard to regulate my breathing! Over the years Bell Lane became so much a part of me that I could sense physically when things were not right.

The Link Inspector asked whether I wanted to put the school into the category of 'cause for concern'. I thought this was a good idea because it would attract support. In retrospect I am not convinced it was the right move because in some eyes I think it created a deficit model that persisted until the next Ofsted. Supply teachers and visitors were still telling me what a wonderful school I ran, but at this time I could only see what was wrong.

From where did I derive support through this difficult time? Locally it was difficult; I used to walk into head teacher meetings and feel that I was surrounded by people who could do it, while I could not. We were allocated a link advisory head from a very different setting whom I could work with, but who several of the staff found unsympathetic. When the secondment ended we were allocated Kris Chowdhry, former head of a similar school to Bell Lane in Haringey, who had been doing advisory work for a while. Kris gelled perfectly. She was able to provide just the right blend of support and challenge; a true critical friend who went on to provide excellent support and guidance to the school and particularly to me in her roles as vice-chair of governors and project manager for our Children's Centre. Every head teacher needs support like this.

I mentioned earlier how fortunate I was that my headship coincided with the opening of the National College for School Leadership. In 2002 I had joined the pilot of the 'New Visions' early headship course. There are advantages and disadvantages to pilot courses. While there may be aspects that subsequently improve, they are usually much cheaper or free. I paid nothing for New Visions, which was one of the best professional development courses I have ever taken. The course introduced me to the work of leadership gurus like Michael Fullan and John West-Burnham and filled in the theoretical background to the leadership roles I had undertaken largely instinctively to this point. New Visions also gave me a fine mentor in the person of my tutor, Pat Clark, who was at that time International Director at the Institute of Education. I had met and been impressed by Pat on the 'Headlamp' training for new heads and was delighted to discover that she was to be my tutor.

A core element of the course was the triads, groups of three who visited each others' schools. We built some very supportive relationships and when the course ended, continued to study together for a while, including a British Council sponsored visit to schools in Melbourne, Australia.

During our period as 'cause for concern' the group was a great source of support, especially when they visited and gave me their honest and more positive take on how things were going.

I also had excellent internal support. This period gave me clear understanding of the term 'blind panic', because when I stopped panicking and began to draw on my training and skills, I began to see the way forward. My first move was to reduce the strategic team to just myself, Sarah and three trusted and hard-working colleagues who between them had a range of experience and skills that I thought could take us forward. We worked very hard, action planning, observing, coaching, and evaluating. There were some welcome resignations and we did some redeployment.

In the summer of 2005 the Link Inspector suggested that we should have an interim review in the autumn term. By this time we felt we had a handle on the strengths and weaknesses and were making progress, but the review report was not particularly encouraging. This was one of the outcomes that made me question the 'cause for concern' decision. I felt that the review was conducted with a negative mindset.

Throughout this period I hoped that Ofsted would not visit. It had been six years since our last inspection and the recently introduced new framework for inspections brought a rash of visits throughout the authority. Under the new system the six week notice period had been reduced to a few days. The call came the Thursday before May Bank Holiday 2006. The inspection team wanted to come in Wednesday and Thursday the following week. On the Thursday the school was scheduled to be a polling station for the local elections, so the visit was brought forward to Tuesday and Wednesday.

Although staff did come in over the weekend it was encouraging to note that there was not a great panic to strip walls and put up displays. The good practice already in place and the work we had done to emphasise the importance of consistency meant that the school was ready.

The inspection was our first experience of the shortened version, using our SEF (Self-Evaluation Form) as the starting point. Although during the two days the focus was very clearly on Maths and English, specifically on outcomes in Y2 an Y6, there was a notable effort to drill down into the results to identify the value-added impact of our teaching.

At the end of the first day the feedback was promising but questions were raised about the effectiveness of middle managers, which would impact on the outcome for leadership and management. The role of subject leaders in primary schools has received much scrutiny in recent years, moving them away from routine tasks like managing learning resources to a much more strategic role in raising standards. We had moved with this agenda, but due to high staff turnover some key post holders were inexperienced and not yet performing as we wanted. I was determined to get at least as good an outcome as my predecessor for leadership and management and was not going to let this go without a fight. I told the lead inspector, 'Whatever you say about middle managers, if we are marked down for leadership and management that means me'. By the morning of day two she was able to assure me that leadership and management were good.

In fact, we came out good in all areas. The lead inspector commented that she felt that the local authority had been hard on us in the review. She laid considerable emphasis on staff turnover in the preceding few years, and it is interesting to note that it is only at the time of writing, when Bell Lane is again working to capacity with greater stability that I can really appreciate the impact. Such a school thrives on stability and consistency.

During the worst of the times described I of course considered moving on. But if things had gone wrong, then I had a responsibility, and had to play my part in putting us back on track. I also needed to restore my own self-confidence and self-esteem, to be able to walk into a room of head teachers and feel again that I was among peers. On a purely pragmatic level, headship, especially of a school the size of Bell Lane, is well remunerated. I could not easily match the salary in a different role, and in an age of uncertain pensions the teachers' pension fund is still robust. Apart from this, I love Bell Lane and had a strong connection to the school and its community. I had worked hard to bring the school to where it was. I was proud of my achievements and I wanted to develop it further.

Shortly before the Ofsted inspection Sarah, my deputy left. It was an excellent partnership and we often used to joke that we had a 'suicide pact' – if I ever left she would, and if she ever left, I would. She would have been very happy being a career deputy, but this changed when her long term relationship with another member of staff ended. The local authority from time to time has vacancies for acting heads and to ease the very difficult situation for them both at school I began to explore this possibility. This has turned out extremely well. With her experience at Bell Lane and having completed her National Professional Qualification for Headship (NPQH) Sarah was more than ready for headship, and is now really enjoying being the successful leader of a delightful local infant school.

The role of Acting Deputy was taken by my wonderful EMAG (Ethnic Minority Achievement Grant) co-ordinator, Julia Hughes. This appointment followed a period of development in Special Needs provision, in response to which we extended Sarah's role as SENCO so that Julia became Acting Deputy and Inclusion Manager, with oversight of all aspects of inclusion, from children with statements of special needs to those identified as gifted and talented.

In the term following the Ofsted inspection we advertised the Deputy Head post and were extremely fortunate to recruit Jason Marantz, a Canadian whose previous experience in this country was exclusively in the Jewish sector. Jason is an ambitious young man who recognised that the experience of working in a Jewish primary school is very different from what he would learn working at a school like Bell Lane. Let me give you an example. Just round the corner from the school is a local Jewish primary. One morning the Head came to visit. It was the same morning that one of our drug addicted parents turned up at school, flashing her breasts at a member of staff in the playground and demanding to remove her daughter from the school. As she left to walk the few hundred metres and light years to her school my colleague replied, 'I'm going back to Paradise'.

We employed Jason with responsibility for Teaching and Learning and Julia, became Assistant Head/Inclusion Manager. This made my role much more strategic. The professional partnership with these two remarkable people, supported by an increasingly competent and confident staff team set the school firmly on the path from good to outstanding.

Readers may wonder how a Jewish Head and a Jewish Deputy are accepted in a multi-faith school like Bell Lane. Though it is in the heart of Jewish Hendon, the school attracts just a few Jewish pupils, usually of mixed faith parentage. The local Jewish population sends its children to Jewish or independent schools. However, because of where it is the school attracts a high proportion of Jewish staff and governors. It is also worth noting that several members of staff are strong adherents to other faiths. I think this is because of the values that compel them to work with the more disadvantaged elements in society.

In all the years I worked at Bell Lane, which included some very challenging times for interfaith relations (the Gulf War, 9/11, three intifadas) my religion never presented a problem. My only discomfort as a Jew was once when talking in the staff room about holidaying in Israel. A local authority advisor who was present commented, 'Oh, yes, I can just imagine them all in their gold lamé bikinis'. I have always had great respect from parents of other faiths. I find it very moving when a Somali or Pakistani mother with her head covered wishes me 'Happy New Year' on *Rosh Hashannah*. One Friday as Jason was about to leave to get home for Shabbat he was asked by the office staff to see a Moslem parent who wanted to take his children early to reach the mosque by sunset. There is much more to unite us than to divide us. My experience is that parents with a strong faith are grateful to have their children in a school with a strong set of values, which seeks to understand, respect and celebrate all faiths.

Jason was never destined to stay long at Bell Lane, he is too good a catch for the Jewish community, Early in 2008 he was appointed Head of Wolfson Hillel Primary, the orthodox school where he was Assistant Head prior to coming to Bell Lane. I look forward to watching with pride the school's future development under his inspired leadership.

A cross-section of pupil population at Bell Lane Primary School.

Good to Outstanding – the Challenges Ahead

Looking forward to the pre-retirement years at Bell Lane, the challenge was to take the school from good to great. In 2006 I attended a course with that title and then invited a local colleague whose school was rated outstanding by Ofsted to address my Leadership Learning Group. In her striking presentation she simply took the school's mission statement and explained each word in terms of the practices and systems they have in place to realise the vision. This then was our task; to articulate and share the vision and ensure that we all worked consistently towards our goals. What follows is a review of some of the areas that present a challenge in achieving this aim.

Extended services

In 2003 Tony Blair's Labour Government launched its 'Every Child Matters' agenda, primarily in response to institutional failings in cases like the death of Victoria Climbié. I remember when I was a SENCO going to national Special Needs conferences which bemoaned the lack of joined-up thinking between Education, Health and Social Services, and such cases were examples of these failings writ large. The ECM agenda recognised that successful outcomes for young people required a holistic approach to their welfare and education.

A significant outcome of this welcome shift was the requirement for schools to offer a range of extended services, ideally from 8.00 am to 6.00 pm. Not surprisingly Bell Lane was identified early on for designation as a Children's Centre. We had always successfully provided a range of after school activities and the Excellence Cluster funding supported us to sustain and develop these, but the Children's Centre initiative had a wider vision. From November 2007, as well as after school and breakfast clubs, we began to offer services for under-5s and their parents such as Job Seekers' Advice, support to quit smoking, baby clinics, access to library services and health visitors.

The Government set itself very ambitious targets for the establishment of such centres, stating in 2005 that, 'by March 2006, Children's Centres are expected to reach at least 650,000 pre-school children in the 20% most disadvantaged wards'. We were in tranche 2, which further extended the provision. To achieve this they provided a very large amount of start-up money to be spent by March 2008, with more to follow.

The initiative was a mixed blessing for me and for Bell Lane. In the first instance, like so many recent initiatives it suddenly appeared among my priorities to be implemented in a very short period of time. This made it very hard to hold on to our existing priorities and I was grateful at this time to have a strong senior team. The money that we were given enabled us to adequately manage the start up, including appointing Kris Chowdhry for two days a week as Project Manager, but future funding arrangements were not entirely clear.

The Government vision for the Children's Centre was 8.00 am to 6.00 pm provision for 48 weeks a year. There was to be more staff, some of whom would be employed on different terms and conditions from the teaching and support staff, and there would be much liaison with other agencies and providers. At no time in the process did anyone come to the heads involved and say, This is the new role and here are the terms and conditions attached to it. So my fellow head teachers and I had to lobby hard to get clarification. Only when some centres locally had been up and running for over a year, was consideration given at national level to the implications for heads' pay and conditions.

In anticipation of the changes I began a new year-long qualification, the National Professional Qualification for Integrated Centre Leadership, alongside early years professionals who work both within and outside school settings. However, the course covered much of the same leadership ground as courses like Leadership Programme for Serving Heads (LPSH), which I had already completed, and there was far less focus on the management aspects than I had hoped. It was the first time in my academic career I had withdrawn from a course.

I deeply believed in the principles behind the Children's Centre, but was very afraid that in the way it had been introduced it was going to be difficult to fully integrate and would be essentially an add-on that would detract heads from existing priorities and increase the burden on senior colleagues.

Building

The history of the Bell Lane building is somewhat strange. The original buildings were erected in 1901, comprising separate infant and junior schools. In the 1960s the infant school was knocked down. No one really knows why, and I have even heard it suggested that it was a mistake. When I arrived at the school there were plans for rebuilding which were subsequently shelved because of lack of resources.

My predecessor coped with the reduced accommodation and with pupil mobility by running the school as one and a half form entry, with vertically grouped classes, which I phased out as an unnecessary level of complexity.

To house the full two forms of entry we added demountable accommodation so that the site now comprises the main building, a demountable Nursery, a two-room Horsa hut which houses the Y1 classes, a two-room demountable for Reception and a new two-room demountable for the Children's Centre. The Sports Hall block was added in 2005, linked to the main building.

During my time at the school the government provided welcome ring-fenced funding to improve school buildings, and I used this to improve the learning environment in line with my vision for the school. I refurbished or replaced all the toilets, replaced a small kitchen with one where healthy meals can be cooked freshly each day, and improved the outdoor environment. As part of the sports hall initiative we moved the office downstairs, and we added disabled toilets and ramps, making the school much more accessible.

In 2003 the local authority identified primary school buildings in need of major improvement and Bell Lane was not surprisingly included. A bid was made for Private Finance Initiative funding which was unsuccessful. This, in view of the experience of PFI in education, might have been a blessing. Then in 2005 the Government announced its 'Building Schools for the Future' initiative, proposing to refurbish or replace all secondary schools. Barnet restated the commitment to rebuild primary schools through the PSCIP (Primary School Capital Investment Programme). This ambitious project includes closures and amalgamations across the borough. Funding comes primarily from sale of land on some primary sites. The Bell Lane site is closely enclosed by housing on all sides, so that we would be beneficiaries of sales elsewhere, but not able to contribute. Until summer 2007 it was also hoped that additional funding would derive from the generous allocation for Children's Centres, but the directive was for this money to be spent before March 2008. Bell Lane's rebuild, including a purpose built Children's Centre was scheduled for 2009. For two years I spent many hours blue sky thinking, preparing outcome specifications and visiting other schools to get ideas for the new building.

In autumn 2007 I attended a meeting at which we were informed that due to a whole set of national and local circumstances and miscalculations the programme had to be altered. Once again Bell Lane came off the priority list and now stands little chance of being rebuilt earlier than 2012.

It was deeply upsetting news. This was my pre-retirement project. So the school continues to make do and mend to provide the best possible twenty-first century education in a deteriorating Victorian building.

Raising standards

When I was interviewed for the headship at Bell Lane I said that I wanted to create a 'target-busting environment'. I am not afraid of targets but I believe that they have to be fit for purpose. Each year in the autumn term we set targets for the percentage of Level 4s (the expected level at age 11) and L5 (pupils achieving above that level) expected from the current Year 5, to achieve at the end of Year 6. These are sent to the Education Department (currently known as the DCSF) and form part of the overall targets for the Local Authority.

Let me describe a fairly typical Bell Lane cohort at the end of Y6. The cohort comprises 44 children of which 61% speak a language other than English; 18% are on the Special Needs Register at School Action, School Action Plus (outside agency intervention) or statemented (resourced individual provision); almost 40% of the cohort arrived since the KS1 SATs tests in Y2 so that we cannot give an accurate progress measure across the key stage; five of the pupils do not sit the tests because they arrived after the start of Y5 with little or no English, so have not been able to access the curriculum at the requisite level. They are not counted in the published outcomes and require a considerable amount of support to have a meaningful learning experience alongside pupils preparing for KS2 SATs tests.

A further six, because of the extent of their special needs, or because of their language needs, sometimes combined with learning difficulties, are teacher assessed at below the level to be entered for one or more of the tests. They are nevertheless included in the published cohort, each child representing 3%. Throughout the life of this cohort 47 pupils have left, or joined and left.

In such a context we can and should set targets. We can set targets for the stable cohort; we can set individual or group curricular targets in different subjects across the year; we can set targets for the rate of progress. A target for how many of the cohort will match the achievement of their peers nationwide is meaningless.

For two years running in 2007 and 2008 Bell Lane achieved the Barnet average for value added. This is a meaningful measure of its success.

A curriculum for the Twenty-first Century

I referred earlier to the concept of 'futures thinking'. Progress in many areas is so fast that we do not have a clear picture of the world for which we are preparing the children currently in school.

The advent of the National Curriculum created a generation of teachers concerned to deliver content. Recent education documents such as 'Excellence and Enjoyment' and 'Every Child Matters' have thankfully re-aligned our focus to consider the role of schools in designing a curriculum to develop creative and adaptable lifelong learners with a range of learning skills. This is the challenge in terms of developing a relevant twenty-first century curriculum for all children.

Creating community

At the very beginning of my contribution to this book I referred to the vital triangle of child, home and school. In my comments about faith schools I noted that they benefit from a sense of community. For me this is a key element in education.

Bell Lane has wonderful, supportive parents, but many of them, whether because of their own school experience, language and cultural differences or pressures of time do not engage easily with the school community. To increase their engagement in the community and in their children's learning is a seminal task. There are some very hard to reach parents. Of particular concern are those with mental illness or victims of drug or alcohol abuse. The school has some superb staff with specific responsibilities in relation to parents who are really moving this agenda forward. The Children's Centre also opens up exciting new opportunities for the relationship with families.

The school is committed to forming relationships across communities, a vital task in our fractured society. We were proud to be featured in a government publication *Faith in the System*[7] for our relationship with a local Jewish

---

7 *Faith in the System: The Role of Schools with a religious character in English education and society,* DCSF, September 2007. For a downloadable pdf of this report see http://www.dfes.gov.uk/publications/faithinthesystem/index.shtml

school. Bell Lane welcomes volunteers, many of them senior citizens from the local community who help in classes. The curriculum features a range of visits and visitors and the school supports international, national and local charities. There are many more possibilities to exploit in our global village.

We can only create community if the staff team provides a strong role model. In 1992/3 we had three part-time 'welfare' assistants and a Nursery Nurse, today there is a much larger and more complex staff team including eleven teaching assistants, two Learning Mentors, three Nursery Nurses, three admin assistants, two site managers, three kitchen staff and six cleaners. Reform of the school workforce and recent staffing restructures have created some tensions in the relationship between teaching and non-teaching staff. As suggested earlier, the different roles in the Children's Centre will add a further level of complexity. The work that we did on Restorative Approaches is supportive of team building but there is more to do in understanding the group dynamics and improving staff cohesion to create the best possible environment for effective learning.

Funding

In 1985, before the local management of schools, my predecessor managed a budget of £6,000. By 1995 this had increased to £570,000 and in 07/08 our budget was over £1.6 million. Every penny of it is clearly targeted towards providing the best possible outcomes for all children.

Under the umbrella of the Labour Government's Social Inclusion agenda Bell Lane has benefited from enhanced funding to address the needs of a challenging context. This is welcome, and must be sustained if the school is to realise the vision.

Staffing

In the worst of times at Bell Lane staff mobility against a backdrop of teacher shortage was a major contributing factor. The school needs a good, stable staff team to function at its best.

As I write, the supply of teachers is reasonably good, but during my time in education a mis-match in supply and demand has frequently presented a real threat. Another threat is the cost of housing, which in the area of the school is high. In recent years young staff members at the school have taken advantage of welcome schemes to support key workers in finding affordable housing in London, and such schemes should continue to ensure that we can retain our finest young educators.

These, then, are some of the challenges that lie ahead. When I was interviewed for the Bell Lane headship I was asked, 'How do you recognise a successful school?' I spoke about the 'buzz' that you can feel in a happy and effective school. Bell Lane today has a wonderful buzz. With a clear grasp of strengths and areas of development, and a talented, committed and hard-working staff I am confident that the school now has the capacity to be outstanding.

Other Projects

Holocaust education

One day in 2006 I was searching on the Imperial War Museum website for an appropriate educational visit for one of our year groups, when I spotted an item about the museum's Fellowship in Holocaust Education. The Fellowship is a year-long programme to develop leading teachers for teaching the Holocaust.

Throughout my childhood I heard from my mother about her gentle cousin Esther from Belgium and her family, whose much awaited visits to weddings and other happy events came to an abrupt end with the war. I learnt about their pleas to the family here to help and the fruitless efforts of my grandfather to do so. I was shown the telegrams from France stamped with the swastika. I helped my mother trace them through Yad Vashem, the Holocaust Memorial Centre in Israel, where we learnt of their deportation from Belgium to Auschwitz. In 1999 I visited Auschwitz and lit memorial candles for them.

These experiences are foremost among many I have had as a post-Holocaust generation Jew that have formed the basis of my deep commitment to Holocaust education. At Bell Lane I learnt that harmonious co-existence in a diverse community can be significantly supported by telling another's story, by an understanding of each other's culture and history, and by finding common links to support that understanding.

Many Bell Lane families over the years were, and sadly still are refugees and asylum seekers such as Somalians, Kosovans and Rwandans. Teaching

Staff at Bell Lane Primary School dressed for the religious ceremony of Eid.

about the Holocaust and linking it to their experiences can provide powerful foundations for educating the whole school community about injustice, bullying, prejudice, and the importance of integrity, fairness and peace.

Thus, it was that in 2006/7 I undertook the Fellowship. In July 2006 I spent a week at the Imperial War Museum where we heard lectures from experts such as Professor David Cesarani, and Stephen Feinberg of the United States Holocaust Memorial Museum, interspersed with fascinating sessions on pedagogy. In February our group of 25 educators from across the UK spent another memorable week at Yad Vashem, the Holocaust Memorial Centre in Jerusalem. There we learnt about the centre's educational philosophy of teaching about the Holocaust as the story of real lives, of neighbours in the twentieth century. We visited sites of different faiths in the Old City of Jerusalem to explore the theme of historical narratives and had wonderful sessions on history and pedagogy from the centre's remarkable staff team. We met Professor Walter Zvi Bacharach, a religious survivor of Auschwitz who challenged us with his personal insight into the theology of the Holocaust, and Marian Gerstenfeld, who told us how honoured she was to address a group from England, the home of the soldiers who liberated her from Bergen-Belsen.

Back at school I worked for just over a term with a group of able Y5 pupils on a project for the course. The group reflected the very diverse nature

Holocaust Project, Bell Lane Primary School, 2002.

of our school community and included refugees and pupils who had arrived speaking no English. I wrote to the parents to ask for their permission for the children to be included in the project. They all readily accepted, some citing their own experiences as a reason for their positive response.

The outcome of our project is a web resource, which tells the story of Bernd Koschland, a former colleague from JFS and good friend and neighbour of the school, who came to England at the age of eight on the Kindertransport. Bernd, a former teacher was wonderfully generous with his involvement, visiting the school for lessons and assemblies, accompanying us to the Jewish Museum in Finchley and even entertaining the children with orange juice and biscuits at his home as he showed them precious artefacts representing his last links with his murdered parents.

I am now in the process of disseminating the resource to other educators, and hope in the future to use the learning from this year to ensure that the memory of those who perished will be, as we Jews say, 'for a blessing' in preparing young people for a better world.

In October 2007 I undertook the final study visit of the course to Lithuania and Poland. We visited Vilnius (Vilna), Kaunus (Kovno), Warsaw, Lodz, Krakow and the sites of the camps at Treblinka and Auschwitz Birkenau.

In Lithuania, where once thriving communities of numerous Jews lived, worked, worshipped and celebrated, we focused particularly on the void. In Vilnius, the 'Jerusalem of Lithuania', which teemed with Jews actively involved in community and rich learning activities we learnt that a handful of elderly men are now paid to attend the fine synagogue.

We visited the sites of mass graves at Ponary and The Ninth Fort and other sites of Jewish resistance and massacre by the Nazis and by their neighbours. We experienced some excellent learning about pedagogy at historical sites. At Ponary we discussed how the survivors could say *kaddish*, the 'orphan's' prayer extolling God, for their murdered loved ones. In the Vilna ghetto, using eye-witness accounts, we debated the motivation of Yaakov Gens, the head of the Jewish council. Was he a villain or a saviour?

Warsaw was a revelation. A thriving twenty-first century city; a phoenix from the ashes of blanket bombing. Here I had scant time to begin to search for my roots. Within the area designated as the infamous Warsaw ghetto I found Zimna Street, where my father's brother Herschel lived until all contact was lost in 1941. I searched unsuccessfully for Solna Street, where my grandparents lived before their inspired departure in the 1920s. But the streets are different now, post-war estates bearing no resemblance to the fine flat that my grandmother kept so immaculately that the local estate agent used it as a show flat.

From his orphanage in Warsaw we traced the journey of Janusz Korczak, the remarkable educator whose vision laid the foundation for the Universal Rights of the Child. We visited the Jewish cemetery where we saw the statue of Korczak marching through the city with his children to the infamous Umschlagplatz, then herded to death at Treblinka.

Among the thousands of stones that commemorate the lost communities, by the one stone bearing the name of a person, Janusz Korczak, our inspirational facilitator, Paul Salmons, challenged our educational vision. Paul, the former Holocaust Education Co-ordinator at the Imperial War Museum, believes that deep learning takes place 'at the uncomfortable edge of experience'.

In *How to Love Children* Korczak writes: 'You will never understand children if you ignore their qualities.' How often, I mused at that time, are we educators driven by what we have to teach, not the individuals whom we are teaching. Is twenty-first century British education able to deliver learning which will create a society in which such events could never happen?

I felt deeply uncomfortable in Kazimierz, the Jewish quarter in Krakow. I think Hitler would have loved it. Helped by the Hollywood hype around *Schindler's List* Kazimierz has evolved as a kind of Jewish theme park. The railings in the town square are in the form of the menorah and while the '*kosher* style' restaurants offer edible and audible 'schmaltz' there is only one place where the food is actually *kosher*. Tourists could go away thinking that the ghetto existed in the quaint narrow streets of Kazimierz, while it was actually across the river, on the other side of the bridge across which the community was herded like animals.

Listening to the klezmer ensemble playing nostalgic Yiddish melodies I felt deep pride in the work of Maurice's Israeli Dance Institute in bringing the authentic diverse richness of pre- and post-war Jewish culture to Jewish communities in Eastern Europe, Turkey and Argentina as they struggle to reassert or maintain their identity.

I had been to Auschwitz Birkenau before on a day trip. But with the fellowship it was an entirely different experience. John West-Burnham talks about levels of learning as shallow, deep and profound. This time my learning, against the background of the study programme, went to a deeper and more challenging level.

In his sincere efforts to accommodate the most observant member of the group, Paul had arranged the visit to Auschwitz overnight on Friday. So it was that we bizarrely spent *Shabbat* in a hotel overlooking the camp. This was also the *Shabbat* before my father's *Yahrzeit*. [8] As our visit came to an end in the gathering dusk I stood by the destroyed crematoria and said together the

---

8 *Yahrzeit* is a commemoration of the death of a Jew by a mourner (the child, sibling, spouse or parent of the deceased). The date of the *Yahrzeit*, which is calculated according to the Hebrew calendar, is the anniversary of the death, not the burial. The anniversary of the death of a loved one is naturally a solemn day, and Judaism helps the mourner experience this pain and and also honours the memory of the deceased via *Yahrzeit* rituals. The main expression of the *Yahrzeit* is reciting the Mourner's *kaddish* prayer. Lighting a *Yahrzeit* candle, a special memorial candle that burns for 24 hours, is another *Yahrzeit* practice. The candle should be lit after dark on the evening before the anniversary of the death and burn for a full 24 hours. Many people visit the graves of the deceased on the *Yahrzeit*, and some people observe *Yahrzeit* by fasting. While Jews have observed *Yahrzeit* since Talmudic times, the ceremony was not called *Yahrzeit* until the sixteenth century. The word comes from the German word *Yahrzeit*, a word used by the Christian Church for the occasion of honouring the dead.

Kaddish for my dear father and the for the souls of all those murdered in that terrible place. The emotion was almost more than I could bear.

Back at the hotel, we Jewish participants invited the the non-Jews (the majority) to join us making *havdallah*, the beautiful ceremony separating *Shabbat* and the rest of the week. We read passages about how the Jews in the Holocaust had defiantly found ways to similarly celebrate. With wine and spices, song and dance, it was a powerful reaffirmation.

There is one more aspect of my involvement in the course that I want to highlight. Opposite our house is the Finchley Catholic High School. Mari Martin, who leads on Restorative Approaches for Barnet and is a governor at Finchley Catholic, heard of my participation in the Fellowship and told me about a play about the Holocaust called *Remember* being produced at the school. This information brought me into contact with a remarkable educational project led by a remarkable group of people. I contacted the school, explained about the Fellowship, and offered my help. They truly did not need it. During 2006/7 the play was performed at the school, and at the local Arts Depot theatre. Not satisfied with this, the visionary production team, under the leadership of Mark Sell, took the play to Poland where it was performed in Krakow and at Auschwitz. The chronicle of this amazing journey can be found on the school's website. [9] Then one day when I visited the production team they mentioned their desire to perform in a synagogue. I was delighted to be able to facilitate this with the New North London, which welcomed them with open arms. The evening was a resounding success. It was a very emotional experience to listen to Catholic youngsters singing in perfect Hebrew under the eternal lamp in my synagogue. They sang the heartfelt prayer Ani Maamin ('I believe') and the song of the Jewish partisans, and through their retelling from the point of view of victims, perpetrators and bystanders indeed, helped to ensure that we will 'Remember'. Rabbi Wittenberg praised their courage.

The following day I wrote to Mark:

It was truly humbling for me as the daughter of Jewish immigrants of that era to see the story of my people's suffering told so empathetically. It is no secret that that period was a very difficult one in Jewish-Catholic relations, and your play brings such healing – I really hope that the encounter in the synagogue will bring together the youngsters of the two com-

---

9 http://www.finchleycatholic.org.uk/music2.asp

munities. Though you pulled no punches in describing the horrors, the evening left me with optimism that especially we in education have the power to bring change.

JCOSS

I have written earlier about the impact of the polarisation within the Anglo-Jewish community. Nowhere is this more acutely felt than in its educational provision. In Greater London there are over 20 Jewish primary schools and about a dozen Jewish secondary schools (I am not being specific because new schools are opening all the time). Three of the Jewish primaries are affiliated to the combined Liberal, Reform and Masorti movements, the rest are under the auspices of the orthodox or ultra-orthodox sectors.

Although schools under the auspices of the United Synagogue, the 'mainstream' orthodox movement, nominally accept pupils from across the religious spectrum, their admissions criteria are such as to exclude those married or converted in the Liberal, Reform and Masorti movements. This has led to real heartache for children wishing to transfer particularly from the three non-orthodox Jewish primaries. There are tales of parents having to search abroad for photos and documentation to provide evidence of their eligibility. Parental choice currently does not exist for Jewish parents who are not able to meet the entrance criteria for the Jewish secondaries, all of which have exclusive admissions criteria. In an inclusive educational environment this state of affairs, the recent target of legal challenge, does no credit to the community. Another notable gap in Jewish provision is for pupils with severe special needs.

In 2000 I was asked to represent the Masorti movement on the Jewish Community Day School Advisory Board, a group which brings together representatives from the Liberal, Reform and Masorti movements to oversee day school development. About a year after I joined we began to support a small but very dynamic group with a remarkable vision for changing the face of Jewish secondary education by providing a cross-community Jewish secondary school.

The vision of the Jewish Cross Communal Secondary School (JCOSS) is described on the website as follows:

> …because of the rigid definition of who is a Jew, there is little real choice for some Jewish families. JCoSS will be different. The JCoSS admission policy will enable students from Reform, Liberal, Masorti, Sephardi, United and Federation backgrounds, together

with students from unaffiliated families, to be educated alongside each other on an equal basis. JCOSS will combine a first-class secular education with a ground-breaking Jewish studies programme. [10]

The Norwood connection is particularly exciting. It is British Jewry's leading family and children's charity in partnership with whom JCOSS, uniquely in the Jewish community, will provide a leading-edge Special Education Needs resource, open not only to the new school but also to the wider Jewish community and other local schools.

In October 2003 I visited Melbourne, Australia with my New Visions group and had the privilege of spending three days living the dream of JCOSS at Bialik College, a superb Jewish cross-communal school. What follows is an extract from an article I wrote for my synagogue magazine on my return:

> As we entered the building we saw around us lively young people in royal blue and yellow tracksuits. The adults in the building included some men wearing kippot (skullcaps), some not, women in trousers and some in skirts and dresses, one or two with a scarf or even a sheitel (wig). My excitement increased as I realised that I had fortuitously found my way to a cross-communal school of the type envisioned by the JCOSS project.

Bialik College is a remarkable institution, whose inspirational leader until recently was Genia Janover. In the 17 years that Genia was head, the school grew, through her vision, from a 350 strong failing primary to a school of 1040 pupils from Kindergarten to Y12, representing 600 families. In terms of ability and special need it is fully inclusive; 1 in 6 pupils does not pay fees. Genia describes the school as 'traditional Zionist non-orthodox, characterised by academic excellence and strong pastoral care'. Having Pat Clark (my New Visions tutor), who has visited schools worldwide, alongside me to benchmark, it soon became evident that Bialik is, from an international perspective, a truly excellent school.

Physically, the campus is impressive. Recent additions include the Early Learning Centre and a Creative Arts Centre, which incorporates state of the art music technology provision. At the time of our visit a sports centre was on the drawing board, which I am sure must now be in use.

There is so much to tell about Bialik, and so much that can inform good educational practice in any school, but I shall focus on the Jewish aspects.

---

10 http://www.jcoss.org/html/the_need_for_jcoss.html; http://www.thejc.com/articles/us-pledges-challenge-court-decision-jfs

We first visited the Early Learning Centre, where the best possible practice for the youngest pupils has been drawn from the model of Reggio Emilia, a centre of excellence for this age group in Italy. In this part of the school each room has two members of staff, one of whom is Hebrew speaking. In this way Hebrew becomes an integral part of the learning.

Throughout the school the Jewish and Zionist ethos is evident in displays and classroom activity. When I visited a member of the Reform movement headed the Jewish studies department, which includes staff from across the religious spectrum. On Friday we joined *Kabbalat Shabbat* (the ceremony to welcome Shabbat) in just one of the classrooms, though it takes place throughout the school. The *challah* (Shabbat bread) bill is impressive!

Logo of Bialik College, Melbourne, Australia.

While such activity may be seen in Jewish schools worldwide, there are more unusual aspects to the Jewish life of Bialik College. One building, in front of which fly the Australian and Israeli flags, serves as a *mo'adon*, a kind of club room. Each year the school brings over three post-army youth workers from Masorti Olami (the world Masorti movement) in Israel. These youngsters, who are housed in a flat by the school, deliver an informal Jewish and Zionist education programme.

In Australia the academic year ends in December and we were able to watch rehearsals for the end of year concert for the *b'nei mitzvah* (confirmation) pupils. This was the culmination of their 'Roots' project. The concert included Israeli and Yiddish songs and Israeli dance choreographed by the school's resident Israeli choreographer. One by one the students told their stories. You can imagine how moving these were in a community which boasts the highest number of post-Holocaust refugees. But it included, too, stories from the more recent South African and Russian immigrations, and the daughter of the United Jewish Appeal *shaliach* (emissary) who spoke proudly of her grandfather's involvement in the Israeli War of Independence.

On our third day we met Karen Morrison. Karen's primary role in the school is to run an impressive programme for gifted and talented pupils. However, when the horrific events of 11 September 2001 took place, her work took a new direction in the creation of the 'Harmony through Understanding' programme. The school, Karen explains, '…has one basic rule – Respect – for self, for others and for our environment'. As part of a whole school focus on '*Tikkun Olam*' (healing the world) she felt that they had to make a response to events in America on that day. The project, for which she originally raised $40,000 Australian dollars, now brings together regularly pupils from Jewish, Catholic, Moslem, government and independent schools for an impressive programme of speakers and facilitated activities. She is inundated with calls and e-mails to extend the programme to more schools.

So it was that day by day we uncovered more wonderful features of Bialik College. On the last day, almost as we walked out of the door, Genia called us over to meet 'Doc'. Doctor Paul Bartrop runs a programme unique in any secondary school in the world, entitled 'Comparative Genocide Studies'. 'The Jewish Studies department teaches the Holocaust', he explains. His course, which covers atrocities such as Armenia, Rwanda and Kosova considers:

> …some of the responses that take place (or do not take place) in the presence of genocide, and what forms of action can be introduced to both ease distress and bring it to an end.

Recently, Genia told us, she and her deputy, Michael Cohen, had a discussion about what the ideal Bialik graduate should look like Jewishly. 'They should', she said 'be knowledgeable, have depth of understanding about Judaism, Zionism and *Tikkun Olam*,(healing the world).

Early efforts by the JCOSS team to find premises and obtain financial support from the Department for Education met with disappointment, but in 2005 a site was secured as part of a project to develop East Barnet Secondary School. Then there was further good luck when the Education White Paper [11] in that year heralded a pilot for parent-promoted schools. JCOSS was invited to join the pilot. By this time I had joined the Steering Group and spent some very exciting times articulating the vision into a mission statement and planning aspects of the building and secular and Jewish curriculum. It all went quiet during the sensitive negotiations with the council planning section, but in August 2007 the school passed the first difficult stage of planning and in 2009 we were all systems go. On a very snowy day in February, Akiva pupils participated in the selection process which resulted in the appointment of Jeremy Stowe-Lindner as the school's first head.

It has been an absolute privilege to be involved in the JCOSS project, which articulates so many of my educational beliefs and values. It is an idea whose time has come and will, I am convinced, change the face of Anglo-Jewish education vastly and very much for the better.

The final chapter?

At times when the complexities of Bell Lane overwhelmed, I often joked with the staff about ending my educational career at an uncomplicated stable middle class school. It was always just that, a joke, while my inner voice told me, 'But you'll be at Bell Lane until you retire'. Until, that is, autumn 2007 at a Barnet Heads' Network meeting when an approach was made by the Head of the latest addition to the Barnet family of schools.

Akiva school was opened in 1981, the first of three primary schools serving the progressive Anglo-Jewish synagogue movements (Liberal, Reform and Masorti). Twenty-eight years on, the school is successful and over-subscribed and in January 2008 at last realised twin ambitions to enter the state system as a voluntary aided school, and to expand from one to two form entry in a beautiful new building on the Sternberg Centre site, where my synagogue is also housed.

---

11 DFES, Higher Standards, better schools for all!More choices for parents and pupils, 25 Oct 2005.

The gruelling processes of rebuild and transfer to voluntary aided status were masterfully overseen by headteacher Sue de Botton. It was Sue's decision to then retire that was the subject of our conversation at the heads' meeting. I knew Akiva well. When I ran the Sunday morning classes at the synagogue we used the school's former premises. Akiva had also always embraced our children's Israeli dance project with enthusiasm and as Head of a Barnet state school I had been enlisted to give some support to Sue during the transition.

When Sue informed me about her plans to retire and asked whether I would consider applying for the post, I at first dismissed the idea with; 'No, not me, I'll be at Bell Lane forever'. But then the idea began to niggle. Without my rebuild and with a Children's Centre for which I was struggling to find real enthusiasm, with the outstanding professional partnership with Jason about to end, would this be a good time for a change? As friends retired around me I began to feel that staying at Bell Lane would probably mean retirement no later than 60. Was that what I wanted? I began to feel that I had one more headship in me.

Plus, there was something more. I had been deeply moved on the Eastern European Holocaust visit so as to fully appreciate the richness of Jewish communal life and Jewish learning that had been lost in centres like Vilnius. Here was an opportunity to be involved in rebuilding post Holocaust Jewish life and learning. A move to Akiva would offer me the opportunity to develop my own Jewish learning, particularly Holocaust education. I could actively involve myself in supporting access to Jewish education for all Jewish children, and to be head of the major feeder school for JCOSS, now finally through all the planning stages, would be a real privilege.

So it was that in March 2009 I rather surprised myself by becoming head of Akiva. I know it was the right move because as well as feeling right it had been greeted with enthusiasm by so many in the Jewish community and the local authority. As Yentl the matchmaker would say in *Fiddler on the Roof*: 'It's a perfect match'.

Leaving Bell Lane was a wrench. I held it together through most of the farewells, breaking down only at the Y5/6 end of year concert and while saying goodbye to some very dear colleagues with whom I have worked for many years, and of course to Jason and Julia.

Takeaways

The title for this section comes from a conversation with Danny, my son and increasingly my teacher about what I would put in the conclusion. 'Well it's the takeaways, isn't it? It's the things you want people to take away from your story'.

Community is central to my philosophy of education. I owe my successes to the many communities to which I have belonged: the loving community of my immediate and wider family; my inspirational synagogue community, and the wider Jewish community and the many learning communities in which I have participated, particularly Bell Lane Primary. I believe that effective teaching and learning is facilitated in the context of a happy and supportive learning community.

I am optimistic about English primary education in the twenty-first century. Personally I have had only positive experiences of the inspection regime, which I believe has made a valuable contribution to ensuring that pupils receive high quality learning experiences.

I welcome moves towards a more creative cross-curricular approach and away from the emphasis on content and the formulaic teaching that characterised the introduction of the National Curriculum and the Literacy and Numeracy Strategies.

I am relieved to see from the highest levels of government down, real efforts to strengthen links between Education, Health, and Social Services to foster greater holistic provision for families. I welcome the 'Every Child Matters' agenda with its emphasis on health and fitness, and safety and enjoyment in learning. I am encouraged that children currently in our schools are much more aware of the threats to our environment. I only hope that it is not too late for them to help to heal our world.

I am grateful that my headship coincided with the creation of the National College for School Leadership. Recently Jason and I had a conversation about 'futures thinking' and I realised that the college has given us a vocabulary and an agenda for educational leadership. With its programmes and particularly the current focus on networks it is providing valuable support for what can be a fairly lonely and isolated role.

I worry about our fractured society. Many primary schools are particularly beautiful examples of real community cohesion and respect for the 'other', but there are sadly too many contexts in which this is not sustained through adolescence into adulthood.

While I understand and respect the motivation in terms of Jewish continuity to create more Jewish schools, there are aspects that make me uneasy. It is a shame that more Jewish children are not included in multicultural classrooms, both in terms of what they could gain and what they could contribute. I worry that Jewish schools reflect and reinforce the polarisation in the community. I welcome JCOSS as a model in which I hope communal leaders, families and educators across the religious spectrum will engage in the interests of greater cohesion.

I am concerned that the British economic climate which has supported development in schools is looking rather more uncertain and I particularly lament Bell Lane's recent removal from the rebuild programme. As Jason noted in our 'futures' conversation, Bell Lane will struggle to provide 'a twenty-first century education with twentieth century trained teachers in a nineteenth century building'.

When Gab's boss, Linford Christie visited Bell Lane he spoke affectionately of the teachers who identified his talent then nurtured it, collecting him from home on a Saturday to take him to training. Recently, I received a letter from a former pupil at JFS. She had met one of my teachers, who spoke warmly of me and of Bell Lane and she was delighted to discover the connection. She wrote:

> When she mentioned your name I couldn't believe it – my Mrs Stone. It was wonderful to hear about you and to hear someone talking of you in these terms. I have such fond memories of you and my early years at JFS. I felt I had to write to you to let you know this and see how you are.

This is the gift of being an educator. A life in education has so far been a wonderful life, as a learner, a teacher and especially as a leader. It is a particular privilege to be in a position to make a difference, and to empower others to make a difference in the lives of young people. There can be no greater joy than to spend one's working life in the company of the younger generation engaged in the discovery of learning. Our duty is to make their learning a truly memorable experience and give them the skills and the enthusiasm to continue learning for the rest of their lives.

Jean's life in education

To my much loved husband, Leslie Philip Lawrence, teacher and educator, who loved young people, and passed his passion for learning to our children and grandchildren, and for chemistry to our greatly missed daughter. He was a fine leader and developed a very successful further education college. Leslie also made it possible for me to have a career, helping and encouraging me every step of the way.

The Early Years

In trying to define what I am, what title to give myself, I am ashamed in a way to have to say that I am not just a teacher. I am ashamed because to be a teacher, to spend most of one's career in the classroom is a fantastic and noble profession and worthy of a life-time vocation. But mine didn't work out that way. For reasons which will become apparent if you read on, I moved through life, getting to know school after school but also getting to know about many of the other activities which lie within the framework we call education. For this reason I would like to call myself an educationist. I think I can make the claim to have worked in jobs and settings, all of which come under the umbrella of education. Of course, most people get to know about schools first of all through the schools they attended in their childhood – though historically this has not always been so until recently, and, alas, it still is not always in so-called under-developed countries. I have to tell you that my own parents, both Polish Jews, never went to school, except to a form of religious school, which taught them Hebrew. When they immigrated to England before the First World War they taught themselves to speak English and my earliest memories are of watching my beloved father struggling with much sucking on a pencil to teach himself to read and later to write English. I have not been entirely accurate in saying that my father 'never went to school' – he went for a fortnight, he told us, but then the school-master told him that he could not attend his school if he did not wear shoes. As his parents could not afford to buy him any, he no longer went to school. But as I have said (forgive the digression) along with my ten brothers and sisters I first knew of schools through attending them as a pupil.

But because I was of school age during the Second World War I went to a particularly large number of schools as I toured around England as an evacuee, moving from place to place to try to escape the bombs falling on London and the major cities. I therefore represent the thousands upon thousands of children whose education was severely disrupted by the Second World War in spite of the heroic efforts of their teachers to try to soldier on, and to compensate for this disruption. Sometimes when I moved up and down the country I would attend school, but sometimes there was no chance for this and in spite of being a bright child my schooling suffered substantially. Indeed it was not until I entered in 1943 the sixth form of Central Foundation School, a grammar school in the East End of London in those days, that I had the chance to settle down academically. Anyway, all this moving from school to school was adding to my experience of what schools could be like and my ability to compare them.

What else have I done in my long career in education, which has given me the right to call myself an educationist? Well, I have taught in secondary modern, grammar and comprehensive schools. I have taught in small and large schools, single sex and coeducational schools, inner city and suburban schools, two colleges of education, and I have worked in four universities. I have supervised students teaching all kinds of school subjects in perhaps I would guess between a hundred and two hundred schools. I have worked at teacher training in an environment which gave me colleagues favouring orientations to teaching that ranged from Marxist to ultra conservative. I have held posts as a research assistant to a university professor of education, and in a local authority education research department. In schools I have been an assistant teacher, head of department and headmistress (in a secondary modern and comprehensive inner-city school), and have taught the whole ability range from sixth form to children with special needs. I hold a degree in modern languages, a Doctorate in mediaeval French, and a Masters degree in the psychology of education. I rest my case. Besides, I am sick of blowing my own trumpet. But I wanted you to know some of the things that this book is about. Forgive me.

* * *

It is my intention to consider in some detail the schools I attended, the colleges where I trained and the posts to which I was appointed in later pages, but first I want to make sense of all this by talking a little of my family background and the settings against which my life first unfurled. The pogroms in Poland triggered off mass immigration by Jews to the west at the end of the nineteenth century. Thus it was that my grandfather's five children grew up against a background of poverty, repression and persecution but within the framework of a loving family and a caring Jewish community. At the turn of the century they moved to Warsaw, where my father Joseph Goldstein married Fanny Kamen, a lovely young dress-maker who left her family home without regret, since her poor, widowed mother had remarried and she was badly treated by her stepfather. My extraordinary mother travelled right across Europe to London to be with her husband who had preceded her, with three young children and pregnant with her fourth. Her husband did not even know that she was coming. It was 1913. The First World War broke out in the following year.

Joseph was a tailor, a very skilled one who, after a period of working for other people, decided to try to make more money to feed his growing family by becoming a master-tailor, and who moved into a house which he rented in Boreham Street, Bethnal Green in the heart of London's East End, where many other Jews had already settled, including a few members of his own family. The house had an attic, which became the tailor's workshop where Joseph could ply his trade. Boreham Street where the Goldsteins lived at No. 21 and where they lived for many years up to the outbreak of the Second World War in 1939, consisted of twelve uniform red brick houses facing another identical twelve across the pavement, each occupied by a Jewish family, or several, thus it became known as Jews' Alley. It ran parallel to the bustling thoroughfare of Brick Lane; meanwhile in the alley the many children could in perfect safety whirl their hoops and swing from the lamp-posts at either end, and play hop-scotch and diabolo.

Boreham Street was perfect for an annual ritual at Passover, an important Jewish festival, when hundreds of children would throng the pavement to play complicated games all involving hazelnuts. The sight was extraordinary, an East End Lowry of tiny people, and a Brueghel of activity. The hordes of children stood or crouched, or kneeled on one or both knees, throwing nuts into shoe-boxes, or rolling them against farthings propped up against the walls, or bargained, exchanging twenty hard-earned nuts for a farthing. They were mini-entrepreneurs! The children were swamped with happiness, and forgot in their noise and commotion that the houses were occupied, except when Mrs Levine opened her first-floor window and poured a bucket of cold water down onto a few unfortunate heads. For a while No. 11 had a wet space in front of it, but it soon dried, crossed and re-crossed by small pairs of black-shoed feet, the Passover 'business'-children of Boreham Street.

When I was born in 1929, the eleventh child in the family, my eldest brother, Lou, was thoroughly ashamed and angry as the six-year gap in my mother's child-bearing had led the family to believe that there would now be peace from this activity. But there I was and they had to adjust to yet another infant. As for me, I had come into a fantastic home with adoring parents and a horde of older sisters and brothers who spoilt me completely. We were never to know hunger, nor to be ill-dressed in spite of the fact that my father's work was seasonal so that we lurched from comparative wealth during the 'season' and hardship during the 'off-time'. When times were bad my mother bought us clothes on tick and paid off her debts when things got better. When there was no work for my brothers in the workshop upstairs and they were lolling around in the kitchen I would watch my mother go to her apron pocket and draw out coins to give to her sons, so that they could run off to the dogs. Dog-racing and horse-racing were much loved in the family and in the whole area, at times with pernicious consequences. Sometimes business went so well that Lou could run around in a car, and for years my mother had two Gentile maids to help her.

In the kitchen there was no sink but a couple of steps down from the kitchen there was one from which water could be fetched, and where we could wash. In the absence of a bathroom small children would be bathed in a zinc bath in front of the kitchen range, and when they were older they would be taken to the local public baths by my mother. I well remember the occasion when I fainted in the baths because the water was too hot, and caused a great commotion. We were extremely lucky in that we had an inside toilet, although I remember it was outside in the yard where the black beetles used to crawl which came in from the leather factory adjacent to the house, and whose hooter woke us up each morning.

Our sleeping arrangements were interesting, there being so many people in the house to accommodate. I slept in my parents' bedroom all the ten years I lived in Boreham Street while there was one bedroom shared by my four sisters (Annie had married and left home before I was born) and one shared by my brothers. You can imagine the noise emanating from those two rooms. When four bodies shared the bed they slept two at each end, feet to feet. So you see I was the lucky one for I had a bed of my own. Bugs infested the beds, and lice and fleas our hair, but getting rid of these was just a fact of life. And there were so many compensations and so many exciting things happening all the time.

The food was wonderful, typically Jewish and *kosher*. There were three sittings for lunch, one for the little children, one for the older ones, and one for my father and the boys who nipped down from the work-shop for a quick meal. When potatoes were cooked fourteen pounds of them needed to be peeled for a single meal. It was helpful that Kossoff's the bakers had a shop just round the corner, so that vast baking trays could be taken round there for baking for a small sum. To Kossoff's too went the trays of *cholent*, the succulent dish of meat, potatoes and beans which has to be baked slowly overnight for its juices to give off its wonderfully rich aroma.

Summer without a garden had its advantages, because everyone pulled chairs out on to the pavement where endless talking went on, and the community of neighbours was strengthened. These were the days when there was real poverty for the widow and the unemployed and the sick, and neighbours who knew you and were true friends were a real lifeline. I am proud to be able to say that my parents were always ready to help and fed far more than one family. Every use was made of local parks such as Victoria Park and Shoreditch bandstand and there were simple picnics galore and wonderful clubs which organised activities of every kind. The synagogues were also there for the young, with their schools and classes and festivals and festivities. I have the clearest recollection of my brother Ronnie's *Bar Mitzvah* in 1936 at the age of thirteen when he took upon himself the duties of his religion (and has carried these out for the past seventy years), for I can feel to this day in my hands the almonds and raisins that I threw towards him over the balcony of the synagogue where I was standing as he recited in Hebrew from the Torah.

Before I come on to talking about the schools that I attended I should like to mention something about an important question that I have thought a great deal about especially in my later years; the question of why I was the only child of all eleven children to go to a university. In 1988 most of my brothers and sisters described their lives up to the outbreak of the Second World War in a book entitled *And Then There Were Eleven*. Esther compiled and edited it and we published it privately, and I have been able to use it for much of what I now relate. But first let me point out that I have known my brothers and sisters well for most of their lives and have in particular watched them through the careers they followed. In my opinion, and having spent my own life in the field of education, all of them, or at least almost all of them were not just clever people but people who were capable of benefiting from a university education. Today, there is no doubt that they would have gone on to higher education. This is clearly to be seen from a study of the way they spent their latter years, from the way they exploited their hobbies, such as writing lectures and fiction, and computing, and from the voraciousness and range with which they read in all sorts of fields. Several of them ran their own businesses brilliantly. If further evidence were needed of their high order of intelligence it is there in abundance in the life histories of their own children, most of whom have written their stories, too, just as their parents did, so that the saga of the family of Joseph and Fanny Goldstein continues.

The author (centre) with husband Leslie (right) and sister Esther (left).

Their grand-children are doing extraordinary things, but in contrast to their parents so many of them have climbed the education ladder. Why, then, did their parents not? I used to think that it was due to lack of money, a problem which had mostly disappeared by the time that I was ready for education. But I was wrong, and the picture is more complicated though money was a contributing factor in several cases. There was, for example, the fact that if you had not been born in England you were not eligible to receive a scholarship entitling you to free Grammar School education. This affected my three eldest brothers and sister. My parents did all they could for them by sending them to private establishments. Annie went to Clarks, a commercial college while Lou went to Cussacks College. Lou later went into machining, as a tailor in my father's workshop.

For other children the explanation is very specific. Thus, Ronnie passed the scholarship exam and went to Parmiter's, a grammar school, but says he didn't like the 'snobby' environment and that the homework he had to do interfered with his beloved club activities, [1] and so he truanted from school. When he was about to be found out by his father, he ran away from home for a while. The next day Mum took him to school and he was 'allowed' to leave for good. So he went to Mansford Street Central School, and eventually into the family work-shop as a machinist. Did the staff at Parmiter's fail him at a vital moment? Did Mum just not know the implications of what that decision was doing to her clever son? Was there no careers work in the school to help her? Probably not. These were the days when Polly just left school at the age of thirteen, and Mick won a scholarship to Regent Street Polytechnic but Dad wanted him to have a trade, so he went into hairdressing.

The histories of Gertie and Esther are also interesting. Gertie passed the scholarship exam and went to Central Foundation School, where Esther had attended a little while earlier. She went to Whitechapel Library to do her homework away from the ever-noisy kitchen. She was a lovely, fun-loving child who fooled around at school and got poor reports. Thus, she wrote all over a weak exam paper: 'That's all there is and there ain't no more', making bad marks even worse and missing her chances of the career of writer which she craved. Mum was ill with glaucoma and lost an eye at this time and sister, Annie, was extremely ill so the family was under acute stress. As Gertie herself wrote years later:

> The notion comes to my mind, the first truly unselfish idea I have ever conceived, to leave school and go out to work to help the family exchequer. Reluctantly my father agrees.

Esther was at Central Foundation School, the same grammar school as Gertie. She was an excellent student and teaching attracted her except that married teachers were then prohibited. She was told by the careers mistress that women had no chance of success in journalism, so she took three months' secretarial training at school and determined to infiltrate Fleet Street as a secretary. Not only were jobs hard to get with so many people after them, but

---

[1] Ronnie's memories of club life at Cambridge and Bethnal Green Boys Club are recorded on a blog, which can be read and viewed at http://candbgoldboys.blogspot.com/

she ran into anti-Semitism in her search. Finally, her careers teacher told her that Fleet Street would not employ Jews. So she took a job as a typist, got very bored and eventually took a good secretarial job where, although she again met with anti-Semitism, the Managing Director was Jewish and she was able to fight against it.

Looking at the lessons to be learnt from these stories of educational advancement, or indeed the opposite, it is clearly vital that schools take special care with careers work with immigrant children and their parents, where they are not familiar with further and higher education. The route to these stages of education remains something of a game and you have to know how to play it. I went to university and the other ten didn't mainly because I was born later in the history of education than they were. I am not saying that they did not in all cases find happiness and fulfilment in their lives but I still feel grief for what they missed. I had it. The eleventh child was the lucky one.

* * *

Virginia Road School was the first I ever knew by crossing the threshold at the age of three through the vast metal gates, turned back, against the railings which hugged the road. Pink brick walls with high windows, handled with the high pole at whose end the metal hook looked foolishly small, and which was the caretaker's task to work. The wooden floor blocks stretched across the hall: a slightly polished empty space, and off the hall began the classrooms; half their walls were tiled, with apple green paint above. Since it was a nursery school, a great feature was 'the sleep', the time, in the early afternoon when I was given a first responsibility – to lay out in rows the canvas beds, simple folding cots of pale green canvas onto which the infants clambered, to lie in peace, eyes closed for most in obedient pretence, while my thoughts ranged over my world.

The best moment was Friday afternoon when my teacher with the fairish hair, slightly waved and banned, sat carefully on her chair and made her kind pronouncement, that her class, being so good all week, deserved the gift of sweets. They were hard and boiled and finely sugared, so that sucking slightly seared the tongue: shaped like fruits, tiny pears and slices of orange and lemon, and my favourite dark one: raspberry, larger than life, had I known the fruit.

This was the fitting end of school, always there, a reward for unknown virtue. Fifty years later, bespectacled and psychologically well-versed, I was to preach before my teaching students the benefits of behaviour modification techniques – at Virginia Road, in the early thirties, my teacher knew them well.

Rochelle Street was my next school, and where now children with special needs, whose minds work slower than the rest, learn what they can from teachers who usually care. In those days children there (many of them bright, without the later 'ethnic minority label', but still a wholesome mix), were brought with the boats from all over the world, mixed in tint of complexion, mixed in creed, and with parents struggling to survive and to achieve. Obesity was not a problem, but for some hunger, and shoelessness and dirt, for the homes were those of torn lino, cold water taps and the occasional poverty of unemployment, or the 'slack season'.

But the world was full of people for these children in their crowded homes and bustling streets, and there were riches to be had in this, and in the schools and in the clubs, population thick as spawn, with their doing and their playing and their acting and their outings, organised and pushing children to extend themselves in this direction and in that. Dedicated club leaders and teachers, often working extra time to feed the open minds of thousands of children, and who would later leave the alleys and poverty behind.

Rochelle Street School was open day and evening, after school for the clubs, and for the Hebrew classes of the Jews who gathered in the hall to recite the *Shema*, the 'Hear O Israel, the Lord our God, the Lord is one'. In the playground, benches lined the walls, under the shelter – no luxury this, for in the thirties children who barely ate needed to sit and rest.

I was seven years old. I sat in the classroom which led off the hall, and where the dark brown of the tiles covering the lower part of the walls was mixed with mottling of cream and shone, all glazed. There was normally a feeling of comfort inside me, in this room, from the companionable movement of the other children and the warm, regulated ambience, but on this day I kept glancing up towards the door.

Finally she came, as I knew she would, the nurse, dark blue and white in uniform, the white starched and with her face with its very white skin and mauveish lips, very straight. She had a paper in her hand which she lifted carefully and read from in such a clear, firm fashion. She read the list of children who were to have their hair de-nitted, deloused – the ones who had been discovered when half an hour ago she had inspected their heads, with the long precise strokes of her oblong metal comb, which flicked the hair back to reveal the parting along which the creatures could clearly be seen. My name was there, of course, and obediently and numb, anaesthetized, hardly conscious of moving across the half-room, I went to line up with the others. The group of children thus assembled at the door, looking up at the nurse occasionally, did not look at each other, not out of shame, just that there was no point in any communication. The act of going was the overwhelming thing, and we shuffled away, to the place with the soft soap whose smell bit into your nostrils, not entirely unpleasant but just very different and strong. My sense of smell was never very fine, but this scent, with the gooey texture of the soap, olive green, and translucently liquid, affected me. The place was tiled too, but unlike those in the classroom these squares held no colour or warmth. Later when I knew the word I would have called them 'functional', for that is all they were, blending with the grey, finely-veined sink over which I bent my hair, for cleansing.

The trouble with the whole process was that I could never satisfy them. I would be temporarily clean, but the nits and lice would return and it would all happen again, so that it was not an experience with any start or finish. It was part of a pattern which was to recur, like living in the midst of a roll of patterned wallpaper.

At home in the small, square bedroom where my bed touched that of my parents, I would sit combing for nits with the square metal comb, looking and finding, cracking them with my thumbnails and crushing with the flat of the nail the occasional still or slow-moving louse, which left its almost colourless smear along the comb. Gradually the nits grew fewer and fewer until the search was futile and complete. It was not bad when it was over: there was a satisfaction there.

Campbell the toffee man sat on the seat of his contraption, in the road just outside Rochelle Street School. It was basically a tricycle with a large square container for his toffee in front of him, the top of it covered with ready-wrapped packets in cornets of coarse paper – and with blocks of the sweet brown sticky stuff, of all kinds, some chipped by the hammer, the rest in smooth, neatly squared, flat slabs. Nut toffee was pale and honey-coloured, but fig toffee was blackish-brown, with striations and speckled with pips. He seemed to me a very patient man, for he was always there when I came out of school. His feet seemed permanently to rest on the pedals of his van, and always he was a picture of blends of muddy grey and brown, with his scarf and his flat cap in rough-textured, vaguely registering, herringbone design.

I usually went straight home, in a safe routine, never questioned. Had I, however, turned left instead and crossed the road, I would soon have been at the bandstand. The bandstand on top of the mound had given its name to the whole area, which went up and up, along tarmacadam paths, up clutches of steps, then flat, then climbing more steps and so forth, to the very top where the empty stand gazed outwards upon the buildings of Shoreditch and of Bethnal Green. The tiny hill was nothing, but to the children and perhaps their parents it meant a great deal, for it had flower beds on the flat, and it had trees. I loved it, for as I mounted it, the openness of the location, in which my body and limbs could stretch themselves, always moving upwards, amidst gasps and tensions, pleased me endlessly. Every now and then, catching my breath, I would glance backwards, focusing upon the downward graveled path, rather than the barely-perceived vista, and at last the bandstand itself was there in front of me, the circular railing with its definite exclusion neither liked nor disliked, but simply marking the end. Running down was more hazardous for knees could be grazed, and then there would be a fuss, but the relief of being again at the bottom was good, as was the level walk home, out of the openness up there at the top.

The way home led past a set of grey 'buildings' on my right, a block of tiny homes – how odd to call them 'flats' or 'apartments', but that, I suppose, is what they would now be called, built on three sides of grey stone courtyard. Their aspect was eerie to a child brought up in Boreham Street, for they were endlessly high, and the windows small as dots, close together, seen from below. There was a hardness about them, a chill, and though I did not recognise the precise nature of their effect upon me, it was a response to ugliness that I was feeling.

My later love of beautiful buildings and environment was incipient in my feeling of revulsion for the 'buildings', and my contrasted affection for the warm red brick of the houses of our street, and their gables in which the tailors, who were fathers and sons, laboured away.

* * *

Summer in the East End was the dusty time, when the litter of crushed cigarette boxes, Players, Gold Flakes and Woodbines and triangular Walls' ice-cream lolly cartons lying on the pavement and in the gutter, stayed with the eye. The dust was brown and heavy on the pavement and the square patch of earth around the rare tree was parched and cracked, and littered too. In the roads it was a quieter time at the weekends than at other seasons, for people had gone if they could, on charabancs, to Hampton Court and other places; and the lawns of Victoria Park were heavy with sprawlers and with picnics in paper carrier bags, no plastic then! One summer, aged eight, I was invited to my teacher's home for tea. Mr Taylor was married and had a daughter of his pupils' age, and lived in a suburb in a tiny terraced house whose rooms struck me with their order, quiet, and regularity, though I sensed that they were small. We had tea at a table pressed against the wall, and over it I observed the tiny, elegant hand of Mr Taylor's daughter, and the way the creamy skin shone, delicately over her prominent wrist-bone. But most of all I felt the shock of the change of place, on my return home to the dusty streets. I had been in a clean and open place and this was different: suburb from town, trees from dust, airiness from dry, oppressive heat. The slim elegance of the child's hand and arm, the skin exposed by the short sleeved, summer dress, stayed with me for a long, long time.

Summer was a world without gardens, whose substitute was the street itself, with wooden chairs parked in front of the door, and easy converse with those seated likewise, across the street. No serried lines of deckchairs, but a chair here, or a pair there, informally and in the shapes of friendship and togetherness. Tizer was the sparkling drink, orange even then but with a different tang, but for me the best was being sent, for twelve o'clock dinner, along the street and down the alley, to the dairy, hand heavy with the big enamel pitcher, to return heavier still, full of sour cream, the smetana. Pour it over the boiled new potatoes, hot under its cold thickness and nothing more was needed. Foaming sasparilla, brilliant raspberry and lemon yellow, hung high in massive glass tureens above the stalls in Brick Lane market – full on summer Sunday mornings, to pass icily down the gullet, while the cries of the man with the ice cart, or the water-melon carrier, the thick slices and chunky halves sitting heavy on the blocks of glistening, slowly melting ice, brought exquisite cool with them, and slaked the thirst of the dusty, paper-smattered streets.

The bugs, the beetles and the baths were all important, in their own way. The bugs were a strictly bedroom phenomenon, very occasionally seen settled on a wall, but almost always in bed. It seemed slightly odd, since there were so many of them, that they were not to be seen on the top of the over-bed, the down-filled, half-fluffy, half-lumpy quilt-like, sheet-shrouded eiderdown which kept you very warm at night. Perhaps they, too, preferred to burrow in the warmth of the inside of the coverings, and might die on top; for whatever reason, they lay concealed for the most part inside, in the folds, and it was constantly a matter for surprise to find one suddenly appearing, moving or still, against the starched whiteness of the sheeting.

There were at least three types of bug. First, the mature, dark brownish-red, adult, large enough for the slight ridging to appear on his shiny carapace, shield-like in shape, with legs too small to see. His junior version was half the size and twice as red, crimson, obviously young, while the baby had a translucence about its creamy, red-edged flesh. Crack the bug and the blood – if blood it was – it looked like blood – spilt and smeared the bed. Not pleasant, but better than a creeping creature, or even a still one, there all the time, to startle you horridly, and to crawl.

The beetles were not mine, like the bugs, who belonged in the family mattresses and presumably on the walls. The beetles belonged to the leather factory whose wall was the same wall which edged our yard, and whose hooter calling the never-seen workforce woke me sleeping in my parents' bedroom. Not surprising after all that the beetles flouted observance of the boundary wall and made free with the yard, traversing the oblong with impunity (or did my brothers kill them? I never thought of that) and presenting a problem. The problem would not have existed but that the lavatory with its newspaper squares on the nail was actually in the yard, and to use it meant crossing the yard and risking the sight of the beetles, hardly habituated to, pressed hard in their long oval against the wall, or stationary, exposed on the yard, or making a jerky way across it.

* * *

Before leaving all description of the inter-war years in the East End of London, I should like to try to evaluate the impact of Rochelle School upon the Goldstein family, because it was crucial to them. I was the only child who spent her nursery years at Virginia Road School, for all the others went straight to Rochelle Street from the age of three to the age of transfer to a central school or grammar school at what appears to be eleven or occasionally ten. I have good information for seven siblings from the 'family book' but in addition I have first class information from six of us able to give it from phone calls that I have just made, about certain aspects of the school. My evidence is therefore recent, and covers the period between the year 1916 when Esther entered the school and 1939 when I left it. I was particularly interested in a general assessment of the school, in the teaching of reading and matters related to it, and in teachers' attitudes to the children.

I found that these former pupils thought extremely highly of their school, using terms that ranged from 'good' and 'forward-looking' to 'excellent' and 'smashing'. Teachers were mentioned by name for various reasons. Gertie remembered Miss Brett as excellent, and Ronnie remembers that Mr King who taught science took them home. Mr King's father was a scientist and his schoolteacher son showed and demonstrated to them apparatus for the making of electricity. Mick says that H. G. Taylor was an excellent teacher who took the class on a holiday to Beccles in Suffolk. The school is said to have had a great reputation and pupils were encouraged to take the scholarship exam. Pupils learnt how to read and write; rote methods were the norm. Polly reports how much poetry was learnt by heart, and interestingly, that her teacher gave her a poetry book at the age of five or six and she was sent round the school to read poems aloud to all the classes.

Great emphasis was put on physical fitness with games using ropes taking a large part. Children were encouraged to go to the local library. I wanted to find out how personally I was taught to read and I asked a number of questions of my family about this. The answers were fascinating. Apparently, there were no books in the house, although Polly mentions that there was one book on the First World War, and another on sex, which she hid and passed round! There were newspapers that were probably there so that my father could do his betting. Ronnie says there were a few adventure books at home such as *Kidnapped* and *Robinson Crusoe* but in general there is agreement that the local public library was the place that supplied your books. This was simply because there was no money for them, just as there was no money for toys. If someone gave you an annual you were the happiest child in the world. The older children did not on the whole teach the younger ones to read or write, and our parents were in no position to do this. I am the exception to this. When I was three years old I caught pneumonia at a period when this was a serious disease. My mother installed me on the soft brown leatherette sofa in the front room to recover and Gertie and Esther visited me as the weeks passed and taught me to read and write. They were amazed at my progress. So, once again the youngest child was the lucky one.

In assessing the validity of what I have said about the pre-war years I accept that memories pass with the years and my informants are now very old men and women. When I began to reflect on this, in mid-2007, I was 75, Esther was 92, Gertie 89, Polly 86, Mick 85 and Ronnie 81. But their memories were sharp and clear. Rochelle was a great school of its time; all honour to its teachers – we owe them a great deal.

* * *

It was 1939 and for months the talk had been of war, now imminent, then unlikely, then just possible; each speech, each day, each newspaper tossing the mind this way and that, while the tension rose from disappointments past and others' keen anxiety, even in the children. I was still nine years old and my school had issued all its pupils with a square cardboard box, on a string for the shoulder; within, a gas-mask, a black slippery rubber thing with the pouting snout of a pig, where the filter was, and the plastic visor for the eyes. During the occasional practice it was donned, slightly claustrophobic but not too bad, and I felt it cling and stick around my cheeks, as I supposed it had to. I put it on but never thought of gas, or war – what was it anyway, but a feeling of nervousness, and Mum and everyone looking worried?

I could have been evacuated with the school, but somehow Mum and Dad (did he have a say in it?) did not want it. Instead, some neighbours on the corner would go to Wales, to Cardiff, and they would take me with them.

The carrier bag was packed, with a whole chicken in it, Mum told me later, when she learnt that they had not in fact given me any! And I went, on the madly crowded train, Friday, 1 September 1939, with the trains leaving London quickly, taking them all away from the capital and the certain bombs. People stood packed in the corridors and in the carriage, and I felt the sad jolt of the train, in the night, black outside the windows, and the strangeness seeped into me.

* * *

My temporary home in Cardiff was a tiny tobacconist's, near the castle, and generous people; and Sunday morning, 3 September, came, in the kitchen, just before eleven, the egg boiled in the little saucepan. I lifted it on the teaspoon, as the chimes sounded and Neville Chamberlain spoke. Hitler had not replied and there was no alternative. As he moved towards his conclusion, far away from everyone for the first time, moved ineffably by the moment, I felt the warmth of the large tears moving down my cheek.

A few weeks later I returned to London to begin the years of travel and return to the safe places, then again to London, which pulled the family back each time, until the warnings, with the air raids and the bombs and the fires threw them out again. Brighton, Nottingham, Derby, Luton, Dunstable, Houghton Regis, this school, that school, this friend, that friend, fields of cowslips, and green-badge blue blazers, it all began.

Brighton had so many London children to cope with in its schools that you went to school half-day; the afternoons I spent with books, and read through three a day sometimes, all you were allowed, from a small library well stocked with 'Dimsie' books, and with Angela Brazil, and Richmal Compton's 'William'. We lived in Esther and Jack's maisonette in Hove, the first flat I had known. It had a garden where patriotic radishes and feathery carrots cohabited with London Pride, and vulgar red and yellow nasturtiums in profusion. I took the 'scholarship exam', but in some muddle someone lost my papers so they sent me to a common or garden senior school where I learnt to knit a fawn string dishcloth, to iron the collar and sleeves of shirt before the rest, and to dance round the Maypole, first under, then over the long, pretty pastel ribbons. I also learnt French: the first lesson, a clever teacher who provided a sheet with mauve duplicating ink; a picture of an elephant and some sentences about him. It seemed good, that as I looked and read the meaning was quite clear, and I saw the accents on the word elephant were lines that went a certain way. I also played table-tennis with Gloria, my friend.

Back in London I lived in Dalston, and with my mother ill, I shopped for fish in the market in Ridley Road, turning the gills back as I had been told, to check for their red freshness under the surprised gaze of the stall-holder at the cheekiness of the small shopper. The raids started till I lay one night, one leg under the quilt, the other dangling down the side of the bed, waiting to be thrust into the slipper, for the dash to the cellar when the warning sounded, as it would. Once there, all in the shared house gathered down below, several families, I played the rummy which each night won me a sizeable sum – once 2/6d, a fortune!

There was the one night when leaving the house with Mum to go down to the cellar the warning siren had been late, and already the bombs had been released. In the dark, the sky was light and cloudy and looking up I saw plainly the large matchstick bombs leaving the belly of the plane. Mum pushed me against the wall and covered me with her body, her breasts squashing me, in total maternal sacrifice. In the morning all the talk was of where the bombs had destroyed buildings, where they had raised the fires, and who had been nearby. So often it was a thankful 'nearly', and in fact the large family, in the midst of all the disaster, lost no one in the blitz.

In Nottingham and Derby I lived with Esther, who mothered me, while I mothered her babies in their prams and changed nappies: there I was promoted to the middle class, with their lovely houses and the bay windows and the gardens in a quiet road or on Cherry Tree Hill. In Houghton Regis I lived for the first time in a country village where my friend was a farmer's daughter with orange-silk hair, and a walk from the terraced cottage led to fields of cowslips, and a pond and brook from which the jam-jar was filled with creatures, newts and spawn, and algae.

In Luton, twelve, and at grammar school, I ate the wartime cauliflower rissoles and dried-egg, scrambled, and saw for the last time my brother Jack, in the blue-grey airman's uniform, with the gunner's patch, standing by the second-hand inlaid-edged bureau with a slight smile on his face. I am looking at the same bureau as I write this. All my other four brothers were in the army,

Ronnie and Mick abroad, and three of my sisters' husbands too, and for my parents, letters became important. My mother wrote only Yiddish but father had learnt to sign his name and write a little English; building on this, and on his reading of the dog-racing columns of the newspapers, he taught himself with frowning to write long letters at the kitchen table on Sunday mornings, white papered and airmail blue, or the 'airgraph' which was photographed, reduced in size for sending. He taught himself to write in English to the point where he liked to write in verse, with his odd scattering of words starting with a capital letter.

* * *

Luton High School was the grammar school, selective and selecting, placing pupils in their special groups, and I began in the class 'two parallel Y', in the uniform, red, yellow and black, with the velour, brimmed hat for winter and the summer Panama. The summer dress was pale yellow with a square neckline, and did not last the week. It was my only one and so on Wednesday I would wash and wet-iron it, and hang it in front of a fire to dry. The lisle stockings, or the summer socks and the sensible shoes completed the picture. I wore my hair in a fringe, loved the swimming in the school's own swimming-pool, and found the lessons easy, though I had missed most of the first year work in the scholarship-paper mix-up and the frequent changes of school.

Being 'clever' I was made to miss the third year and proceed direct to the fourth, to the class called 'special' where I started to accumulate on my breast the row of medals that would jangle as I walked along the corridor; honours medals for good work and the junior swimming championship. You walked along the left hand side of the corridors, which were very long, and I became conscious of success. I did not realize just how strict, just how starchy and how hierarchical in approach the High School was until the family returned to London in 1942 to Manor Road, in Stoke Newington and I went to Spital Square, where my sisters Esther and Gertie had been before me, properly called Central Foundation School, just off the market of Spitalfields, with the rotting cabbage in the kerb, just outside the playground where the old building jutted into the solitary netball pitch, which was its 'grounds'.

This was an old school, centuries old with a history proudly told in assemblies by the heads, and the dark honours boards with the gold lettering of pupils' glories past. Half the children were Jewish, and Jewish prayers were sung in separate state. Here were no jangling medals (I took mine off) but informality among high standards.

Most of the teachers were superb. Blonde Dorothy Colmar, tall and straight in bearing, with a drive and a passion for French which carried to her pupils, crystal clear in exposition, and with a precision in pronunciation which begged them to copy her. Music was Miss Colmar's other love so that songs were taught in French to her piano and her voice whose words would last a lifetime, rounds and jingles and the sterner stuff, the Marseillaise and the songs of Lorraine. Kathleen Roberts, of the kinky greying hair and the love for English of the truly gifted teacher bringing into the small sixth-form room the bundles of little sheets of paper with the meticulous hand-written notes on Milton and Wordsworth, on Dryden and Keats. Miss Brady with the mauve tweed suit for Latin lessons and the fashionable purple blouse, whose red hair should have topped a tutu, always wishing she could have been a ballet dancer. Miss Brown, the science teacher, of the voluminous floor length skirt, and Miss Gray the banned historian, with the house where Cromwellian coins had been found in the pond, as she told us whilst having tea with the cut-glass jam-pots and the linen serviettes. Their teaching was committed, with a quality of richness and of accuracy, of seriousness that revealed their own delight in what they would transmit.

* * *

These were the years of poetry, romantic, yes, but rich and beautiful, lying in bought books, the fruits of pocket-money, bought pages relished with their subtle words, their lines and limpid verses, blending to a poem. Quiet moments, anywhere, in street or room, where the words were spoken, carefully, to extract the essence of a message, alone or with a friend. One of those was Harold Pinter, known through meeting at club; nice boy, a thoughtful cove who joined with me in relishing our books. He took me home, and round a lamp post where Bouverie Road joined Manor Road, he twined himself, reciting Prufrock: 'I grow old, I grow old, I shall wear the bottoms of my trousers rolled'.

We were sixteen, and the words, and the moment had meaning. Harold borrowed from me books: a complete Shakespeare and a Rupert Brooke never to return! But recompense was taking me to Hackney Downs, his school, to see him black leather-coated, as Macbeth in a modern-dress version. He was good, I thought; I knew that drama was his thing. I met his mother, shook her hand, with his father in the kitchen background, more educated than mine, who had never been to school.

These were the months of bombing, of Vls, things that whined in the air and suddenly stopped, while breath was held, only to fall and damn to smithereens some place elsewhere. I took my Higher School Certificate in a room whose windows looked onto a brick wall built to forestall the blast, and in the middle of one exam the warning siren wailed and we all left our half-written papers to file down to safety, mouths sealed by the promise not to talk and cheat. The war ended and my exam results were out. Outside the houses the banners proclaimed the return of fathers, husbands, sons, and inside hearts burned and plans were made.

Pupils at North London Collegiate School, where the author's late daughter, Nicky, taught science and which Nicky's two daughters attended.

The Teaching Years

All sorts of things happened at the end of the war. Our house in Manor Road emptied as Jack Rosen came home from the forces and Esther moved out and Alec came home and Debbie moved too. The house was empty of children and for the first time I had a room where I could study in quiet and that I could decorate as I wished. I had done well in my exams and took the decision not to do a degree in law at University College, London, but to follow my strength in languages and go there to study French and German though it meant doing the German almost from scratch. It was to prove a happy change of mind; my Latin was to be a great help in my study of the history of the French language, and led to an interest in mediaeval French, in which later I was to take a PhD Years later my son Jonathan was to become a lawyer, having followed a joint degree course at Cambridge, where he took a year of French and German followed by two years of law. My daughter Nicky also went to Cambridge, to Girton, and became a science teacher at North London Collegiate School.

I decided to take a gap year before starting university and managed to get a three-month London County Council travelling scholarship, which meant I could go to Belgium to improve my French in 1946. I lived with a Jewish family just recovering from the German occupation, during which the husband had never been able to leave the flat as he looked Jewish. His wife looked Flemish but every time she went out to shop he was afraid that she would be picked up by the Germans, never to return. I had some happy experiences in Brussels. I met the daughter of a ritual Jewish slaughterer and warden of Anderlecht synagogue and helped her carry out the job of emptying the spittoons in the synagogue! There were lots of spittoons, one at the end of each row! And Henry Wyman, a boyfriend, travelled from Germany while on leave from the forces to see me, and we danced together in the Bois du Cambre, the woods outside Brussels, and I ate my first Truite au Bleu and potatoes coloured pink.

I spent the rest of my gap year working as a clerk in an engineering factory in Shoreditch, East London. The factory manufactured the metal bits and pieces that belonged to the making of ladies' brassieres and corsets! I had an interesting time. I learnt to type, and typed hundreds of Woolworths invoices. I even managed to misfile an invoice for a thousand pounds on a

Friday afternoon, when the final accounts for the week were being made up, to everybody's consternation. But they gave me a rise, which made my wage up to a magnificent £2.7/6d a week, so they must have forgiven me.

My first day at university was one of the happiest in my life. I remember the thrill of walking along the path into the administrative building and sensing deep inside me that I was in the right place for me (I later felt the same emotions when I walked along a path to get to a classroom in the first school in which I ever taught as a fully trained teacher). They were blissful days at UCL. The war had just finished and the intake of students was full of mature students with great experiences behind them and so happy to be where they were. The lecturers were, so many of them, inspirational. Dr Tancock, with his incredible lectures on literature, Dr Walker and the Renaissance, Mlle Schlumberger, and Professor Woledge and Mlle Coustenoble. Elizabeth Wilkinson and her fantastic teaching of German literature. There are simply too many to name. I was transported. In addition, I was encouraged to follow the certificate course given in the phonetics department in the phonetics of French. What an experience that was.

The method of teaching was stunning in its effectiveness. They literally destroyed the French that you had spoken, by teaching you scientifically to form every single French vowel and consonant. Only then would they teach you the intonation of the language and put the whole of the learning together. It was like magic. You started the course with French that sounded like that of an Englishman talking French and you ended up speaking like a Parisian. I learnt more about the teaching of skills from my phonetics course than I have ever done elsewhere.

When my degree course ended, I was accepted onto a doctoral course in mediaeval French which gave me the opportunity to do 'real' research and to spend another very happy two years at UCL, researching a fifteenth century Arthurian romance under the supervision of Professor Brian Woledge. It was exciting to be able to spend days reading in the library of the British Museum and in Paris at the Bibliothèque Nationale. In Paris my evenings were deliciously crammed with visits to the opera and ballet, and the Comedie Francaise, made financially possible by dint of living in a youth hostel and watching performances from the gods. By then I had met Leslie Lawrence at a university 'hop' and had decided to train as a teacher at the London Institute

Leslie Lawrence, 1945, in Vienna, where he served in the Intelligence Corps interrogating war criminals.

of Education. I quite enjoyed my introduction to education studies, though no sparks flew for me until I got onto more advanced studies in philosophy and psychology, which I had long wanted to take.

My first teaching post was at a co-educational school, Downer Grammar School, in Queensbury, North London. By this time I had married and was living in Hampstead, in a rented flat with a view of St. Paul's from the attic window, which had a flat roof on which we would sun-bathe in the nude. Downer was the first grammar school to be built in the country since the war, so it had beautiful new buildings and the staff was mature - many were ex-servicemen, and staff-room life and teaching were a joy. Staff did all sorts of things together like play-reading in each other's homes. I could not have been happier and to crown it all, within two years I was asked to take over the headship of the modern languages department. Two years later Leslie got a job at Bolton Technical College, as head of department; I was pregnant with Nicky, our first child, so we moved to Manchester where she was born. When she was a few months old I became research assistant to Professor R. A. C. Oliver in the School of Education at Manchester University, not far from Whalley Range where we were living. I spent a fascinating two years there. I only saw the Professor half a dozen times while I was working for him. He would leave his research instructions in my pigeon-hole, and I did the necessary work either at my desk or at home, and returned it when complete to his pigeon-hole. This was a perfect arrangement to have since I had a small child, who was looked after by an NNEB-trained nanny from Monday to Friday, and who became a firm friend. My research projects were varied and very stimulating, and I learnt a lot. In the gaps between the researches I took advantage of the fact that the library I needed was just across the road and I completed my PhD research.

One research project was a study of the predictive value of the General Studies A-level exam for success at university and beyond. Another was to edit the very first book on hospital schools, written by a Matron on a fellowship, at a time when work in such schools was uncoordinated and their staff had to use their own brilliance and ingenuity to design and fabricate necessary aids for hospitalised children with disabilities and needs of all kinds. I also researched the comparability of examinations at school certificate level. I did this by comparing the exams in French of two exam boards both of whose papers had been taken by the same set of children at around the same time. I compared the papers themselves and the children's scripts and results. I learnt a great deal from the work that I was doing, obviously. Computers were in their early days at Manchester in 1958: they looked like vast kitchen cabinets when I visited the large rooms in which they were housed. I wanted to explore the possibility of using the computer for the rapid dating of mediaeval texts such as I was myself studying at that time. I was told that this was entirely feasible, but the necessary magnetic tape was not yet available, and I left Manchester before it was.

On our return down south, to Surrey, in 1959, following Leslie changing his job, I decided that I had had enough of working in grammar schools. After all I had attended two of them, taught for four years in one, and trained as a teacher in another. What I needed now was to work in a different type of school, which would widen my experience; so I looked for a post in a secondary modern school in Surrey. French was not taught much in secondary modern schools, so I offered English as my main subject. I was very lucky to be able to apply for a suitable post at St Mary's School, a small secondary modern Church of England school, surrounded by the sort of housing which we could now afford to buy. I was granted an interview at which the Rural

Dean chaired the committee. When I pointed out that I was Jewish he replied with a smile that if I didn't mind coming to them, he certainly didn't mind having me.

I worked at St Mary's for four years and they again were wonderful years. When teaching French I learnt how to adapt my teaching to the strengths of the girls and found that a mixture of spoken French combined with the reading of specially abridged simple novels like Simenon's, which at that time were readily available, suited them best, and they were able to achieve a high degree of success. On reflection, I am concerned about the restriction of teachers' autonomy in choice of curriculum brought about with the introduction of the National Curriculum. There is nothing better than lessons where a teacher teaches what he or she enjoys best, and therefore teaches in a stimulating fashion, for engrossing children and getting them to learn. Teachers should be given maximal choice in what they teach or learning can lose its magic and risks becoming ineffective.

In the middle of my years at St Mary's my second child, Jonathan was born, but when I returned to teaching the pattern of our lives was again straightforward. I had a daily nanny, and I walked Nicky to her school then popped into mine and walked home to lunch when I wasn't on duty. I taught even French occasionally to General Certificate O-level, and English for various certificate examinations, and was appointed Head of English. The Head, Miss Blake, and her deputy Miss Berg, were fine teachers as indeed were the staff in general, and good and caring organisation led to minimal disruption of teaching. I loved the teaching and ran a small library, and remember writing and producing a Christmas play and an Elizabethan pageant together with the Head of Music. One experience, which I valued greatly, was accompanying my class to St Mary's church each week. Admiral Nelson had attended this church, and one is shown the post to which he tethered his horse. It is a lovely old building and I was always moved at seeing the shy expressions on the faces of the girls as they exited from the pews at the end of the service. Dwelling on this emotion, I am reinforced in my opinion that there can be little joy in teaching unless you love children, not in sentimental fashion but with respect for their uniqueness as young people and often for their beauty.

From St Mary's in 1964 I was appointed Head of a Secondary Modern Girls' School, Norbury Manor, in Croydon, which had getting on for three hundred girls. It was a good school, which had from all reports been lovingly looked after by a fine headmistress and deputy. I know full well that when schools were streamed at age eleven into Grammar and Secondary Modern there were very good grounds for abolishing this system and for developing instead the Comprehensive system. There was the difficulty of selecting on 'ability' at age eleven, the possible development of 'sink' Secondary Moderns, and the need for large schools, which could offer a wide choice of curriculum and a viable sixth form. But my own experience of two Secondary Moderns showed me that such schools are often good, small and peaceful schools with the advantages of learning that can flow from this. It seems to me that their main disadvantage is that although there was always the possibility of transfer of pupils to Grammar schools, in practice this possibility was not often, for various reasons, sufficiently exploited.

Norbury Manor taught me something about the influence of architecture on school control which has stayed with me ever since and which is important today. It was a newly-built school which had been built with the administrative block overlooking an empty area along each side of which was built one of the two teaching blocks. What this meant was that the Head's room overlooked all the classrooms and that the Head was able to know at any time what was going on in them. If in a large school this principle of visual supervision could be extended to apply to senior staff then obviously control advantages would accrue.

I stayed at Norbury Manor for only a couple of years, because the deputy Head could never be reconciled to her not being given the headship when I was appointed, and a jealous deputy can make a Head's job very difficult, but in this short time I was able to do two things at least which were worthwhile. For example, when I arrived I discovered that a number of girls were complete non-readers. Staff saw the need to help and one-to-one tuition was arranged which quite soon transformed life for these children. We now had no more illiteracy. Furthermore, I became aware that there was no youth club in the area and so I arranged to open one for the girls, one evening a week on the school premises. Staff and parents were generous with their time, and we soon had a committee that I chaired, and a rota of supervision. We consulted with the girls at each stage and it became clear that all they wanted was somewhere off from the streets, where they could meet their friends and have a soft drink and talk. True, even in 1964, we had to confiscate knives (not too many of them happily) from their boyfriends as they came in, but the club worked and eventually the powers that be took note of what we had done and opened a proper youth club for them.

I next applied for the headship of Norwood Girls' School, a comprehensive run by the Inner London Education Authority, the largest authority in the country. This was to change my life completely. The fresh post was advertised in exciting terms, speaking of the future when the school would grow and move into new buildings, and I felt that I could wait for this, could make a long commitment, which I could work towards. My energies were there and would be used: at the age of 36 in 1966 I felt them to be strong and good, and having now experience as a head, I could work fast and build some solid years. My mood then was entirely optimistic.

Before I finally decided to apply I went with Leslie to look at the school. The name was elegant – Norwood Girls' School – though this did not impress me as much as it was, I later found, to impress many of those who heard it, bringing to mind visions of trees, dignified and tall, in a leafy suburb of good houses, when they did not know the truth. There were, in fact, not too far from the school, such houses and such trees, calm and dignified, in avenues, all broad, where the middle classes in ex-Edwardian splendour, or in new 'town houses' lived on the edge of Dulwich and paid owners' rates. Some of my teachers lived in such houses, like the home tuition teacher in the large and beautiful home in Dulwich Park Road, who would receive into it the backward reader, to make scones with her in the vast kitchen, or to read with her in the corner of the long lounge with its view of the willow tree. This was the house where the Inspector and I had sat, initiating the tuition scheme, sipping our tea from the porcelain cups, in bourgeois contentment with the teacher, doing our good deeds while the devastation and the disaster of the school lay up the road, unknown. For the beautiful houses and the lovely roads belied the ugly truth about the state of the school. The school looked like the kind of school in which I had been taught many years before, in the East End. It was a late nineteenth century building, on a medium-sized road where council flats and terraced houses adjoined a small parade of miscellaneous shops, and led to slightly larger, cheapish, older houses, some divided into flats. Down the road was the local Technical College, with a park not far away; in general it was a fairly mixed neighbourhood, with some poorer connotations, but lying near to wealth. A long wall fronted the school, along the narrow pavement, for there were two schools, not one, on the same site: the secondary school, to be mine, and also a primary school. Some of the primary school girls would cross the playground in between, when they grew older, and become my pupils. The wall was high, of yellow, grey and blackish brick, quite clearly old, with the original arched doorways, referring above in cement to the first children to attend the schools. The big wooden boards gave the names and degrees of the Heads. All those responsible were thus duly announced, for all who wished to know.

Just inside the secondary school gate, on the black asphalt playground, with its netball court marked out with white-painted lines, all tidily straight, lay the horrendous large rubbish container, oblong and high, dusty and showing its grubby contents. The odd bit of litter lay nearby, but there was more on the road, outside the entrance, not too much but some. You should expect it, it could be argued – children and schools have litter.

The playground was empty and quiet. I noted the two sets of buildings, with the line of prefabricated huts between them, at the back of the area. I would later learn that my school shared a building with the primary school: the top floor was mine, up the winding staircase to the very top, up the echoing, shouting stairs, lined with the large brown tiles, and where litter had endlessly to be picked up. I was not sure, as we just stood and looked; I had some thoughts that this might be a new and different type of place, of school, of job, and so Leslie and I talked. We said and believed, 'A school is just a school', and thus I made my firm decision to apply. One point I noted. There was no notice showing where one might enter the school; no sign which helped the visitor or parent to know how access could be gained to those who would receive them, no clear words of welcome, nothing at all.

I went for an interview on a day when I could slip away unnoticed from school and met the Head, a lady of middle years, but who had been unwell for a while. The retiring Head was dignified – extremely so – and when the applicant asked her questions of all kinds designed to enquire into the nature of her work, the replies came smoothly, pointing to the 'fact' that all was well, that nothing serious or untoward was there to occasion anxiety. And at the interview with the school governors all was 'hail fellow, well met', good cheer, bonhomie and laughter, and an air of ease and satisfaction with the whole situation. The school was closed that day so there was no teaching in action to be seen, no noise to disturb the quiet of the meeting. Such a pity not to show the school as it was to those who might well lead it! The second interview took place at County Hall on the Embankment, that place of massive, endless corridors with its arches of marble, standing so substantially by the Thames, those solid halls which governed and surveyed so many schools, some good, some very bad. And once again the tenor of the hour was one to imply that here, was a splendid school with few problems, a perfect gift, an honour that they might bestow upon some deserving soul to further elevate a new height. They who gave were ignorant of the gift, those who by virtue of their responsibilities might have known, knew not, those who might have enquired did not enquire, or if they did were appeased by the show, and blinkered to the reality.

*   *   *

I was appointed, and some months later arrived at the school. I went into my room, to take up my duties (it was several months since the previous Head had taken early retirement through ill health). It was simply furnished, with a fine mahogany knee-hole desk, an easy chair opposite, a few bookshelves, and some rows of painted shelves containing files. I looked out of the window, to the other school, with the black playground in between, empty, for term had not yet started. My hands rested on the radiator below the window – it was cold. I turned and looked inward into the room; after a few seconds I moved towards the desk to start my work. Behind the desk were the rows of files, and I leaned back in the chair and placed the first one before me. I took the top sheet out. It was a letter about resources, with a County Hall letter heading and the date was five years before. The second sheet was a copy of a completed enquiry form from a juvenile court: the date was three years previous. The third was a copy of an alphabetical list of equipment for Housecraft, undated, and with the last sheet missing. The fourth was a letter, to a parent, one year before. I felt deeply shocked, for I had an immediate sense of what this meant. This was no mere disorder, no mere muddle.

In gross dismay I knew that this must signify serious disorder, and that certain unknown factors and the illness and absence of a headteacher had bitten deep into the fabric of the organisation of the school. Within the file lay the business of the school: children, teachers, those who worked in support of these, parents, books, rooms and rules, buildings, neighbours and community, hospitals, clinics, police, administration, exams, careers, and information, learning and money, and again the teachers and the children. Without form, without system, the papers jostled each other in shapeless confusion, and the mixture of dates was merely yet more proof of the chaos. Order had been lost and sequence forgotten; no one could have known, or found, or worked with all that lay there. How any school could have functioned amidst such chaos was less the question than how it might have functioned in security and relative peace. No mind could have called such a file a system, system had gone and piles of miscellaneous papers were all that remained. Before I closed the box I knew that the second and the third would contain the same, and so indeed it was. My first task was then to carry home, on the back seat of my car, bit by bit, the voluminous hoard, so that in the peace of my home long hours might be spent in reading and sorting, in discarding and storing in a new established order the correspondence and data of the years past. By the time the work was done I saw, as if through a broken kaleidoscope, the shape of things at Norwood. Bit by bit, a letter here, a document there, laid out before me the substance of my job; a parameter here, a problem there, and so I started to find sense where none had been apparent. Had it not been for working through the files I would have experienced even greater shock than I did, when later such unusual events occurred in the school.

I found another piece in the jigsaw of the school on my first day of term. I took my papers, and my bible and the book of hymns and left my room. I went down the stairs, which led to the platform of the hall, and moved to the front of it where I put my papers on the table, and waited to take assembly. Leading directly on to the hall were two art rooms used as form rooms, and from these rooms girls moved in irregularly formed groups of twos and threes into the hall, where they moved along a row. From a corridor on my left other girls in a file moved into the hall, vaguely ushered into rows by a member of staff from those who stood at the left of the hall, as I faced it. Gradually the hall was two-thirds full, but what struck me was the general air of disorganisation, a laissez-faire which left the rows crooked, on a slant, with gaps here but crowding there, and a harsh reprimand on occasion, which did not still areas of noise, scattered and unexpected. But the faces of the children were good to see, many black, with dark hair of rich depth of colour, shining, in plaits, or bounding on a shoulder, or clustering round a sculptured head. Some were bright blue eyed or bright brown on a brilliant white, while the high cheeks and the curve of features were beautiful. A few Asian girls, and a few African, but one in three Caribbean, and the rest white. I knew without doubt that my girls were poor. Though they mostly wore the school uniform, dark red and grey, which might have concealed any indications of poverty, yet they were there, in the small but potent signs: in the scuffing of the shoes, and in the over-washed fabrics which had lost their sheen, in the cheapness of the detail, the occasional tear or stain. But more than that I saw the faces of the poor, the occasional paleness, where the skin is grey or translucent over the bone, the lack of fat under the skin, or the bloating of cheap starch. For I could recognise the faces of my youth living as I had in the 1930s in Bethnal Green. The physiognomy of the poor working classes betrays itself, and with their clothes, stares at you, incontrovertible. These were the children of Norwood, mine to teach, and so many of them with a bottomless need, as I would find.

When the prayers were over they sat down on the floor, and I felt anger that they should have to do this. To me it seemed a symbol of their enforced degradation, and I worried long afterwards that they should have to sit on a floor made dirty by their shoes. They should have dignity, and should not be demeaned. I felt the same as I walked through the playground and observed that the almost total absence of seats meant that the girls sat on the asphalt, and I quickly ordered playground seats, to raise them from the ground.

Bit by bit, during my first weeks at the school, I constructed the pieces of paper, the forms and the tick-off lists, where they were needed to bring systems into the working of the school. I find it difficult to remember procedures in great detail and find lists on paper a comfort: properly completed, all necessary steps for carrying out processes are taken, and everyone is informed who should be. An illustration was the 'visit form'. Very often, at Norwood, children would not appear for a lesson and, on enquiring, the teacher would be told that they had 'gone on a visit', to some firm, or to a sporting event, or the Tower of London, or some entertainment. With a 'visit form' to complete, the teacher organising the visit would be reminded to inform the teachers whose classes the children would miss, and confusion would be reduced. For my own purposes, I had checklists; for example, relating to staff appointments so that all ran smoothly, so that candidates were well looked after and appointments could be made promptly and efficiently without snags arising in the school. I saw administrative structures as essential to the well-being of the school, and checklists help. Memory is fallible and confusion leads to insecurity in the environment. I spoke once, years later, to Mrs Sibley, hard-working secretary of the school for many years from its inception in 1958, and she laughed as she recalled that her first task on my arrival was to label my files and start filing. My first full knowledge of the peculiar state of my teachers' control of pupil behaviour also came on my first day, when a knock on my door revealed a teacher who in pleasantly accented English asked me to help her as she was having a problem with some girls, who were proving very difficult. Slightly surprised at this direct approach, but thinking that the situation must be very grave and that the teacher must be *in extremis* I followed her downstairs, expecting either to be faced with two or three girls waiting below, or to be taken to some classroom, where I would be confronted by the villains. How surprised I was, then, on passing from the stairs onto the platform of the hall, to hear the teacher explain dramatically, with a large-armed gesture pointing to an endless row of girls lined up, 'There they are!' For she had brought for reprimand not just a clutch of culprits but some twenty girls! The bizarreness of the act and the silliness of the teacher's expectation made me angry, though I did not show it, wanting to be kind to her, and also busy with my attempt to do the impossible being asked of me. Teachers just don't bring whole classes to a Head's room, for reprimand. That this had happened was a symptom of many things: that some teachers in the school had reached a point of sheer explosion at their inability to control their pupils and classes, and that with the coming of the new Head there was a naive belief that she would immediately solve their problems. But it was a symptom, too, of lack of teacher knowledge as to how to deal with control difficulties, so that solutions were attempted which would tend to make the problem worse.

At Norwood anything could happen, for this was no ordinary establishment, no planned community, with no stable ethos of peace and security. Staff reactions could often not be foreseen, for lack of expertise and experience in some cases made teacher behaviour erratic and dubious. In other schools such teachers might have coped, and later would, but in this school where the demands on even the highly skilled were inordinate, the fragile crumbled, made mistakes, and failed, at gruelling cost both to themselves and to the children. The task for such good senior staff as there were was to support the weak to such a degree that they themselves were strained. So the stress passed, through the children, who brought so much of it from their homes, through the hierarchy of teachers, to those at the top, there to rest.

Norwood School girls and a member of staff outside the entrance to the building where the author had her office.

The behaviour of many of the children was the lynchpin of the difficulties of the school, as I very quickly found. This was clearly reflected in the abuse of the buildings, where one extreme was the faeces occasionally soiling the floor of the outdoor toilets, which I would pick up on a spade, out of shame and kindness, not wanting to ask a caretaker or cleaner to do this task. Or the lighted toilet roll plunged into the lavatory basin, whose burning caused the pan to explode and crack, inflicting expensive damage. Or the blood-stained sanitary towels that could be found anywhere: in the toilets or behind a radiator, or by the playground wall. Or the gouging of the wood of the desks or doors, in scale more than just 'time-honoured tradition', or the endless litter. It was not the dirty object, or place, nor the dramatic event, which was the worst – these can be dealt with, removed, repaired or cleaned. It was the underlying malaise in the community, among the girls, and in their relations with those meant to teach them, that such filth reflected, and which it became my biggest task to deal with. It might be thought that some fault lay with those whose work it was to keep the school clean. On the contrary, the caretaker was splendid, hard-working and well-organised, and faced his massive task with exemplary patience and goodwill. I became used to being called to deal with vandalistic emergencies, what in another school would be a rare event for me became 'not unusual' and, as with the staffs' problems with misbehaving children, so my work in dealing with alarms and excursions came to be expected. I had to force myself, after a while, not to over-react. Thus, on one occasion being told that a bench had 'been broken' I went to see it, quite expecting to find that a girl had taken some implement to break it with, only to find that all that had happened was that a bolt had loosened, and I had to remind myself to hold my nervous system in check, to stop my imagination running rife.

The repair and maintenance of the buildings became a priority, in the attempt to reduce vandalism, for it was obvious that broken objects begged for further abuse, but mainly because I felt strongly that the personal dignity of the children in my care was at stake in the environment which the school provided. It was with this in mind that the playground seats had been ordered, and I roused the authority's gardeners to do what little could be done to improve the few spaces around the school. Tubs planted with shrubs and flowers came into place, at entrances, and where there were flower beds, roses and shrubs were planted. A programme to cheer the corridors up with paintings and children's work was started, while the needs of staff were recognised by the complete refurbishing of the staffroom. At the same time, in an attempt to create a positive environment, I instituted a series of parties for the children at the end of the school day: a simple get-together for the children in each year, with food and squash provided, and some music and some simple games, just so that they felt that school was a good place, where there was pleasure, and simple goodwill towards them. You could call it naive, call it bribery, but in this situation of dirt and malevolence and misery, I felt, with Margaret, that some simple routes might help towards the change in attitudes that were needed for any improvement to occur.

Margaret was there from the beginning. Margaret Tucker, acting deputy Head and acting Head before the new one arrived, who had been head of English. The most gifted of teachers, she saw the school as it was with keen clarity, and with courage and love dared to apply for the post of deputy Head. Her compassion for the children and her standards of professionalism were a strength on which I could call, and we both found, to our wonder, an identity of view and aspiration for the school that was to forge a friendship and a stream of laughter on which we could rely and from which we drew strength. Margaret's room was in the 'other' building (the primary school building) where she was surrounded, as we later arranged, with the younger and the less able. Here she worked an endless day, with the patience and the care of the most dedicated; here her room was never just for her. Instead it was a world of problem days and problem people; here a mother would sit bemused by some great sorrow, which involved her child, or a father, greyly penitent, shared remorse with his disobedient offspring.

It was to Margaret, too, that reports came of Doris who was frightening her peers by her behaviour. The corridor at the top of the primary school building, used by the secondary girls, was long and straight with half a dozen classrooms leading directly off it, on each side, so that it was a hub of girls' activity in lesson time and out of it. Doris was backward, black, a mild child, but with her mind in sick disorder so that she started, in a room with windows closed, to have clear visions of bats flying about her. Her friends, dismayed, were further shocked, along with others, when she crawled on all fours along the corridor, butting her head against the classroom doors, opening them, and frightening the children inside by her wild behaviour. Juvenile schizophrenia, for this is what it was later diagnosed as, is rare, but I wondered at the lack of care and love which caused a parent not to know that she was ill, or to ignore a sickness which thus rampant could disturb an 'ordinary' school, until I learnt the details of the household: it was later alleged that the child was in moral danger and that her mother would not stay at home to nurse her child, who later fell into the risk of prostitution. I soon learnt, too, that the chaos that was in the school was reflected in the press of problems on the social and medical services in the area, where a shortage of hospital places and facilities for disturbed adolescents from disorganised homes added to their suffering.

It was through Margaret, who had worked within the situation that I learnt how the serious disorganisation within the school had come about. The school had had no structure in that there was no clear system for whole groups of children to refer to senior members of staff responsible – be it for a 'Year' group or a 'House', and for organisation, behavioural control and pastoral care. Therefore, all problems of such kind would pass along informal channels straight up to the Head.

The second half of the 1960s was a period when the need for teachers in expanding secondary schools was great enough seriously to accelerate the staff turnover in schools. In some inner-city schools a turnover of 50% or more in a year was possible. Teachers moved on to seek fresh promotion, and others were needed to fill their place. The scale of change can scarcely be imagined, so that a Head could spend week after week in simply trying to fill his or her staffing vacancies. The door was open to many problems as a result of this. There was a tendency for almost any teacher to be appointed when the crunch came, when all was desperate, when if one did not appoint, then a class might be left if not without a teacher, then at least with an endless series of supply or temporary teachers. So staff were appointed, who often would never have been granted a permanent post had the situation been normal; once there they could not, of course, be shifted, for to reject a teacher from his or her appointed post is almost impossible, unless their behaviour is totally extreme; incompetence is very difficult to prove. There had come, and came, into Norwood School some staff with standards, which were low in all sorts of ways. These included staff who arrived late, not by odd minutes, not just once or twice, but like the teacher who not having to register a form first thing in the morning, as she later explained, was coming in forty minutes late each day, sidling into the school via a classroom door which opened onto the playground near the gate. There were staff whose attitudes to children were in my opinion despicable, like the teacher who would ask her West Indian charges, in a fracas in the playground, why they did not go back to the West Indies? Quite the most blatant form of teacher racism with which I had to deal.

Some teachers were appointed above their capabilities, where the need was urgent; they would do their best, and often better than expected, but there were still cases where the job proved quite beyond them, or at least the routine work was done, but the opportunities for imaginative developments which might have taken place were sadly lost, and the education of children suffered. The schools seized upon teachers coming fresh from college, and though many were excellent, not only did schools have too great a proportion of these for easy absorption, but they also came into schools with staff in a state of flux, so that they often reeled, and did not receive the support they needed.

All these things happened at Norwood, though it was far from alone in suffering them. For me, as a new Head, the high level of staff turnover had two serious consequences. Firstly, it took up so much time that there was less left for other urgent or important matters. Second, but far more important, the effect upon the children of constantly changing supply teachers was terrible, whether they were good or bad teachers. Already insecure from their personal and educational history, their minds were buffeted by change after change; no sooner had a teacher established some sort of routine, of pattern for their work, than he or she was gone, and another came to take their place, with an attempt to fix some other routine, some other pattern. The change of teachers often took place so rapidly that all continuity of teaching was lost, and in the end, for some children, no real teaching took place for months. The loss of potential, the loss of learning, the loss of chances of growth was inestimable.

To make the matter worse, the massed confusion had its obvious impact upon behaviour, and so vicious circles were set up in which the frustration of the learning (or rather 'non-learning') environment led to behaviour problems that made it even more difficult for the child, and classes of children, to learn. For, given the disorganisation, problem behaviour was not just a matter of individual children misbehaving, but was the phenomenon of group behaviour, that most difficult of problems where the dynamics of the clique, the gang, the class, the school, become the spider's web that will not yield, though the struggling flies push against it. The line goes direct from the constant change of teacher for the child, to that same child in the mob in the playground, busy in the fight, angry with the unconscious feeling of betrayal by those who should have taught her. And that fighting was there, frequently, in the playground, during breaks where a scuffle or a push would flare up in seconds into real attack, where the limbs would thrash. Small groups would move to where the noise attracted them, a crowd of twenty or fifty or sometimes more would gather round, excited, and vaguely pleased at a spectacle to enliven the hour. The sight of the mob or the noise of calling to the pair still fighting would attract the teachers who would push through the crowd to the assaulters, and with shouts and efforts to control would pull them apart, and try to disperse the crowd which would dwindle slowly. They left behind a sorry sight, in the torn blouse or skirt, grazed limbs or blood-stained face of the two who fell upon each other, who would limp towards the building, and be taken to Margaret's room or to mine, there to sit outside to calm down; or perhaps they would be removed for solace and first aid, but then brought back for counselling so that the origins of their anger could emerge and steps be taken to avoid a repetition of the fight. This was a very long and slow task, the questioning and establishing who had done what, and why and when and why again. Each enquiry had elements of a court-room scene, but was carried out with kindness in a search for fruitful justice, while around all this the school went busily on with its French and Music, Maths, and History. Sometimes the fight would start up in the staircase of the primary school building where the hollow tube of the stairwell sent echoes up and down, and where the tight crush of girls on steep, stone stairs, made it a dangerous event. I would marvel at how serious hurt was regularly avoided, though chances of it were always very high. I learnt to warn the staff that when they came across a fight, they should send quickly, if its scale was large, or if the physical stature of the girls was large, for other help – a child could bear the message to another teacher – as they might by themselves be overwhelmed. And when the fight was over I might be further saddened by a child who said, in answer to my strictures, 'You only say that 'cos I'm black', at a time when bruising words had been thrown by one child to another and had whipped up aggression and spite.

Another reason for the school's disorder, and a main one, was the hidden selection process, which brought together in one school too high a proportion of children with personal problems of such character, that their disturbance fed into the maelstrom. In those years, a fair attempt was made to share among the schools children whose ability was of a certain order, and Norwood had, on paper, a fair balance of its children in the higher, average and lower bands. But what had clearly happened was that tucked within these bands were children some of whom had background and personal factors of instability and some who had no clear sign of them. When advice was given as to where those first, vulnerable children should go, for example, by the child's primary school head teacher, sometimes with good intentions, the advice was that the child should apply to Norwood School. Competing badly with other local schools in newer, modern buildings, or with 'better' schools in the public's eye, it had become a 'sink' school where those who misbehaved or had undeserving parents, or were vulnerable in some way merited to go. One could always tell a doubtful parent that this school had developed special skills in handling such children as theirs – not true, but perhaps it was reasonable enough, for those advising and for those thus advised, to credit it.

Research from the Cambridge Institute of Criminology would years later suggest that in part these hidden selection mechanisms would account for certain schools containing undue numbers of delinquent children: they were right. In Norwood School they brought together children whose emotional disadvantages predisposed them to difficulties in learning and behaving. The disturbed child's problems interacted with those of other similar children, exacerbating her own and theirs, and building an unhealthy whole, a disturbed school, a maladjusted school of vast dimensions.

You might think that, in an all-through school, with pupils from eleven years to eighteen, you would find peace and all quite well among the children who went on into the sixth form where relative educational success would be the norm. But in the sixth were some strugglers, whose fight against themselves had turned inwards, whereas the healthier child might strike out. These children had fine, able brains, but were adolescents who were mentally ill. Two I will never forget, the first for her growing sickness which would lead to her removal from home to Cane Hill Hospital, and the second, the thick-haired, beautiful Janet who never faced her teachers, but who would sit at her sixth-form lessons, gaze averted, looking downwards over her shoulder, but listening. This child came to see me, and sat before me with a length of white string in her hands which she entwined among her fingers, round and in and out, endlessly, obsessionally. This was the tragedy that, years before no one was alert to these girls' pain, nor had they seen it, been willing or able to take steps to help them. Such was their ignorance that such children would suffer for many years, until a point when it might be almost too late. It was their tragedy to come into a school where what disorder they brought with them would be fanned, rather than calmed.

Philip Graham, one of our finest child psychiatrists, then working at the local child guidance clinic, would say to me, when visiting the clinic for a case conference on my long list of disturbed children, that there must indeed be group factors involved: the school itself must be partly responsible for the quantity of disturbed behaviour arising within it.

Pupil turnover was another factor that added to the lunacy. Although in general the population in the area was quite stable, for fifty-three children, for example, information about number of previous schools was not available and the area was serving as a reception area for new immigrants. The area was one where families were moving in and moving out for many reasons: some were recent immigrants; others were being re-housed, whilst there were those of parents who were permanently transient, the adult waifs and strays of our society, in temporary accommodation, short-stay hostels. Or they were children in care, now here, now moving on, for Norwood School received many children in care, from several local children's homes. Such children were a feature of the school's intake, constant in their need for considerable emotional support from the staff, constantly to be remembered as 'special cases'. The children came and went, so that a teacher never had a stable class, but always someone had left, usually with no goodbyes said, rupturing her friendships, leaving children hurt and bewildered, without time for the loss to be acknowledged, before others arrived. With the children constantly changing, teaching was made very difficult, as the newcomers so often had not done the same work as the rest of the class: either the class was held up, for explanations to be given, or the child's need for extra tuition was ignored, or a skilful hard-working teacher would somehow satisfy it. The class registers told the tale of the turnover, with their deleted names, and their additions, a story of passage, rather than rest, or rupture and frustration, rather than strongly woven webs, excessive novelty bringing anxiety for all.

The task of those administering the school was a demanding one and a large apparatus had to be created to ensure that each child coming in was fully integrated, helped in every way to settle, with her parents informed of all that they should know. The simplest way was to arrange that at the child's entering the school the interview would centre round a massive form, several pages long, where the teacher interviewing could record in full as much as possible about the child, her background and needs, and which would remind the teacher to offer the parents all the forms of help which they could have. Two details here suffice: the teacher would ask whether the girl had ever been in hospital as an infant, for they had found that this might be important in adding to the vulnerability of the child, and she would ask for details of the immigration history of the family (otherwise very difficult to obtain) for the clues this might offer to the situation of the child. I still laugh when I remember one case that occurred before this careful structuring of interviews became routine. There was a child whose school behaviour was absolutely impossible. She was frequently agitated, often threw temper tantrums, and in general was most difficult to control; thus the question arose whether she might be clinically maladjusted. I discussed the case with the local school psychologist who then arranged for the doctor's medical examination, which routinely preceded discussion and diagnosis of maladjustment. After the examination, the psychologist said, 'We must first deal with her toe!' This child had recently arrived in England from Ghana where she had lived in a rural community, never wearing shoes. The big toe on one of her feet was unduly large, so that coming to school in England meant not just wearing shoes, but the pressure of the shoe upon her outsize toe, and unbearable pain. Little wonder, then, that she was misbehaving!

Some of the children in care had been taken into care for reasons of truancy from school or absconding from home, so that particular alertness became necessary to ensure that they felt happy in the school, lest they run away again and compound their problems. As part of this side of my work I liaised with the various children's homes, met the children's house-parents, had tea with the children and sat in one Head's room, with a small infant on my lap, clinging, arms round my neck in the pathological, compulsively tight hug of the emotionally deprived. I valued the work of those who ran the homes and came to know their sadness and their limitations, too.

Norwood had only one in three children, of its 700, with parents from ethnic minority groups, and many of these children had lived in England from birth or for many years. This was, however, a period when an influx of children and their parents came into the country from the Caribbean islands and these children were part of the high 'turnover' of pupils that the school knew at this time. For the staff this meant, as for indigenous white migrant children, a large task in settling the children into the school, interviewing their parents and explaining to them the various social benefits that they might be entitled to, such as a uniform grant or free meals. But more significant than this was the fact that a number of the children were vulnerable, feeling lost at the shock of coming into the school and country from a very different sort of environment, and different style of schooling. For example, there were shocks in coming from a semi-rural or rural community to an urban one, in coming from schools with tight, authoritarian discipline to those where the style of discipline was less tight and more relaxed. These effects were added to by all sorts of difficulties, in food for example but undoubtedly the biggest trauma came from changes in their home environment and circumstances. Thus very often a girl who had been living for many years in the country in the West Indies, with her grandmother looking after her while her mother and possibly father were living in England with a new family, suddenly found herself transported into the midst of this new, differently functioning family, in often cramped and cold accommodation, in the midst of a city.

It was small wonder that children in this position became slightly or even substantially emotionally disturbed, or at least registered in their reaction to their new school and their general behaviour something of the shocks which they were experiencing and had recently experienced. It was not simply that the reaction was that of difficult behaviour: more insidious was the depression some went through, sometimes obvious in withdrawal and solitariness, but in others more difficult to perceive, because it was concealed behind restlessness and extrovert behaviour. What became clear to me, from my work with such children, was that it was often not just the child who was suffering from depression, but also the child's mother, whose life was overwhelming her, so that at home the depression of each of them exacerbated that of the other. Fortunately, the child guidance clinic where such a child could be referred would also, via its psychiatric social worker, be able to help her mother, if she were willing.

Sometimes recent immigration led to merriment, as with one Asian child, involved in Housecraft. Her teacher came to me and explained that at the end of a cookery lesson her plates and cutlery were not to be seen, and were eventually recovered – in a table drawer, where they lay unwashed. The explanation was really quite simple: she was of high caste, and back home she had certainly never washed up, and at that stage saw no reason why she should start doing so in England!

Among unhappy incidents at this period was one concerning a West Indian child, who became involved in an argument with another child in a

Needlework lesson, seized a pair of dress-making scissors lying on a bench and moved in on the other child. Happily the teacher in charge saw was happening and intervened, and with a struggle managed to control the girl and remove the scissors from her hand. She brought the child over the playground and up to my room, where the girl sat, sullen faced and shoulders bowed, whilst the teacher described what had happened. It was clear to me that the child had to be excluded from the school in view of such dangerous behaviour, and I decided, since her mother was not on the telephone, to take her home myself. The girl was still in paroxysms of anger, bitterly protesting, and throwing things to the ground, so that the senior teacher now helping with the case was worried for my safety, but I went to my car, with the child, carefully, feeling my way, and we travelled safely to the house. There, at the top of the flight of stairs, was her mother, in her simple kitchen, frowning and angered at the event. It later emerged that this child had come to England and the school either without the required medical examination, or if she had one, it was not detailed enough to elicit the highly significant fact that her intelligence was not just sub-normal, but severely sub-normal – hence her difficulties in coping with events in the needlecraft room, and her total lack of control and dangerous assault. Once examination had elicited this information, it was possible for her to be placed in a suitably protective educational environment where her special needs for security and support would be met.

Thus it was, that to the difficulties the school was already experiencing were added these other factors of teacher turnover, pupil turnover and hidden selection processes. These combined in a potent mix, each interacting with the other to create a school of super-ordinate difficulty.

The knowledge of all this came to me piece by piece; sometimes a day would pass where the events came thick and fast in an exhausting mass; sometimes a day would bring a single incident of such a startling kind that it would stand alone in my mind in its implications, as when a routine fire drill would show total confusion, noise everywhere, and a head of department who refused to leave the building! Or a day where a teacher, unable to cope and roused to a frenzy in a quarrel with a girl, went nearly berserk and pinioned her in paralytic rage against a wall. But week by week the facts began to grow in number and fall into patterns: some patterns would shift, but then re-form into others until I could feel I had a clear picture of what was there, and what was wrong. I had not spoken up, had not revealed my thinking to my seniors; an invitation to visit County Hall had remained unaccepted, for I felt there was too much to do, there simply was not time to leave the school. Besides, I was not yet ready to speak, my mind was not yet firm in what I wanted to say, and so I worked and waited. Only to my husband and Margaret did I talk of what I saw, and of my anger and disbelief that such a state should exist. In those first months I had a visitor, one of Her Majesty's Inspectors who seemed to me to sweep in, full of camaraderie, to praise my predecessor, drink his tea, and then sweep out, a happy man, without seeing the school, without one serious question. I could only sit, and marvel. This was the only time to the best of my recollection one of Her Majesty's Inspectors visited the school in the four years I was to spend there.

By the middle of my first term I felt I knew what I would have to say, and made a resolve to put the facts on paper, in a report, which I would send to the Divisional Education Officer. When I told Margaret of what I planned to do, she said how glad she was, that she would then 'feel clean'. So I wrote a long report full of such serious complaints that I could not sensibly ask for it to be written even by my own school secretary, so I had it typed outside the school. The report made it clear that I considered that a grave situation had arisen within the school, and gave a list of how this was reflected in the behaviour of pupils and of some staff. It listed factors such as staff incompetence and stress, and dereliction of professional duties. It listed late staff arrival at the school, and absence for no good reason. It noted that such weaknesses were found not just among some inexperienced or junior staff, but that some heads of department also were gravely incompetent. It pointed to the problems of the children, needing better teaching than some were giving them; it made it plain that their indiscipline and disorder were unacceptable, that abuses against buildings were common, and that staff were frequently disobeyed. It pointed out that the special needs of the children were simply not being met, and suggested that improved staffing and facilities for remedial work would be essential. It stated that the whole matter was most serious and urgent, and that resources would be needed, if it was to be coped with.

At the time that the report was sent to Divisional Office the disorder in the school reached a new peak in the junior school building where Margaret had her room. Case after case occurred of girls whose disobedience flared, who chased around the building, out of lessons, totally defiant or who stayed in classrooms to abuse the teacher grossly, and disturb the other children. At Norwood, children would commonly hang about the buildings, out of lessons until some patrolling teacher would pick up the truant here, or there, in an empty room or some outbuilding. But this spate of wandering difficult children was quite different from the norm, and even Margaret began to wilt under the onslaught. The moment came when she too had to speak, coping with a room full of recalcitrant pupils and besieged by endless complaints from staff. She told me that we had to restrain the three arch culprits who were racing about the school, disturbing classes, defying all authority, and whipping up disturbance, and we agreed that I alone as Head could keep them under some control if they could work in my room, all day, every day, for just a while. We did consider exclusion from the school, but there were good reasons for not doing this: the moral danger into which one would fall, the second with a mother suffering from acute depression, and the third with the mere boisterousness of a maladjusted child of low intelligence who would be alone at home all day. And so I worked in my room, running a school of 700 girls and some 50 staff, with three problem pupils in there all the time, to teach and supervise, and who were beyond the control of the staff designated to teach them.

When my report reached the Divisional Officer he acted promptly, consulted with the District Inspector and informed the Education Officer for Schools of the Authority, who arranged a meeting for all of us to attend at County Hall. We met one afternoon at the end of winter in a small room where greyness entered from the sky above the Thames, invisible beyond the window from where I sat, nervous and tired. The three men talked among themselves most of the time and I was not asked many questions. Most surprise seemed to come from the smooth-skinned, sharp-eyed Education Officer when I described the situation in which I had been working, with three disturbed and disturbing children in my room, trying to run my school in spite of this. Was this really so, could it be so? I was asked if I really had no one on my staff, who could do this work? And I replied, 'No'. I left the building and walked towards where my car was parked. I got in and held the wheel and wept.

* * *

In a little while, a fruit appeared from the meeting. I was offered the chance to have the school inspected, either by a full inspection of Her Majesty's Inspectors, which would take a long time to arrange, or by a 'visitation' of the Inner London Inspectorate, which would be achieved more quickly. I chose the second. A date was duly arranged for the week-long inspection and I began to assemble all the information which would be needed for it, all the descriptions of the work of the school, its pupils, its curriculum, its staff, their qualifications and experience, and the details of what they were teaching and the rest. Amidst this work the senior remedial education post in the school was advertised: there could be few more important posts in a school where learning difficulties, unmet by help, could so easily spill over into behaviour problems, and where so many special needs existed. Furthermore, such a teacher could teach others how to view the needs of children and promote all education in the school. By wonderful chance, and recognition of her qualities, the person now appointed was Judy Mariani, whose splendid training and experience had fully equipped her for the work she came to do. With her quick perceptions, her intuitive appraisal, she assessed the situation, defined the children's needs, and immediately planned a strategy to meet them, assessing staff and how best to deploy and support them.

Judi Mariani, Head of Remedial Education at Norwood School.

Even before she took up her post, she was able to help me in a direct and simple way. She came to visit the school, to meet her colleagues and to see some of the children, and before leaving, came to see me. She said that she had noticed, in a class of second year children, one child who stood apart from all the others, in that she was achieving virtually nothing. She had observed the child's general demeanour as well as she could in a short space of time, and she had spotted, apart from her severe learning difficulties, the very great influence that this girl, Maria, had on others, whom she appeared effectively to control. In Judy's opinion Maria had an intelligence which was in fact sub-normal (tests later confirmed, indeed, that this was so) and this, combined with an unusually dominant personality, led to bullying and abuse of power. Now, about this time the school had been plagued by an outbreak of mass pilfering. Someone, or some group, had been going through the school cloakrooms, rifling pockets and bags, removing everything of value, and efforts had failed to detect the culprits. Judy's observations led me to reconsider the group she had observed to be under the influence of the girl Maria, and the enquiries were successful. Maria – ironic that one should call her 'sub-normally intelligent!' had been the leader of this gang of thieves, highly successful for a long time!

Judy was to make a massive contribution to the work of the school, not just through her rich personality and mind, from which others could draw ideas and much support, but through her thinking about the work of less able children. It was she who was to develop the idea of an observation class for children whose precise needs had not yet been established, and who needed time with thoughtful teachers so that this might happen. More than this she revitalised the content of the teaching for all less able pupils, bringing it to life with colour and with art, making worthwhile accomplishment possible, with vision and with skill. Detailed curricula were carefully drawn up and copied for all her staff and others who were interested. An exciting inclusion was a course in child development, for backward pupils, for she recognised their special need for this: both now, when they should understand and say just how they felt, and later when they would themselves have care of children. Throughout, she used imagination, as when, knowing that adolescents who find number difficult have need of basic learning apparatus, she understood how they might feel if other children saw them use it and said hurtful, sneering things at their infant-like learning. So she found a room somewhat removed, where these activities could be pursued, without risk of being seen. She understood, too, how important it was that she should teach all the teachers in the school about her work and about the children in her care, and she was patient and understanding with those for whom remedial education was an inferior thing. She worked closely with me, and when she left, she was to become a headmistress herself, of an infant school in Brixton.

* * *

The week of the 'visitation' arrived and the band of Inspectors descended on the school, and scattered into the departments which were their special interest: English, History, Maths, Modern Languages, Crafts and all the rest. They talked to staff, and watched them teach the girls, sitting in lessons and wandering round the class. They walked around the school from time to time, and talked together in rooms specially set apart. The days were fairly quiet, as you can imagine, since the presence of so many serious-looking visitors had a slightly cowing effect upon the community of pupils and, of course, the staff who knew how much their careers depended on the impression now received. Yet their presence did not curb everything or everyone; thus it was that one event occurred when the District Inspector with one of his colleagues was sitting in my room with Margaret and I. Suddenly, I looked out of the window, my eye caught by a movement opposite, and I drew the others' attention to the sight. A child had opened a hall window on the second floor of the primary school building opposite, had stepped out onto the narrow ledge of the false balcony outside, and was moving along it, step by step, hands flattened for support on first the window and then the wall. Nothing stopped her but this, and the lowest black iron balcony railing, from falling fifty feet or more, onto the asphalt covered area below. At that distance, I knew there was nothing I could do if that child slipped. I looked at Margaret, who smiled slightly and said loudly in angry despair to the Inspectors, 'You see, Norwood is running true to form'. Happily, in response to someone calling her from the hall, the child relented and retreated, disappearing from view. The child was Mandy, whose school record showed a dozen different surnames so confused was her life history; a sweet and twisted girl, with courage and a sense of fun, a distorted sparkle, who had won the friendship of another disturbed girl called Valerie, a depressive, middle-class child who would later throw herself, in spite of psychiatric help, from the balcony of a theatre. These two would at times go on the loose, untracked and wild, and lock themselves in toilets or such places and cavort, in an extreme disorder, so that one hardly knew what to do to help. Margaret did what she could, and knew them well, spoke with their mothers and understood their needs, without being able (nor was anyone) to satisfy them.

The visitation proceeded on its course, and it was clear that the problems had been seen, until one day, walking along the corridor with me, a staff inspector of the Authority turned and spoke to me of his concern, adding, 'It may well be that this is one of London's difficult schools'. On the Friday there was a large meeting of almost all the Inspectors, and myself, addressed initially by the District Inspector. He spoke in grief-laden tones of the fact that the report earlier submitted by myself had been justified and vindicated in all respects by the inspection. It was all there, just as I had said, the weaknesses in the school and in some of its staff, the need for change. In fairness to the Inspectors, during the week they had done their work well and had already greatly helped to bring about some changes. For seeing where the staff weaknesses lay, they had brought pressure to bear upon the poorest staff, to bring about a move of school for them in various ways, such as by pointing out their failure in this post. Thus, at the end of the year amongst those teachers who left were some who were deemed incompetent.

At the meeting one quite tiny thing angered me beyond all measure. In talking about the condition of the building, with its damaged fabric and derelict appearance, a comment was made about the fact that the children had chalked lines and marks for 'hopping' games upon the playground and that this looked very untidy and should be forbidden. I was hardly able to contain the explosion within me, at their inability to see the worst of all: that here were children whose school lives were empty, who had nothing to do, for whom there was no rich provision – not even playground seats to sit on – so that I was happy that at least in the playground they had made for themselves an activity. Seeing my anger, the Inspector took fright and suggested that I might like to have lines painted in, on the asphalt, instead of the chalk! (I shortly arranged for the provision of plenty of lunchtime activities, boxes of games of all kinds, which helped counter the emptiness). A further result of the inspection was that it established for the period of my headship the special needs of the school in terms of staffing and resources, and my later requests for help in these directions were met with considerable promptness and generosity.

During the inspection I had taught the classes that I usually taught: they were two, at either end of the wide spectrum of abilities and ages, so that I could experience the same range my teachers had to teach. First, I took the girls in the sixth form for General Studies, so that I could teach them along a wide front, and discuss with them issues of many kinds, philosophical, psychological and political, amongst others. I enjoyed the wonderful experience of talking with keen lively adolescents on significant matters, in which their novel slant and fresh ideas would constantly amaze me with their breadth and maturity. As well as this, I taught a class of first year children, who were the least able of their age, a class of 20 girls. I shall never forget my first lesson with this class. As I became absorbed in teaching, listening, observing and replying, controlling here, suggesting there, arranging and organising their work and their groups, and came towards the end of the lesson I found that I was using every ounce of skill that I possessed, that the demands on me as a person and teacher were inordinately heavy, and I walked away from the room at the end, amazed, that I, with my years of experience as a teacher and as a head teacher, could feel so taxed. This was a most valuable experience, teaching me what it was like for my staff to work with such a class.

My immediate problem was what now to teach these children that would so absorb their interests and energies as to reduce the problem of control and encourage them to learn, and I decided upon the simple project of letter writing. There was little contact between the girls and the small children in the next door primary school, except for meetings in the playground or, in some cases, brothers and sisters who attended that school. So it was decided that my class would write weekly letters to a class of junior school children, who would write back, and get to know them. In this small way, they would be stimulated both to read and write, and at the conclusion, they would meet the younger children, by arranging a party for them as part of their Housecraft lessons. It did the trick, created a lot of interest, especially for two or three girls who had never used an envelope, and found putting a letter into one and sticking it down a mysterious, satisfying experience; and likewise for the girls who acted as postmen, and for the whole class, as they designed their party invitations.

My main task after the visitation was to try to fill the vacancies which would be left by the departure of staff some of whom the inspectors had put to flight. Hence, an endless round of advertising, of considering applications and of interviewing suitable candidates now began. Whole days went, sometimes wasted, as the indifference of one or the total unsuitability of another gradually became apparent. My criteria had now to be stringent for the future of the school depended largely on the quality of those chosen. By chance after chance some wonderful teachers did apply to the school, and who would spend years working for its benefit. The first was Mary Scott, who by a rare professional hazard was without a post, but who had been head of Modern Languages in an august, independent school. The staff Inspector, knowing her to be available, and knowing Norwood's need, invited her to look at what it had to offer in the way of a head of Modern Languages post. So she came, and I came face to face for the first time with someone who was to make an enormous contribution to the school as head of department, then as head of year, then as deputy Head, and finally as Head of the school itself.

On talking to her, it became apparent that she was no ordinary teacher, able to work on a limited front or perhaps with just one kind of child, but someone who could span the whole range of educational experience. Another to come on board was Marion; once again a teacher who would spend a decade in service to the school, first as head of Housecraft, then as head of year, then head of lower school, when she would become a deputy Head of one of London's most prestigious schools and later be appointed to the headship of Prendergast School. Miss Perry had just come from Fiji where she had done voluntary service, in keeping with a career in which so much of her free time had been devoted to the service of young Guides. A dedicated teacher, her boundless common sense and store of practical skills, together with her energy, were to prove a constant boon. Kay Lynn came too, very different from these others, with her yearning to teach children to dance, with her aesthetic strength and imagination, with vision and skill which she was good at communicating. Head of Physical Education, and teaching more mundane skills and games, she was to infuse the school with musical movement, and would

Older pupils from Norwood School on a Home Economics residential holiday, organised by Marion Perry.

liaise with Art and other departments, to create performances which left an audience breathless with the excitement of seeing the young in dance.

With these new staff to join the many good staff left in the school, good things could happen in the curriculum. The work in Housecraft and Needlework had always been strong, but Marion would now expand the horizons of the girls, taking them away on residential projects where they could learn to live and work together. Thus, these town children would come to live in Girl Guide huts, large and black painted, in the middle of a field, and from which the view was of horses and soft fields. Their great excitement at dormitory living would meet the tussles of their life together, and girls would learn, and some would change, or show confusion at their days of close cohabitation. They would plan their common meals with thought and calculation, and would cook, wash up and clear together, and would also gain in the humour and the closeness, a wider learning of socialisation. The school had been one of the first to teach Metalwork to girls, but now it would be able to offer courses in Car Maintenance, so that the sight became common of open jalopies, unheard of in a girls' school. The valuable work of the Commerce department under Miss Farmer was now extended, to develop the work in Commerce itself, as well as shorthand and typing. And the work of Sheila Ferguson, a splendid History teacher and Jenny Dunn, who had become Head of English, in teaching an integrated course together, on local history, was to continue. As a result, children of eleven and twelve could study the history of their families and communities, talking to grandparents, neighbours and the like, could walk about the paths and adjacent streets and blend the whole historically true past into their speech, their reading and their writing.

Our work in developing the curriculum was further shown in its enrichment for the older children's work. There were already some good and interesting choices made available in activities for fourth and fifth year pupils. They could already skate, ride, ballroom dance and play judo, and to these were added others, but we now created a general option scheme, around a central core curriculum, so that disgruntled, 'turned-off' adolescents might have some choice in what they were to do. We knew how crucial the development of the curriculum was for the school as a whole, how much it would raise staff morale, and how much it could contribute to the intellectual, social and emotional growth of the children. Others, like Joan Biggs in her splendid pottery work, and Janet Hancock in her work in Religious Education, also knew how curriculum content can help children. But still one main preoccupation was the need to cater for those children who were showing serious behavioural disturbance.

* * *

I took the chance, when it came, to spend a weekend at the Inner London staff residential centre, at Stoke d'Abernon, where the psychologists were running a course on emotionally disturbed children. The manor house stands on the edge of a river, and the high rooms which overlook the water are quiet and the armchairs deep. I came to stay there in a grey depression, not in the clinical sense, but in the depths from weight of working, and because there was so much still to do, so many children needing so much help. It seemed ironic that the teachers and psychologists could be there, in such tranquil surroundings, while the substance of their talk lived in a remote gloom, among tired houses. While I listened to the talks and lectures, the theories, the types of problems, the types of behaviour, I noted often, in the left-hand margins, the names of my pupils, to whom each description referred.

Shortly after my return, knowing of the dimensions of the problem, Marie Rowe came to talk with me: senior psychologist, she would later become responsible, as inspector, for all children with special needs, in the Authority. This meeting gave me the chance I needed to talk through the general picture, and to speak of the long list of disturbed children in the school of which no two were the same.

The local psychologist now gave lots of help, and the child guidance clinic offered its staff too. Thus, for example, the clinic staff came into the school, to take a seminar for the whole staff, in which they went through a complete case study of one of their children. At another time, the senior Brixton clinic staff came to help the senior school staff talk through their anxieties about juvenile suicide, for on the school's roll were no fewer than nine pupils who at one time or other had attempted – seriously or not – to kill themselves.

Another factor needing staff's attention was child abuse and neglect. It was clearly necessary for teachers to be alert to any sign that this was taking place, to keep eyes open for dirty and ragged clothes, for signs of malnutrition, and for signs of bruising and of any hurt. It was important, for a case to be proven, that a doctor should see the signs while they were evident: happily the school doctor was usually in attendance each week and one of her tasks was to see such children as were thought to be affected. I was also in regular liaison with the officers of the NSPCC, although by now I had arranged a scheme for pastoral care in which this work would be taken up more and more by the new heads of year. The doctor, too, would help in cases of pregnancy, though sometimes the bulk of this work fell to me.

The school relied heavily upon the excellence of its school doctors, of which Dr Alice Potter deserves special mention. It was quite obvious that in matters of health the school really could help its children, and medicals and their follow-up were always taken seriously. When Mary became deputy Head and even later when she was Head, she gave medicals priority, usually being in attendance herself while they were conducted so that any care or follow-up which was deemed necessary would be sure to take place. The school knew that matters of health were basic to good learning, that apparently routine tests of eyesight and of hearing and of weight could reveal crucial needs, and that it was useless if remedial action was not checked by the school, where parents might themselves be negligent or need advice and support.

There were, of course, some cases in which all that medicine could do was not enough, and very occasionally, as indeed in all schools, there would be a funeral, which I would attend. In any big institution, in which there are large numbers of people, this will arise, as indeed would the telephone calls telling again of the death of a father or a mother. The school set up the channels of communication and support so that some help might be given even though it felt its inadequacy. I tried to arrange for a counsellor to be appointed so that children could talk through their problems, but this met with difficulties, as did the requested appointment of a school-based social worker. Some cases were long-term, with death their end, as in the case of a fourteen-year-old, ill with serious kidney disease, which became gradually worse. I would call and see the child always lying on the couch, a knitted blanket over her thin body, and her mother, who in her desperate need and confusion, took refuge in a rare religious sect. The school could help, with books and play materials, and little gifts, and visits from her classmates.

Dr Alice Potter, Norwood School doctor.

On a larger scale, the school could turn outwards, and it would help with an old people's home nearby, whose elderly would sometimes be invited for a party, or for a school performance, while sometimes the girls would invite themselves in, to provide some music or perhaps a play. At Christmas, there would be a party for local old folk, and also some gifts to those who needed them, in boxes carried with enormous delight by the girls delivering them to the various homes. One year, one family on the list of those in need was that of a girl whose father was in prison; it so happened that no pupil lived nearby who could volunteer to do the delivery, and so I opted to do this myself. I parked the car opposite the house, and went and knocked on the door, which was opened by a pretty, well-dressed woman. I explained my visit, and passed over the parcel, but not before I had looked into the room. Sumptuously furnished in velvet and brocade, just oozing wealth, its sideboard held a dazzling array of bottles of spirits! Before Dad went off to prison, he had provided more than adequately for his family; in confusion, free of my 'parcel for the needy' I stumbled back to my car and reflected wryly that there must be a lesson for me, here, somewhere!

On a more serious note, the school had to take on, with the various voluntary and paid agencies serving it, a large welfare task. It was in an area of immense housing need, and many children suffered from their bad housing, like the child who had literally nowhere to sit to do her homework, but had to lie on her bed doing it, at an age when she was attempting to study for external exams. Another child, Vera, lived with her mother and her educationally sub-normal elder brother in an ancient house whose walls were soaked with damp. Her mother was chronically ill with asthma and related chest problems, and the fire in the living room grate which had to burn constantly, competed with the ever open window which helped her to breathe. I visited this wonderful family, wonderful in the placid cheerfulness and love of the three of them, very close together, and hardly complaining. Vera, too, was attempting to study for her exams. The madness of the deprivation struck me so forcibly that I unashamedly pulled strings. A member of the school's governing body was an influential local councillor and I raised the family's plight, with its implications for the girl, at a Governor's Meeting. Within weeks the family was re-housed.

My predecessor had started a store of second-hand uniform, which in the capable hands of Edna Kirk helped many families to bridge the gap between the far too small uniform grant and the girls' actual needs. Whenever girls left the school they would be asked to give or sell cheaply to the store any items they did not need. Shoes, however, still remained a problem and occasionally when a girl was absent persistently, a visit would discover that the absence was due to lack of shoes.

By the middle of my second year I knew firmly that the school community in which I was working was in its rarity clearly to be explained by the nature of the children coming together within it, so l decided to undertake some research, based on the pupil records lying in my files, which now contained a mass of data mainly gathered since my arrival in the school. I designed a profile for each girl which would include the most significant facts about her, details of her home background, of her previous school history, and of her career at Norwood School, both in terms of her work and her behaviour, as far as it had been recorded. In this way data could be assembled which would then describe the features of the groups of girls, and of the school itself. When I was ready, I wrote to County Hall, to Alan Little who was head of the research and statistics division, to ask whether he could offer me some help in the collection of the facts. In the event, he became so interested in the idea of studying the school in this way that he offered to take over the research entirely, to carry it out and to report on it. He had in mind that such a whole-school study, of a school now known as disadvantaged, could be used to point to all the Authority's needs of various kinds. There would, it was surmised, be other schools like this one, in this large Authority, and there were lessons that were worth learning. Thus, it was that in the following summer, in the quiet period of the school holidays, several researchers came into my room, outside which the files of records stood and carefully picked their way through the detail. Back at County Hall they counted and wove together the information into a sort of sense, a story.

There were other 'stories', of course, which could have been written, all true, about this self-same school - the story about past and present teachers, and about myself, the Head who now had come to the school. To what extent did I exacerbate the situation? Certainly it seemed, for a while, that when my controls were put upon the school, disturbance showed up more clearly. Was I the best to do the difficult job? But, in a way, the story of the teachers had been told in the report on the visitation. Another story which could have been written was that about the Authority itself and about such of Norwood's problems as came from the actual administrative structure. One has to assume, however, that after the visitation, such blame as there was had fairly been apportioned, and lessons learnt.

In general, as you would expect, the report revealed little which was unknown to the staff and I, but it did make some important points:

Although it is accepted that deprived children need additional attention and help there is no record of the incidence of deprivation in a school and what this would mean in terms of staffing and additional resources. In Norwood a frightening proportion of children exhibit behaviour problems which are the result of the children living in homes under great tensions, either materially or emotionally.

The importance of medical examination was confirmed. One in five children had a slight physical disability and 1 in 20 (32 girls) had a gross disability. The latter included curvature of the spine involving the insertion of a metal splint: a collapsed lung which made all physical exercise unavailable to the girl, and which had made her timid and shy, so long had she spent in hospital with her illness; and an intelligent girl who was totally deaf. There was confirmation of the abnormally high incidence of disturbed behaviour among the children, already known to myself and to the child guidance clinic, not just aggressiveness turned outward in all ways, but the sad burning inward of the punishment against the child herself, the 'no one cares if I die' and the obscene sensual preoccupation. The cultural shock of immigration was noted, leading at times to withdrawal, at others to attention-seeking.

A few girls were thought to be in contact with groups taking drugs; the school knew that soft drugs were exchanged and taken at school, but only very rarely was evidence found to support these suspicions. The police suspected a group of girls in the fourth year of being involved with drugs, and a letter was sent to all their parents, warning them of this. Some girls were in contact with boys taking mainline drugs, and one girl received a letter from a boy being treated in a sanatorium for liver disease and septicaemia which was caused by mainline heroin. He did not appear to have been severely affected by the illness, since he was arranging with the girl for a meeting at the weekend so that he could get a fix. Girls in moral danger were documented; the sexually precocious twelve-year-old, and the girl found in the park at three in the morning; but mainly the older, disenchanted, for whom the school held nothing. Or the unstable Nigerian girl who had to endure racial prejudice from some West Indian children, who ran away from home with her brother and slept rough for three nights before being found by the police. Official delinquency was low.

What was most striking was that the general ability of the girls in the school was as good as it was found to be; this was not a school of unintelligent children, but a school with a balance of ability normal for London, with a roughly 'correct' proportion of able, average and less able pupils. It had children of good intelligence, who could learn and achieve beyond their present achievements. There were goals that could be reached, skills that could be learnt, a whole education which could be received, if only their world at school was calm, secure and positive, an antidote, for some, to their rough world at home. This was the bitterness, and this the hope. What was of importance, also, was that the general intelligence of the girls was not matched by what they had achieved in English and Mathematics at the age of eleven. This confirmed that their problem was one of schooling, rather than ability; of schools and teachers, rather than of mind.

The report showed, too, that when children came to enter their secondary school, Norwood was not as popular as some. In the more popular schools, the head teachers have to reject a certain proportion of the children.

In Norwood it appeared that an unrepresentedly high proportion of the children who were rejected from their first choice had disturbed home backgrounds, as expressed in the (primary school) character profile. This selection is not a class one, as Norwood had a fairly normal distribution of children from different socio-economic groups, especially as it was in a predominantly working-class area. Within the groups however, there appeared to be an abnormally high proportion of disturbed children. By distributing the disturbed children more evenly at eleven, some of Norwood's problems would be solved. However, if Norwood was going to have large proportion of disturbed children, which it had at the time, the school required additional staff and resources to cope with the problem.

At the time when I was asking for the research to be done I became ill with debilitating glandular fever, which meant that for six weeks I had to be absent from school and lie in bed. Margaret did all that she could to cope, but the school was in a desperate condition and her workload threatened to be overwhelming. So it was decided that I would continue to deal with paperwork at home, and each day the postman brought a heavy envelope to be dealt with. I lay and worked my way through all the letters, queries and the long reports, in a fatigue that made it take me hours more than it would usually have done. I was finally better, and on return to school I was to have a change of deputy Head, for Margaret was to leave. Instead of going to be Head of a school, tired and needing revitalisation, she went 'backwards' in her career, to become again head of an English department, and was to postpone her eventual appointment to a headship. The years at Norwood had taken their toll on Margaret and on those who worked for a long time at the school, by the gruelling stress that distorts lives and careers. To replace Margaret, Mary was appointed, whose energies and firm determination combined with a flair for practical innovation. Consequently, the work of the school developed, and a slow progress came, with time, to be made.

* * *

An Open Day may be a routine, regular event in some schools. At Norwood it was poignant in its implications. First, by the very decision to have one, knowing as I did the work involved for staff already tired by the hassle and strains, but a decision nonetheless taken so that the school could make to all outside a statement of what was positive and good in its work. Secondly, it would also act as a form of self-assessment both for the children and the staff, so that they might draw upon what was creditable as a source of energy for future tasks.

The task of straightening the school for its exposure was formidable, as indeed it is in most schools, with caretaking staff working overtime at sealing and polishing floors and clearing playground litter. The girls emptied and tidied desks, polishing the desks with dusters and smelly polish and disposing of crumbs and rubbish of all kinds, until the brown and green metal bins in each classroom overflowed. Walls hitherto negligently empty suddenly bloomed with coloured sheets of card, on which were proudly shown pristine children's work, in multi-lined drawings and perfectly inked writings. On the desks, the scoured surfaces were unnoticed, covered as they were by tidy piles of pink and blue exercise books, inviting parents' hands to open them and see all the hard work, all the knowledge, seated on their pages.

School closed early and the cleaners did their last impressive wipe. Staff who lived nearby went home for tea and change of clothes, while the senior staff and I stayed on for a last inspection, a last check. I reflected on my wander at the stillness of the school, at the bleak, old fashioned building, with its beamed ceilings and its clumsy, echoing stone staircase, waiting. One could see the effort poured into preparations by children and teachers, but more than that there was the sense of dignity in all the work displayed. It came from the fact that this was a school like others, standing for the care of the young and the development of potential, and for the transmission and development of ideas and knowledge. These were rooms for doing and learning, a house of study and though this dignity was mocked by transient events, it took its sense from this. It took meaning, too, from the opening of itself to parents of its children. They were too often on the fringe, too frequently not involved, as if their child was sent away from them when she went into school. There is too often an absurd, great chasm between the two environments, home and school, seldom bridged except in problematic crisis, or complaint, or routine events. At least tonight the parents knew that they could enter without constraint and any expectation except that they would see, enjoy, praise and be welcome.

The Open Evening included events, displays and demonstrations of all kinds. Here parents could join in a Mathematics lesson, and there applaud fine gymnasts; there was dance to see, and scientific experimentation. It was a splendid few hours, but best of all was the perception by many of those who saw it that in so many areas of the school staff were teaching well, along original lines, or new ones, bringing good curricula and up-to-date techniques to bear upon their teaching tasks.

Among the visitors who attended was the Divisional Education Officer. He expressed his amazement at what he had seen; frank surprise that so much that was sound and innovative was going on in the school. What struck him forcibly was the contrast between the image of the school presented by the Open Evening, and that which came to him by other, daily channels. He knew of the school largely through its problems and difficult pupils, neighbourhood complaints, its stresses and strains, yet here was its other, lovely side – its work, its potential and its successes.

Through all this time, one of my delights was to cross the playground and go up into the primary school, to talk to its headmaster, who became a friend. Dapper Ron Abbot, of later Schools Council fame, would always listen, an ironical smile upon his lean face, and in the homely order of his small office, we would work together as colleagues. The other Heads were also good for me, in the quiet sharing of their views and needs.

Parents were an important focus of my work as they were seen as crucial to the school. From the first admissions interview, through regular meetings of all sorts and kinds, contact was striven for, not always successfully. Some were absent from the evening meetings because school meant to them a foreign place, where feelings of anxiety and inferiority from their past history would predominate; and so they stayed away, when they were needed. But many came, to talk, to argue or to justify, and some to plead for corporal punishment – 'You hit her, Miss', as though that were the answer, when all the girl knew was this standard reaction, and our aim was to help her to control her own. Some came depressed with all that life was doing to them, or angry at some small affront, like being asked to wait. Another came, very early in the morning, straight from her night-shift, with the grey face of fatigue on her, because she loved her daughter.

The school tried to bring its parents into knowledge of the school, and of the girls' life there, and Mary developed the parents' newsletter, which took home news for everyone to read. More work was done on girls' careers, too, with every child studying careers as part of lessons, from the fourth year, under Mrs Hughes, and efforts were made to involve parents in career discussions and events.

Thus, there are the three phenomena: the difficult child, the difficult class, and the difficult school, all inter-related, as at Norwood, where the effects rippled outward from individuals into whole classes and groups, so many that it could be said that this was a difficult school; and then the impact rebounded from the whole school, onto the classes and the individual children themselves, in a monstrous, wild dynamic, where disorder for a while was the norm. Dealing with pupil misbehaviour took up much of our, especially lesson time, for teachers might have to stop a lesson several times, or it might never get off the ground in the first place. An atmosphere of conflict and aggression might be generated, and destroy the children's chance of concentration, and the noise or bother created by a disruptive group or pupil might compound the situation. Since disrupters will often behave in this way, it is quite clear that loss of learning can build up seriously over time, and in some instances can become decisive in a child's attainment. Where teachers crumple in the face of such problems they may stay away from school or suffer from some psychosomatic disorder which impairs their work and health.

Such absences from school may merely make it harder for their pupils to study as they should. In difficult schools, too, the work of controlling misbehaviour takes up a large part of the time of senior staff, and leaves them without energies for the other part of their work, fostering the learning and well-being of all children in the school. Mere supervision of disruptive pupils may use up valuable staff resources. The result, therefore, of large-scale misbehaviour in a difficult school is this: that its pupils suffer from a form of educational disadvantage, which is compounded by any other disadvantages to which they may already be subjected. Consequently, the child who by virtue of her birth and environment already has the educational cards stacked against her, who may find difficulty in learning even in favourable circumstances, is buffeted in the lesson by interruptions from the others, the general disorder in the class, the door opening and shutting as people come in and out, and the constant requests of the teacher for quiet. If hopes of social mobility are very slim, at the best of times, they are annihilated in an atmosphere such as this.

I can remember, amongst others, a case of 'whole-class' disruption, where a group of fourth year girls presented a very good part-time teacher of Commerce with a serious problem. She was at her wit's end, desperate for help. Commerce had only just been introduced as an examination subject and she was anxious that the group should succeed. In spite of all her efforts to teach well and to make the subject stimulating, the girls were difficult, would not obey her instructions and would not settle to their work. Alas, I knew precious little of group dynamics in those days – did not think of analysing the situation in terms of pupil leaders and followers, nor in terms of group goals. But I knew I must do something drastic and immediate. I clutched at the fact that as Head I had massive power, and decided to break the problem up and tackle it as a predicament of 24 recalcitrant individuals. I arranged to go into the classroom with the teacher present. I spoke to the group peremptorily and sat down at the teacher's desk, grim-faced. One by one the girls came up and sat beside me, the record of their performance in front of me. The rest of the class were 'getting on with their work', but, of course, their ears were extended in our direction. In a deliberately clipped tone I charged each girl with failure to live up to the expectations of her teacher in matters of behaviour or work, and pointed out the career implications of that failure. She was given a few weeks in which to show improvement, after which consideration would be given to her losing the opportunity to continue her secretarial training. Looking back on the technique now I shudder at its crudity and cruelty, but I could think of no other way. Over the next few weeks I kept in close touch with the teacher. Magically, it worked. She had no further trouble. Instead of throwing up her job, as she had earlier threatened to do, she stayed and made a major contribution to the work of the school, later working full-time and becoming a head of department.

The days passed, with their events, like going to church at Christmas for carols, like architects visiting to discuss plans for the new school building, and like the day girls came in after lunch, drunk on cider, too freely sold by the villain at the local off-licence! Teachers worked, large numbers of them, immensely hard, in day-by-day plodding devotion, excited by success, and girls grew up, and learnt and often won, in spite of handicaps of a dozen kinds. Gradually the situation at the school improved, but during my fourth year, as the time came for the school to move into its new buildings, I felt that I lacked the energies which at best I should have, to see the school into what was tantamount to a complete reorganisation, with the existing buildings to be used by the first two years of the school, and the senior school in the new premises. I had, with Mary, helped to plan the new arrangements but so much would remain to be done that I felt I should relinquish my post for another. After two periods as a head teacher I felt I should embark on something new and yet related, and so I accepted an SSRC Fellowship which would allow me to train in educational psychology, and to research the subject of disruptive behaviour in schools which had occupied so much of my time over the past four years. I made my preparations to leave the school, full of grief at a break with the children. At my leave-taking, part of the farewell was a performance of dancing, in the hall, by children who had come from different countries over recent years. In the final dance the tall and beautiful black-haired Indian child, arms above her head, in the folding, flowing, scarlet and turquoise chiffon, circled, heels clapping on the floor, with the sweet bells tinkling round her ankles and her wrists, in the dance of honour.

Studies in Indiscipline

What lessons, then, can the story of Norwood tell us? Firstly, that the analysis of a difficult school cannot be done hastily, just on the basis of what people say about it, even when they think they know why it is difficult. The growth and development of a difficult school is complicated, involving the past and present history of the institution, for Norwood such factors as the Head's illness and absence from school and the strenuous domestic problems off the deputy Head. The recent history of the catchment area was very important; its development into a place into which people with children in need were re-housed, with a consequent lot of change of schools for those children and, importantly, the influx of children from the Caribbean as part of mass immigration for a better life, over a period of years. Migrant and immigrant children need settling into a new environment and this takes time, as well as being at least temporarily a drain on welfare and schools' resources.

The reasons for the development of a difficult school include obviously its pupils and staff. Pupils have school records and I believe that I was the first to recognise the importance that these have in the analysis of the disruptive school. I initiated a piece of research into the pupil records at Norwood by drawing up a list of the type of facts in the files which I considered to be relevant to school difficulty, for example immigration history including Government definition, number of schools attended, family size and history, housing, indices of poverty such as free meals and uniform grant, and need for remedial education. Also included were physical disability, mental illness in family, psychological disability in child, behaviour problems exhibited at school, length of separations from parents through immigration or hospitalisation, involvement in court cases or community behaviour problems, persistent truanting, and referrals for learning and behaviour problems to child guidance clinic or domiciliary tuition, remedial class or hospital treatment.

As I have already mentioned, Professor Alan Little, who was at that time Director of Research and Statistics for the Inner London Education Authority, became so interested in the proposed research and its eventual application to similar schools, that he took over its implementation, sent his researchers into the school during the summer holidays, supervised the screening of records and analysis, and wrote the report on his conclusions, which I have already summarised. Norwood's problems were in the main attributed to an overload of disturbed children in the school, so that by distributing the disturbed children more evenly at age eleven some of its problems would be solved. My deputy and I had already found that Norwood was actually recommended to children who were rejected from their first choice, and who had disturbed home backgrounds. They were recommended to Norwood almost certainly in good faith by primary school heads who told them that Norwood had a reputation for 'doing well with children such as yours.' The bad result of this was the large-scale clustering of disturbed children.

So I recommend that difficult schools need careful and skilled analysis of records. Ofsted inspection is not likely on its own to be adequate. And without proper diagnosis treatment may be superficial and remediation short-term, as is sometimes the case when schools go onto special measures. Needy children must of course be correctly referred for all the help of various kinds which is available to them. The other major factor which Norwood highlights is that staff change may be essential in a difficult school. Either that or massive staff support is indicated. Incompetent members of staff who teach poorly are anathema in such a school. So are those with poor professional standards, who arrive persistently late for school or lessons, who are racist in attitude, who are themselves disturbed, who are absent for no good reason, or who are ceaselessly disobeyed. Help is needed by the school in replacing such teachers or placing those suitable in an easier setting. Such steps should become available via the Inspectorate. At Norwood the London inspectors who had visited the school for a full week, were extremely effective in bringing about staff improvement.

After Norwood I went to train for research into deviant behaviour thanks to a Conversion Fellowship, in educational psychology, in the Psychology department of the London Institute of Education, where I was awarded a Masters Degree. The department was run in 1970 by Professor Thelma Veness, a wonderful person who died young whilst I was there and who supported me generously in my work. I studied psychology of learning and child development, and research and statistics, and wrote a dissertation on the way women teachers look at their most emotionally- and behaviourally-disturbed pupils. The 31 teachers I studied were all highly experienced, and came from all kinds of secondary and primary schools of various sizes. They taught boys and girls mostly aged between 10 and 13. The study tried to find out what sort of pupils they found the most difficult to control, and also what techniques they used to control them. There were some interesting, statistically significant findings; for example, the teacher response seemed to be an emotional one, with the response to boys' behaviour being particularly so. Primary teachers seemed more anxious about boys' behaviour, while secondary teachers were more worried about girls. Can this over-anxiety about boys' behaviour propel them towards delinquency or greater disturbance, one wonders?

As for the types of behaviour which teachers had witnessed in their most difficult and unusual children, those which caused the most frequent and serious difficulties were very clearly, disobedience above all, followed by poor concentration and quickness to fly off the handle. Where two or all three of these were found in the same child, the frequency and the seriousness of the difficulties escalated. I was particularly interested in the actions taken by the teachers to deal with the difficulties, and gathered in all no fewer than 36 techniques used by skilled teachers to handle such problems from communicating with other staff about them down to altering one's plan for the lesson.

The usefulness of such a list of handling techniques was obvious, and I developed the idea of a longer list which a school could use, by including its own suggestions. Entitled 'A Behaviour Problem Checklist' it was developed in discussion with groups of teachers attending courses on special needs or disruptive behaviour. It includes two parts, one for techniques used by classroom teachers and the second for those used by senior staff. The list is of proven utility to schools. Not only can it help systematise work with difficult children but it aids memory, and in pointing to the very wide range of procedures open to teachers singly and in combination, it can be a source of considerable encouragement.

* * *

My one-year Fellowship was extended for a second year so I decided to study misbehaviour in classes of children, by developing a method of analysing the difficulties of behaviour within any classroom. No-one had done this before although classes are often spoken about by teachers in terms of their difficulty.

I did this by developing a grid on which each teacher taking the class would record how easy or difficult she found that pupil. It worked quite well and showed, for example, the pattern of difficulty in the class, and which children related well to certain teachers though they behaved badly with most of the others. It can also be used to explain the behaviour of certain children and to measure the general difficulty of a class, so that its improvement or deterioration can be measured. I tried the technique out in three urban schools. On leaving the Institute of Education I wanted to continue studying indiscipline in schools, rather then returning to school-teaching, so I turned to work in colleges of education which would allow me time for this. Eventually, after two years at Furzedown College I came to Goldsmiths College, now known as Goldsmiths, University of London, where I was to remain for fourteen years and was very happy and busy in a department led by a smiling Welshman, Jack Nicholas. The staff represented a very wide spectrum of political opinion from Marxist to extreme Conservative, which made for a stimulating environment! The students were graduates of high calibre and potential for teaching in secondary schools and I had great joy always from my seminars and tutorial work with them, and from helping, with their method tutors, to supervise their teaching practice in a wide variety of schools. I was very lucky to have the privilege of discussing education with groups of students who had trained in many disciplines. They buzzed with ideas on philosophy, psychology, and sociology and were eager to debate them. If I often thought that teacher training should be more school-based, well, this is now happening. It has to be carefully managed of course, or students may miss out.

I was also most fortunate to find in the department at Goldsmiths Pamela Young, who specialised in educational administration, and David Steed, historian and sociologist. We formed a triumvirate who together would pursue research into disruptive behaviour which we saw as becoming an increasingly important subject for schools. We were the first in this country to note that such behaviour was coming to affect younger children than hitherto and began to highlight this, with a study of primary school teachers' opinions, backed up by descriptions of incidents of disruption. We also looked at the phenomenon in Western Europe mainly through a study of questionnaires and publications in French and German-speaking countries, from responses given in French and German. Even as early as the 1970s, the causes were seen similarly in Europe and the UK, as residing in society and the environment with their values, and in the structures and practices of schools.

But the most developed work the three of us did together was our two studies of the utility of the monitoring of incidents in secondary schools; the first a boys' senior high school, with 800 pupils and 56 staff, and the second an all-through 11-18 co-educational school with 1200 pupils and 101 staff. We studied the patterning of indiscipline by monitoring incidents in the first school over two separate weeks, and in the larger school over a period of a week. We defined disruptive behaviour as:

> ...behaviour which interferes seriously with the teaching process and/or seriously upsets the normal running of the school. It includes physical attacks and malicious destruction of property.

As well as monitoring incidents via an 'incident form' we interviewed many staff, and in the second study a number of children, too. We analysed our information, issued reports on the analysis to all staff, and discussed the report with the staff both informally and at meetings. Suggestions for improving the situation came not only from staff but from us. In the second school we were invited to carry out the study by an advisor who had become interested in our work on the first study. Hence, funding for the study was made available as was permission to interview pupils who had taken part in some of the incidents. It was extremely interesting to be able to compare teacher and pupil versions of the same incident.

Many findings from the two studies were extremely pertinent to the control of disruptive behaviour. In the first, the staff reporting incidents were young and less experienced and the key, immediate problem was the difficulty of engaging the boys in worthwhile learning experiences: 'a general refusal to be taught'; but also important was a rigid, 'automatic' disciplinary system leading straight to suspension. Time of day affected the number of incidents, as did the imputation of malicious intent in the boy, physical danger in science and craft lessons, and the teacher's interpretation of black children's behaviour as deviant or non-deviant. Timetabling emerged as significant. Several incidents suggested an escalation towards a disruptive incident during the course of double lessons.

In the second study only one teacher preferred not to participate. Again, the need for a better understanding of cultural differences was highlighted.

Minor, continuous disruption (what is now known as low level disruption) was stressful. Corridors were mentioned as a disproportionate source of stress and noise, running and talking back were found critical. Limited pupil choice of optional subjects for less able pupils caused disruptive behaviour. Staff decided on the basis of the monitoring of findings on the morning break period, to stagger the time of break for upper and lower school. Early morning was time for many incidents, so a school tuck shop before school and at morning break was advocated. Incidents clustered at the end of the afternoon so an afternoon break was advised for a trial period. Clearly monitoring of incidents is useful in generating all sorts of ideas for reducing them. The school, in proof of this, asked that the dialogue between staff and researchers should continue after the study had concluded. Computer analysis would of course now be feasible for the routine analysis of incidents over a long period, and schools could monitor their situation themselves in this way.

Author with her late daughter Nicky, and grandchildren, celebrating Chanukah.

* * *

As I look back over my years in education and forward to the next decades, I am left with anxieties which have prompted my work on indiscipline. There is a magic in teaching, especially successful teaching, which is intoxicating. Education is a wonderful field, as far as both theory and practice are concerned. But difficult pupil behaviour on a large scale can annihilate successful teaching, and conspire to increase the stress of teaching to highly undesirable levels. Unless we work at making schools lively but peaceful places, teaching will be impaired. Peaceful does not mean dull. On the contrary, good teaching makes children lively, but with a healthy liveliness not a disruptive one. There is much work to be done. Let us hope that the United Kingdom Observatory for the Promotion of Non-Violence will help, and that the study of selection processes which lead to the clustering of disturbed or violent children in certain schools, will also assist. Let us hope that in the inner cities Academies will work their charm and improve behaviour as well as standards. Truancy might well be reduced if we develop techniques for helping children who have missed schooling to make up missed work. And techniques for supply teacher support need to be put into place. Ofsted inspectors need more expertise in behavioural control, and the help of psychologists. There is indeed much to do. Schools must, above all, professionalise their approach to indiscipline.

During my years at Goldsmiths, my family grew up in Croydon and our marriage and children brought us great joy. We lived in lovely homes, enjoyed wonderful holidays, most of them camping and caravanning in Western Europe. Leslie spent twenty happy years as Principal of Carshalton College of Further Education, in Surrey. Both children married, but when Nicky's first child was born with cystic hygroma, I retired early from Goldsmiths, to live near her in north-west London. I have never regretted the decision, especially since Nicky was to die later at the age of forty from breast cancer. After retirement in 1987 I had two part-time posts, one as research assistant in the educational department of a local authority, and one running a unit for dyslexic students in a new university. I now live close to Nicky's two daughters and Jonathan and Caroline and their three sons, and am deeply grateful for them and the happiness that they, and my wider family, and extraordinarily varied career have brought me.

Bench at North London Collegiate School commemorating the author's late daughter, Nicky.

Jean's Postscript

Education for old age is not on the curriculum, but in a way it is everywhere in the curriculum. For much of what we have learnt at school and in the lives we live after it, whether in colleges or homes or careers, we carry into our old age. We remain very much ourselves but with a few differences. Insufficient is written about old age. Insufficient is done about it too. But it is a great period for self-education. There is normally time for reflection on important matters: our own lives and the lives of those we know, our families and friends, and those who share this extraordinary world with us. It is a time for evaluation when we question the worth of our past deeds, and see ourselves as people who have made a life-time's worth of choices in our own particular way, even though some seem to have been forced on us by our genes and birth, and chance, good or bad. We have time, if we are so inclined, to think about some massive questions, which have baffled humanity since the beginning: what brought us here, is there a God or just a creative force, who designed the creatures of the world, the arts and sciences, the emotions, suffering, happiness, hatred and love, and living and death? All this I have found time to reflect upon in retirement. I have reasons for wanting religions to survive in spite of their causing mayhem at times and, importantly, I understand better the role of love in the development of the human spirit.

As for my main field of study in education – disruptive behaviour in schools, and children and young people in relation to this, I feel sad at what has happened to life in many schools, as the violence endemic in society has washed in to school on an increasing scale, fuelled with major social ills such as drugs, and violence with weapons. We have terrible difficulties with which to cope. People are trying hard, but our coping strategies are too often inadequate. The most important document in recent years, bursting with ideas designed to meet the school situation is the *Steer Report, Learning Behaviour* (2005). [2] If its recommendations are really exploited a great deal will be done that will help teachers and children and their families. It needs reading in full and painstaking implementation. But I am left having it read it with these questions about the wrecking of teaching in numbers of schools by deviant pupil behaviour. So much needs doing, and soon. Is sufficient being done quickly to tackle disruptive behaviour in schools on an international scale? The *Steer Report* recommended that the OECD [3] should undertake international research into behaviour problems in schools. I had published an article in the *Times Educational Supplement* in 'Talkback' [4] suggesting the OECD repeat a European study I carried out with colleagues in Europe twenty years ago, to ascertain developments, and Jacqui Smith, then an Education Minister, arranged for my letter to be sent to the Permanent Delegation of the United Kingdom to the OECD before 10 March 2006. It is now 2011 and I have still not received a response! I was told in early July of 2007 (after chasing them) by an administrator in Paris, that I would receive a reply to Jacqui Smith's original letter 'in two weeks'. It is now far longer than that and I am still waiting. I hope that all recommendations of the *Steer Report* are not taken up so very slowly! I am ill now and cannot pursue the matter but someone is seriously at fault.

Why have we still got only a fraction of the educational psychologists we need to help teachers in coping with disruptive behaviour, which has been

---

2 *The Steer Report. The Report of the Practitioner Group on School Behaviour and Discipline*, (HMSO), 21 October 2007.
3 Organisation for Economic Cooperation and Development.
4 *'Fifty years on, behaviour still holds us back'*, *TES*, 27 January 2006.

a problem faced by the teaching profession for so many years? As it is, educational psychologists are a scarce resource, when they should be plentiful, training teachers, and a regular part of Ofsted inspection schemes, which leads me to my next question.

Why is there no teacher counselling service when for years there has been an obvious need for one? For some teachers behaviour control constitutes a major stress, and they can be diffident for various reasons about obtaining support from colleagues. This can lead to considerable suffering, trigger mental health problems, and lead to withdrawal from the profession.

Why is training for parenthood paid merely lip-service in the school curriculum, and by society as a whole? The media in particular should do more, and headteachers and government explore it as a vital part of the curriculum. Behaviour is taught first at home so many parents, present and future, need training.

There are lots of issues relating to types of school which are relevant to disruptive behaviour and these currently focus upon the establishment of Academies, on the growth of faith schools, and on the question of the retention of independent schools. In retirement my information about schools comes to me via reading, the educational and other press and media, from my family, for I have five grandchildren at school (all at independent schools, one a faith school), and from former colleagues and friends. What of difficult pupil behaviour and different kinds of school? This is no easy or brief topic to discuss seriously, leading as it does into fields of politics and economics, but

Cricket at Haberdashers Aske's Boys School, Elstree - an Independent School attended by the author's three grandsons (David, James and George).

I would say this. There can be little doubt, as far as faith schools are concerned, that the clarity of goals in these schools, and adherence to the precepts and essence of the faith concerned, will lead in almost all cases to conformist behaviour ranging from satisfactory to excellent. Teachers and pupils are, as it were, intrinsically working with parents, in the same direction for the most part.

As for private, independent schools, many factors lead to good behaviour with a low level of disruption. These factors operate also in grammar schools and the many good comprehensive and state-governed primary and secondary schools, where standards of behaviour are high. The central factors firstly, are material resources made available to the children by parents, either because they are affluent, or because they deny themselves to provide resources for their sons and daughters. These include resources such as decent housing, a healthy style of living incorporating good nutrition and exercise, time for talking together and for mentally and physically stimulating experiences. In these schools, classes are relatively small and pupil and staff turnover relatively low. Priorities of conduct through the various elements of school life and teaching are made clear, and teaching is of a high order. Extra-curricular activities absorb energies and talents and are highly developed. It is sheer madness to advocate the destruction of fine schools. The wider education service should be funded and developed so that all children can enjoy such benefits. Centres of excellence such as my fortunate grandchildren attend are to be cherished, and the education they offer be generalised as far as possible.

As for the development of Academies, yes, if inner city schools can be helped through their establishment, it is worth trying them. Already we know they are not always the answer, but they are trying to deal with, amongst other things, a major societal problem – the development of difficult schools within the stresses of disadvantaged, urban communities. The violence and underachievement, the cycle of poverty that is among the great curses of our age need tackling with innovation, and resources; and Academies, with the right sponsors, could help.

I have the chance now to see my life in education in perspective. My years at Norwood were the most formative, determining the rest of my career an impairing my health to the present day. I was 'into' 'difficult' behaviour when it first constituted in some inner-city schools a foretaste of the current

A teacher with pupils at Immanuel School, Bushey, Herts – a Jewish faith school attended by the author's grand-daughter Alexis.

situation of disorder in many more schools. I was among the first to record the life of a 'sink' school, and with colleagues to note the onset of disorder in some primary schools. We were also amongst the first to note difficult behaviour across European schools. I was amongst the first to try to develop simple coping strategies, such as monitoring incidents of disruption, with staff finding solutions from their own professional expertise. In one sense I am a pessimist – social forces are exacerbating teachers' and pupils' problems, but I am also optimistic; solid attempts are being made to cope with them. But still I am concerned that we may not always be hearing the truth. There are vested interests and sometimes good reasons in keeping quiet about the dimensions and severity of the problem, as it affects learning and the mental health of schools.

In 2009, the then Schools Secretary, Ed Balls, [5] has said there would be a crack-down on bad behaviour, that Ofsted would monitor disruptive behaviour, and teachers would be encouraged to order after-school and weekend detention for repeat offenders. Quite what will arise from these statements remains to be seen. What he did not say, and which was immensely

---

5 Rt. Honourable Ed Balls, MP for Normanton, was appointed Secretary of State for Children, Schools and Families in June 2007 as part of Gordon Brown's first Cabinet.

important, is that a body would be established to ensure the implementation of the *Steer Report*.

Thirty years ago in a letter published in *The Times Educational Supplement* I advocated the establishment of a national centre for the study of deviant behaviour. We haven't got one. I think a few of our current problems would be of a different order if we had, but we do have something – not well enough advertised perhaps – better in some respects, in its scope and use of the modern technology, called the UK Observatory for the Promotion of Non-Violence. [6] It deserves nothing but praise. As an online facility it disseminates, for example, rigorously tested research techniques for the development of teacher strategies for coping with difficult behaviour such as bullying. Developing new techniques for diagnosing conditions in schools, it has an international approach and is set fair to help children and teachers and society enormously. I would be proud if I could think that the Observatory's work is being done in a similar spirit to my own, many years ago. I hope that the Department of Children, Schools and Families will make full use of the Observatory's findings, and that the Observatory will work in close conjunction with an effective, fast-moving permanent United Kingdom delegation to the OECD.

Since 1993 when I retired I have seen 'disruptive behaviour in schools' as a topic change to 'violent and aggressive behaviour'. I am greatly saddened by the development, but so, I believe, are many in our society, and we are not alone in the world in this.

---

6 Based at the University of Surrey. To view website see http://www.ukobservatory.com/

Michael's life in education

To the many people who contributed to my personal and professional development: close family, who sacrificed much; colleagues and role models, particularly those I mention; and the tens of thousands of students who came under my care. But most of all to my beloved mother, who devoted herself to ensuring her children had a better life, and to my father, who gave his life for his country and whom I was never able really to know; for they made me.

A Wartime Child

I was born in Stepney, so I'm a true Cockney, which is what I used to tell some of the 'snobs' I had to meet in my later professional life. At some point we had lived on the Sandringham estate of King George VI, or maybe that was before I entered the very troubled world of 1939, five years and a few days after my sister, Leila. My Mum, Sarah (known to everyone as Sadie) once wrote to a newspaper complaining bitterly and with rightful disgust that we were thrown off the estate when war broke out because my Dad was an 'alien'. This was a particularly cruel experience for her to bear a few years later, when Dad, her Jack, was killed in action in the very last days of the war.

Both my parents were of Polish-Jewish origin. Dad, whose name was Jacob but always known as 'Jack', was actually born in Poland, coming to England as a young child in the arms of his mother (Feigele, known as Fanny) and with his two older siblings, Levy (later known as Lou) and Annie, just before the First World War. They came to join my paternal grand-father (Yosef, or Joseph), who had made the journey from Warsaw a short while before. They settled, as did thousands of refugees like them at the time, in the East End of London, in Boreham Street. Amongst their neighbours were recently married Gedaliah ('Joe') and Leah Goldberg, to whom was born a girl, Sarah in 1913, my mother. It was not unusual for marriage to occur within the close-knit Jewish community, crammed together in poor quality tenements. In due course, there were eleven Goldstein children and six Goldbergs.

Both the Goldstein and Goldberg parents committed their lives to making something better for their children, while seeking to retain their heritage, culture, and religion in an alien environment. They had a deep sense of family and social values which they handed down through the generations, and which I know have had a profound effect on my own being.

Life was hard. I can see this best in my mother's side of the family. Her mother died, aged about 44 in 1929, a few days before my mother's sixteenth birthday. There she was, left with a sick and distraught father, to bring up her five siblings: Freda, aged three; Morry (later to change his name to Ray), aged four; Sid, aged six; Ralph, aged nine; and Ben, aged 13. Disease was common in those pre-antibiotics days. Freda died in 1944, aged eighteen, from tuberculosis; she also suffered from Addison's disease.

By the time I was born, war was imminent, and all the boys of both families would soon be fighting for their country. No, it was for much more than that. Their deep-rooted beliefs, their culture and values were under attack like nothing ever before. Although the tragedy and horror of the Second World War were yet to unfold, they knew what was happening in Nazi Germany; anti-semitism was not unknown, even to those born in England.

My first recollections are pre-school, living at 60 Fairholt Road, in the Stamford Hill area of North London. It was an imposing three-storey semi, where we rented a few rooms. We had two bedrooms; Leila and I slept in the same bed in one, and Mum slept in the other using a Rexine-covered 'Put-you-up'. I say Mum because Dad was away at war, in the RAFVR.[1] I have only one very fleeting memory of him, but it is very precious one, as I will recount later.

Author's mother and father, and sister Leila, c. 1943.

We shared a bathroom with the landlords. Two pennies in the slot gave enough gas through an old geyser to warm half a bath-full of water, which had to be shared. We had a tiny living room and a scullery off, looking out

---

1 Royal Air Force Volunteer Reserve.

onto the garden. Our landlords were pretty awful to us. We were not allowed in the garden, and we had to creep around the house so as not to annoy them. One summer holiday I decided to try to make a pin-ball bagatelle as we didn't have money to buy toys. I got a wooden apple box from the local greengrocer, and bought a few pence-worth of nails in Woolworths. I set to work with a small hammer in the scullery, as quiet as I could possibly be. It was not long before I was in trouble, and my mother received much verbiage when she came home.

Author's mother and father, July 1944.

Our landlords also resented Leila and I having keys to the house – we had to wait for Mum to come home from work to get in. Mum had to work, of course, when she lost Dad, and probably through the war in any case. For a while we had a key attached to a piece of string hung inside the letterbox, so we could pull it out to gain entry at will, but this was stopped. It all made for an unpleasant atmosphere, although when the air-raid sirens sounded to let the neighbourhood know the V1 or V2 'doodlebugs' or bombers were coming over, we all went into the cellar. What a frightening place that was for me: a pile of coal held back by some boards at one end; a dirty work-bench with an evil-smelling glue pot at the other, and a single, bare light bulb hanging from the rough ceiling. I think I would rather have risked the bombs than stay there!

My only memory of my father

I never really knew my father. By the time of my first recollections of anything in this world, he was already away fighting in the war. He had enlisted when I was not yet five years old, after several unsuccessful attempts on account of his being Polish by birth; it was not until the Government decided to bring into service all 'friendly aliens' that he could join up. I don't remember him personally at all, except for one fleeting incident which, even over sixty years later, I can still see in my mind's eye.

It was the occasion of a birthday – either mine or my sister's. Our birthdates are only six days apart, so it was the end of April or the beginning of May. It must have been 1944, because Dad enlisted on 22 January 1944 and was killed in action on 16 March 1945. There was a knock at the door. It was Dad, on leave. I rushed downstairs. As I opened the heavy street door, I caught a glimpse of my Dad, but in my anxiety the door banged against my forehead. An immediate cry, and I was in someone's arms (I like to think, my father's), being comforted. Out came the cold penny and the knob of butter for the bump…

I have no recollection of anything else that day. Just a brief glimpse of the person I was never to know, never to play football with in the park, never to share growing up or being a man. But how that brief glimpse remains in my mind and in my heart.

The traumas of evacuation

London was being bombed every night. How dreadfully frightening it must have been for mothers in London, left to look after their children while their husbands were away, somewhere, fighting the war.

I was about five years old, holding my mother's hand, at a point between Stoke Newington Railway Station and the still famous Egg Stores, outside Vale's (private) Library. We had stopped when my mother met a woman she knew. I heard the friend say something about Church Street School. It was where 'they' were arranging evacuation – whatever that meant. Within five minutes we were at the school.

Some days later, wearing my raincoat with a buff-coloured tie-on luggage label bearing my name attached to the lapel, and a 'Mickey Mouse' gas mask in a box around my neck, I was with Leila on a train bound for Blackpool – although I don't think I even knew that at the time, and certainly I had no idea at all where it was! I doubt my mother knew that much about it either, as she had hardly been out of London all her life.

After the train journey, and overnight crammed in a community hall, came the bus. All the other kids had got off, leaving just me and my ten-year-old sister Leila with the person in charge. The woman must have been anxious, for as the bus moved on a bit, she got out and knocked on a door. After a brief conversation she was back in the bus and off we went another short distance to another house…and another…then another… It would have been typical of my mother if the last thing she had said to Leila was not to let me out of her sight, and the dutiful daughter stuck to that resolutely. But not many would take in two young children of different sexes and five years apart in age. Eventually we found a childless couple who were up to the challenge.

It seems incomprehensible now. A young loving mother, separated from her husband by war, putting her two young children on a train to an unfamiliar town hundreds of miles away, to be looked after (she prayed) by strangers, for…who knew how long? It is unimaginable by today's standards, where parents are reluctant to let their kids out of their sights, even to play in the street outside their home. By all subsequent accounts we were lucky. We were indeed looked after, and even loved. I have a clear memory of lots of tears as we finally left to go back home to London.

It is curious how one remembers little cameos of life so far back. The house number was 60, the same as that of our rented accommodation in London. The couple we stayed with were entertainers by profession, one was a singer and the other played the piano, but I can't recall which was which. The mother of one of them lived with them too, and she certainly became my 'Grandma' for the time we were there. I was a bit frightened of their dog, which I think was called Bruce.

The first days at the local school were horrendous. I had only just started school in London – more of that later – but at least back home I was with friends. Here I knew no-one, and for the first time in my life was an outsider, and seemed to be the only Jewish person in the class. Boys and girls were segregated even at play-time; I remember my sister and me standing either side of a huge wire fence in the separate playgrounds, crying our eyes out.

But evidently we got by, and soon began to do the things that all children do; like chalking on a wall on the way home, for which my sister received a roasting when she was reported by a neighbour; collecting shells (never seen by either of us before) on the beach; my first experience of being stung by a wasp, and the blue paper remedy.

Author with Leila, c.1943.

Mum came up to see us on occasional weekends. It must have been dreadful for her. Travel (by train, of course) was not easy in those days, and how she could afford it I don't know. And how heartbreaking it must have been for her to return to the London bombings, leaving her children behind? I know that this experience was repeated many thousands of times across the country, but that doesn't in any way lessen its deep impact on me.

Leila and I must have been several months in Blackpool. When it finally came to leave, we went to buy Mum a gift. Where else to go but to Woolworths; but what to buy? For whatever reason I do not know, but we eventually decided we could afford…a wooden rolling pin! No doubt this caused great amusement, tempered of course by a wish not to offend us. We thought it was a good idea, anyway.

Leaving the family who had taken us into their lives proved a trauma. For us there was the pleasure of going home and being where we belonged, with Mum.

But for the family which had nurtured us for several months it must have been heart-wrenching. I know that the mother, who regarded me as her adopted grandson, cried her eyes out when we finally waved farewell at the door. How I wish we had kept in contact with them. They were kind and generous beyond belief, and yet I know nothing of what became of them, and have never been able to repay them in any way at all. I feel very bad about that.

Other war-time memories

Mum had four brothers: Ben, Ralph, Sid and Morry. Ben must have been married by the time war broke out, because his eldest son was only a few months younger than me. I am not sure about the others, but as Mum had brought them up when her mother died, they regarded her as their mother and came 'home' to see her when they were on leave from the Forces. I remember the excitement when two of them managed to get leave at the same time. Morry always amused me, grabbing a kitchen chair and sitting on it backwards, reading my comics. He was full of typical East End life and humour – always doing something funny to amuse me, like saying silly things or waggling his ears! After the war, one of them, I think it was Morry, brought home a suitcase of German memorabilia, and for a while I was the envy of my friends. The one item I still have and treasure is a German field compass.

Dad was away, of course, and no one knows what that was really like for him. But I do have some indication of his thoughts around that time. I have a very well-worn letter which he wrote to his eldest brother, Lou, whilst he was on a few days leave. Like my father, Lou was born in Warsaw, Poland; as the two eldest boys, they were particularly close. The letter is dated 'Wed 13th'. Between the date of Dad enlisting (22 January 1944) and being killed in action (16 March 1945), the 13th of the month fell on a Wednesday just twice – September and December 1944. In his letter, my father says that on return from leave he was being posted to another station; his service record shows he was posted to 166 Squadron of Bomber Command on 5 January 1945. He also mentioned the possibility of getting more leave around Christmas, so it is likely that the date of his letter was Wednesday 13 December 1944.

The text of the letter is as follows. I have left the grammar, punctuation and spelling as in the original, but added some comments in square brackets:

Dear Lou

Thanks a lot for your letter which certainly came as a surprise, but was nevertheless welcome. I'm afraid letter writing is not one of my strong points, and if there is one who writes less than you, it's myself.

I am glad to hear you have found yourself a job which must be more in your line than drill and P.T. and that you are feeling quite well [Lou was a Lance-Corporal in the Royal Army Service Corps, serving from 1941 to 1946]. I, myself, am feeling O.K and at present am writing this at home, where I am on leave for a few days. It's a pity your leave does not coincide with mine, but I may possibly get some more leave round about Christmas, and will certainly see you if I possibly can.

I hope your family are in the 'pink'. Leila and Michael will be coming home this Saturday, so don't forget to pop round when you come home and bring the family with you. [This must have been the time of our return from evacuation in Blackpool].

I have been doing a fair amount of flying lately, but nothing very eventful which is how I want it to be. I'm pretty confident I'll get through it all O.K. [Tragically, this was not to be so]. We've got a very good crew, which is half Canadian and our pilot believes in taking no unnecessary risks. If I had to choose it all over again, I'd still prefer this to the army.

The reason I haven't written my address on this letter is that I am being posted to another station when I come back from leave. I shan't be sorry, as Sandtoft [Lincolnshire], my present station is miles away from anywhere and we hardly leave the camp. We spend most of our spare time playing 1d [one (old) penny] Solo ['Solo' is a card game rather like Whist, commonly played within my father's community], or going to the camp Cinema.

I'm glad to hear you manage to get a bit of time off and visit Brighton dog track, but believe it or not, I've lost all interest in the game and I'm…[words not clear]…certain it will never hold any attraction for me again. [Gambling on dog- or horse-racing events was a frequent past-time for the older Goldstein boys and their father].

I visited the workshop this afternoon and they have twice as many workpeople, but turn out less than we used to. [The 'workshop' was the clothing factory my grand-father owned, and in which all the boys worked]. Sadie tells me Dave is rowing [arguing] all day long. [My mother was an accomplished self-taught seamstress, and worked in the family workshop during the war. I do not know who 'Dave' is]. They sure miss you on the machine. However, it won't be long now.

Sadie sends her love to you and the family.

All the best,

Jack.

Many years later, I met one of the men who flew with my father, Ted Hull, and his wife Betty. They were an incredible link to my past. I will mention them again later.

The night my father was killed in action

Dad was 27 years old when the Second World War was declared. He joined the RAFVR (service number 2235812), volunteering for flying duties. He was posted successively to No. 3 Air Crew Reception Centre, No. 15 Initial Training Wing, No. 1E Air Gunners' School, No. 8 Air Gunners' School, No. 28 Operational Training Unit, and No. 1 Base Unit (1667 Heavy Conversion Unit), before being assigned to 166 Squadron Bomber Command at RAF Kirmington in Lincolnshire on 5 January 1945. In all, he flew 15 operations as mid-upper gunner in Lancasters from Kirmington, including the major raid on Dresden on 13 February 1945, plus several exercises and aborted missions.

I am forever indebted to my uncle, Dad's youngest brother, Ron Goldstein for carrying out the extensive research into how my father was killed in action. I have written a detailed account of this, and the period immediately thereafter, and posted it on the BBC's WW2 website 'The People's War'.[2]

Crew of 166 Squadron Bomber Command in front of their Lancaster bomber, with author's father kneeling centre front.

---

2 I do hope readers will visit this site at: http://www.bbc.co.uk/ww2peopleswar/stories/90/a8452190.shtml. For a full list of my Second World War stories see http://www.bbc.co.uk/ww2peopleswar/user/17/u2883517.shtml

Suffice it to record that my father was the only member of the seven-man crew not to survive the war. After VE day on 13 May 1945, all six survivors returned to their loved ones and began to re-form their lives. Just eight weeks earlier, my mother had learned that my father was 'missing' by means of a telegram on 17 March 1945, as I describe in the next section. I took her many weeks, even months, before she accepted that he was truly dead, and to her dying day at the age of 87 on 7 January 2001, she never stopped grieving.

A few years ago, Leila and I made personal contact with Ted Hull, the flight engineer, and his wife Betty. We visited them in their home in the village of Martin Hussingtree in Worcestershire. Pictures of Lancaster bombers line some of the walls, and there are other memorabilia. Ted did not want to speak too much about the war, but described an intriguing story about how he met Betty. Ted and my Dad had been out on the town and arrived at a station fairly late to get back to base. But there were no more trains that night. They began to walk, but Dad noticed a young nurse also waiting for the train. He spoke to her, and then introduced her to Ted, who rather took to Betty.

Sadly, Ted passed away in June 2001, but I keep a semblance of contact with Betty.

The telegram

It must have been the moment everyone dreaded…the knock on the door…the peaked cap…the telegram. My mother took it into the scullery, the only source of natural light in the tiny living area in our rented rooms. She kept her back to me so I would not see her tears. I must have asked what was wrong, because she said (and although I was only just coming up to six years old at the time, I really do still remember the words, more than sixty years on): 'Daddy's missing…go out to play'.

Of course I did. I wanted to tell my friends.

The trauma and significance of that dreadful message were not understood by me for a long time, but obviously it had a deep and immediate impact on my mother. Years later, one of my father's sisters, Debbie, gave me two well-folded and much-worn letters, which my mother had written some weeks after that fateful day. They were addressed to my Uncle Lou, the eldest of all the Goldstein boys, and with whom my mother, like my father, was very close. The first is dated Sunday 10 June (1945). Half of one of the three pages is missing, but the sense of the desperate hope still comes through:

Dear Lou,

I am slipping this note to you in Dad's letter, as I feel I must tell you that there is now a little hope for Jack's safety.

I received a letter from Mrs Smith (the children, you remember, were billeted with her). She has a brother, a Ft/S, who is now stationed at Kermington and knows Jack. Mrs Smith tells me that her brother has had 'secondhand' information that Jack is OK and is now back in this country since last Tues. from a P.O.W. camp.

So far I have had no official confirming this, but I went up to the Air Ministry on Friday, had an interview with a Flying Officer there and was told that only one…[missing half-page]…plane. This is all I know at present, but I'm trying to contact Mrs Smith's brother at Kirmington and find out a little more.

If you have any spare time, write to the Air Ministry (Casualty Branch) 73-77 Oxford St W.1, and perhaps you can find out a little more about things.

Cheerio! then for now, hoping this finds you well, all the best.
Sadie.

The second letter was sent a few days later, on Tuesday 19 June 1945. It is less complete than the first one, but the messages are clear:

Dear Lou,

I don't know whether you are still in England, but I hope you will eventually get this letter, so here goes.

On my visit to the Air Ministry yesterday, I learnt that all the crew, except Jack are now back in England and according to the P/O and W.O.P. Jack was killed by German ack-ack ground fire while baling out. The plane was hit and caught fire before even reaching the target and the crew eventually all met in the same P.O.W. camp in Germany, nothing was seen or heard of Jack while they were there.

I feel deep down inside me, that Jack is somewhere in hospital over there and I am still hoping and praying he is…

I have…the children…yet, in fact.

You…only one in…who has really…helpful during…anxious period…I give you my heartfelt thanks and deepest gratitude.

Jack will always be alive in my heart and I'm sure in yours. Here's wishing you all the very best for the future.

Sincerely,

There must have been countless thousands of families in this state; still praying; clinging on to hope of some mistake, some miracle. I grew up with such secret hope, believing that one day my Dad would knock on the door again.

Reflections 1

It is impossible to say how much the experiences I have related have really affected my character and outlook, but I like to think they have made me value human relations both in local environments and globally. War has always been an appalling waste in every conceivable sense. I was too young to be traumatised or damaged, but I know how much my mother just hated the word 'war'. When the first Gulf War began it made her physically ill. She never spoke to me about the wartime, or even about my father; and I knew that she did not want to concern me about such matters. I guess it was her way of protecting me, and herself, from the sadness and hurt. She grieved all her life for her dear Jack, and did not want me to grieve. The fact that we never spoke about my father might seem odd to some, even sad. But it was our way of dealing with our distress.

Jack Goldstein's grave, Durnbach, Germany.

I sometimes ponder how my life would have been different had my father been one of those who returned from the war; and also what life he would have had. More often than that, I wonder what he would have made of my life as it has turned out, and sometimes this has been a great motivator; after all, we all wish our parents to be proud of us, don't we?

The Immediate Post-war Years

A new normality

The period after my father was killed must have been incredibly traumatic for my mother. We two children were a handful; I was not yet six, and my sister Leila was just coming up to eleven years old. It was ages before my mother came to terms with the fact that her husband would never come home again, and that she had to bring up two children by herself. It must have been distressful just to wake up.

None of our relatives was able to help financially. But my mother was able to work in the Goldstein family clothing factory, where all five boys had learned their tailoring trades. Mum was a self-taught whiz with the needle, and this provided the means for her to have an income.

Mum going to work meant that Leila and I had to fend for ourselves after school, before Mum came home from the factory. We played in the street in all weathers; it was safe to do so in those days as there were few cars on the streets – I didn't even know anyone who had one. We amused ourselves playing with an old tin can, a box or a ball. I remember we used the 'pig bin' (into which everyone put their food scraps for collection and transporting out to farms) as a cricket wicket. Skipping was fun and exercise, for the boys too. In the spring we collected butterflies, and in the winter we played in the snow, especially in the famous 1946/7 winter. The 1948 Olympics, held in London, were a stimulus to organise our own races round the block. What with collecting conkers, plus a bit of scrumping, we passed the time creatively.

Leila took me under her wing. She had already taught me to read, tell the time, add up and so on, well before I was of school age. Looking back now, I realise how much I owe her for giving me such a great start and a thirst for learning.

Family support

Both sides of the family had their problems after the war, and struggled to rebuild their lives. It was a comfort to Mum to have my paternal grand-mother, Booba, and grand-father, Zaida, living no more that 10 minutes away in Manor Road. I know that some of their children, my uncles and aunts, lived there too from time to time. I certainly recall Jean, Polly and Ronnie being there.

Ronnie, the youngest of the Goldstein boys, was very special to us. He tried to fill the huge gap in our lives which had been created by the loss of our father. I have wonderful memories of him taking us out for the day, after the war was over. The visit to Madame Tussauds remains vivid in my mind. But the most memorable trips were to the West End to have tea in Lyons Corner House. In those days there was a piano playing and the table linen was crisp and white. How the other half lived. Most of all, I still drool at the thought of our favourite 'sweet': apple foam and Melba sauce!

It was Ronnie too who struggled to help me to ride a two-wheeler bike. Not that we could afford one, but once more it was part of his wish to help fill the gap left by the loss of my father. Again, it was Ronnie to whom Mum turned to lend me long trousers and a trilby hat to wear for my part as a juror in the school's production of Gilbert and Sullivan's *Trial by Jury*. I was quite a sight, with two copies of the *Daily Mirror* in the hat to keep it falling over my eyes, and baggy trousers with concertina turn-ups!

I went to see Booba and Ziada about once a fortnight. I did not enjoy the experience of being squeezed tight and kissed all over, and in any case I couldn't understand some of what Booba was saying. We didn't speak Yiddish at home, so it was a struggle. But the half-crown in my hand as I left made up for it. All of us also went there for seder night, which was quite bewildering for me. No one had ever explained what it was all about, and I guess that was when Leila and I, as young children, most felt the absence of Dad to guide us in the traditions of being Jewish. As a result, we both know so little about the customs and laws, and as deeply proud as we are of our heritage, we practise not.

Of course, I went to *cheder* classes, to learn to read Hebrew. I was sent to a Rabbi in nearby Bethune Road. This huge man terrified me; he seemed to be all beard and gruffness. I hated going, but I knew Mum wanted me to. So I cheated. I left the house to go there, but doubled back and hid in the front garden (remember, we were not allowed in the back!). From time to time I had to creep out to the street to ask a passer-by the time so I knew when to knock on the door and go in. I was not happy deceiving Mum and felt terribly guilty about the waste of money, but it all came to an end when one day I was caught. I still hated the lessons, and even then realised it was a poor approach to education. Learning by rote has its merits, but the hours spent in *cheda* reading unintelligible Hebrew passages out loud, and then being told what they meant in English, was pretty pointless.

Going to Goldstein events such as weddings was also frightening, and the prayers embarrassed me. One experience, though, gave me great excitement – cousin Leon's *Bar Mitzvah*. I was collected by a taxi, the first time I had even been in a car of any kind, and when the cab drew up outside the house I felt important for the first time in my life.

Holidays

The school holidays were a particular problem, with Mum at work. Leila recalls we stayed one summer in Frittendon, near Chatteris in Cambridgeshire. But my better recollection is being sent to a farm in Kent for two successive holidays. I can still see the layout of the farmhouse with the fields and wood vaguely in my mind's eye. The family had a son, I think named Colin; Leila, who was 12-13 by then, had a crush on him. As a young lad brought up in Stamford Hill, I found the very nature of a farm presented a huge adventure. I had some memorable experiences there: crossing the deep pond in a barrel; sleeping overnight with Colin(?) in a (poorly) cleaned-out pigsty; getting lost in the woods which were full of huge rhododendron bushes in full bloom, and finding grass snakes.

Author with Leila, 60 Fairholt Road, c. 1946.

I also have some recollections of going to an RAF base in Bungay in Suffolk – why else would I have the name of such a place so firmly planted in my memory? I can visualise myself in the back of an open Land-Rover speeding through country lanes, holding on in excited fear; and getting up early one morning to go with some men with shotguns to shoot rabbits, but coming back with a pigeon instead.

Back in Fairholt Road, life was getting back to 'normal' after the war. I had a group of good friends: Stanley Liebovitch, whose father died early from 'consumption' and became Stanley Solovitch when his mother re-married; Irving Deal and Tony Bernstein, who both went into ladies' hairdressing; and Brian Silver, who had leg irons and had to endure the cruel taunt of 'Brian is made if iron!' for many years. I had a tricycle, which I used all the time, including to carry the shopping bags of an old lady who lived a good way from the shops, and who gave me sixpence for my trouble.

New family, new home

In 1948, someone new came into our lives, as Mum met Alf (Aaron) Hyman. It was difficult for Leila and I to adjust, and I confess to not having been adaptable. But we knew that this new phase in our lives was for the better, and so it proved. Mum married Alf later that year, in a Liberal *schul* near Stamford Hill, and a new phase of our lives began.

I was not sure how to take to Alf, but I don't think it was easy for any of us. There was never any suggestion of calling him 'Dad', and that might have been hard for him, but it was an important principle for me, even then, and I'm glad I was never asked to do so. I don't recall either actual resentment or warm embrace, but we were a more complete family, and Mum must have had great comfort from that. Clearly, her children had a more secure future.

Alf's introduction to me was not auspicious. I remember receiving a book from him as a gift. Inside he had written: 'To Mick. Be a good boy and more will be on the way'. I remember resenting that immensely. Not only did I dislike the name 'Mick', a name he persisted with, but I hated the bribe. Then there was the pair of boxing gloves he bought for me, and being forced to 'fight' with my best friend, Stanley, in the kitchen. It did not help that Stanley was deemed to have won! So my relationship with Alf did not start well, but I guess he did not really have a chance.

Soon we were off to a new block of 'luxury flats', dreadful by today's standards, but hugely welcomed after Mum had nagged the life out of our local Councillor, using the fact that Leila and I (now coming up for ages 14 and 9) were sharing a bed. Binyon House, at the other end of Stoke Newington, was indeed a great improvement on what we had, but I was away from my friends and the culture was entirely different. We were the only Jewish people there, and it showed. I never felt at ease with the neighbours, and often had to suffer abuse and taunts. It rarely came to physical violence, but I had to learn to run pretty fast and to keep a low profile. Unbeknown to anyone else, I carried a small domestic screwdriver in my pocket – just in case I was attacked – something which would get me arrested these days. I was followed one day, with horrible, abusive shouts, on the way to *cheder* classes at Shacklewell Lane *schul*, and from then on walked there a different way each time.

My half-brother David came along soon after. That made it more cramped in the flat, and there would have been a bedroom problem had Leila not left home before David needed more space. As it was, there were some tensions, and I am sure that I did not help too much. I don't recall feeling any resentment at David's arrival, but I could well have behaved in an unhelpful way at times.

Reflections 2

Mum's second marriage clearly brought much to my life, and allowed a near-normal childhood. But, paradoxically, I think the circumstances probably made me more of a loner. David became the centre of attention, and the locality to which we moved was hostile. So I kept myself to myself. I guess I became more inward-looking. I knew my limitations and lacked self-confidence. Relationships were such that I did not have fatherly guidance, and I lost touch with both my religion and my friends.

Growing Up

Montefiore House School

The primary school to which I went, as did Leila before me, was Montefiore House. It was a large Victorian house, adapted for use as a school on an emergency basis during the war by the then London County Council. It stood on the main road known as Stamford Hill, a few hundred yards down from the Hill itself, about half way towards Stoke Newington railway station to the south. In the evenings it was a boys' club, and also where the local cubs and scouts met.

I began there in 1944, at the age of five. All my street friends went there. It had a family atmosphere and was staffed by truly great teachers. It was a single form entry, with a total of less than a hundred children.

Thanks to Leila, by the time I started school I could already read quite well, write a bit, count, perform simple sums, and tell the time. I can't say I really appreciated this at the time, as Leila and I quarrelled a lot, to the extent that Mum had to keep us apart at meal-times.

Even after the end of the war, materials were very scarce. Toilet paper was available only from the Headmaster, an imposing man named Mr Quint. Oh, the indignity of having to go to ask him for some toilet paper, and to be given only two sheets!

At 'break' we all lined up to get a spoon-full of malt or a tiny bottle of milk. Because there were no kitchens at Montefiore House, for dinner (who from our community ever heard the word 'lunch' in those days?) we were marched, crocodile style, towards Stamford Hill to some place or other. The teachers made sure we ate every scrap, including the ever-present gristle.

Assembly was in a hall which was an add-on to the original house. We sat cross-legged on the wooden floor, which always seemed to be as cold as ice to bare legs and young bottoms. The vast majority of us were Jewish, although I don't think any of the teachers were, but the hymns were chosen with great sensitivity, so we sang and enjoyed ourselves. Don't we all of that generation remember *All Things Bright and Beautiful*?

Special mention must be made of two teachers. Mr Rowan was a large man, who reminded me of Rupert Bear's father, except he also had a moustache (unfortunately, rather like Adolf Hitler's). He remains firmly in my memory for encouraging us to use our imagination. His method was to get each pupil in turn, over the course of several weeks, to sit on their desktops, facing the class, and start a fictional story about anything they wished. Others had to continue the story in the same mode. It really did engage everyone. No one was excused, but remarkably no one tried to be excused! It was so very good for us, using our imaginations, communicating to peers, learning from others, engendering confidence, and so on.

Mr Rowan also encouraged us to learn poems. At the time I had a couple of very battered volumes of Arthur Mee's *Children's Encyclopaedia*, and I selected the longest poems in them that I could find and committed them to memory. How I loved those books! One poem I still remember, from beginning to end is *How They Brought the Good News from Ghent to Aix* by Robert Browning. I was motivated to find other long poems, so I went to Stoke Newington library and found one which I then learned by heart: *Barbara Frietchie* by the American author John Greenleaf Whittier. These poems still enthral me, and give me great comfort in times of stress; I often recite them to myself during times of anxiety.

But Mr Rowan went further by converting poems to plays for the whole class to enact. In my year with him we all learned the whole of *The Pied Piper of Hamlyn* by Robert Browning, and every child in the class had a part to play, often rotated from the previous week. I am sure I am not the only person from that school who still remembers every single word of it.

The second teacher from Montefiore House who stands out for me was Mr Cousins. Each year he adapted and taught the top two classes one of the Gilbert and Sullivan operas. In my two years with him we performed

Mr Cousins' class, Montefiore House Primary School, 1950. Author, front row, second right.

The cast of Pirates of Penzance, Montefiore House Primary School, 1956. The author (the 'Pirate King'), second row, fourth left.

Trial by Jury and *The Pirates of Penzance*. He personally scribed all the words and music on to a duplicating device, which consisted of transparent sheets, mounted one at a time on to a glass platform. The technique was to scratch the image on the transparent sheets, and transfer it using a thick black ink roller onto one sheet of paper at a time. It was a painstaking task, especially as he had very poor sight, but he succeeded in giving every child a full copy to learn in class and rehearse at home. Children were not initially selected for particular parts to play, so that by the end of the year the whole class knew the entire score and all the dialogue. Although I was a mere juror in *Trial by Jury*, I was elevated to the role of Pirate King in *The Pirates of Penzance*, but the remarkable thing is that I still remember large amounts of all the parts in both operas. What a fantastic experience.

Then it was time to think about the dreaded 11-plus examination. We were given a book, which I still have, entitled Attainment Tests by Haydn Perry, full of the kind of questions which we could expect in the 11+ exam. The whole class worked its way through it over a period of about a year, including having to undertake regular homework. Here is a small selection of some of the questions:

1. An egg dealer buys eggs at 5 for 7 1/2 d, and sells them at 1s 8d a dozen. How much profit does he make on a gross?
2. 24 men wrecked on a desert island have provisions for 84 days. How long will the provisions last if 4 other castaways join the party?

3. Find the cost of glazing a house with 100 panes of glass at 1s 6d per pane. Putty costs 4s 9d and the workman who is paid 2s 9d per hour takes 8 hours.
4. Here are words that are usually seen in pairs, but they have been mixed up. Put them in their correct pairs: tried, go, nonsense, far, beck, sugar, touch, true, call, stuff, away, spice.
5. These everyday words are really shortened forms of longer words. Write the words in full: exam., plane., photo., gym., pram., specs.
6. Change into the possessive form by using the apostrophe: 'the tips of the arrows'; 'the bullets of the rifles'.
7. Which of these orchestral instruments are woodwind instruments: flute, banjo, oboe, trumpet, bassoon, trombone, harp, piccolo?
8. Study this example: "teacher is to pupil as doctor is to patient". Now complete the following:
(a) Nursery is to plants as incubator is to…?
(b) Paddington is to trains as Croydon is to …?
(c) Hangar is to planes as garage is to…?
(d) Alps is to Switzerland as Himalayas are to…?
(e) Columbus is to America as Captain Cook is to…?
(f) Lawn-mower is to grass as sandpaper is to…?

This all seems rather quaint now, and how things have changed. But I enjoyed the challenge, and became quite good at such things.

These were hugely formative experiences. They give some insight into the communities in which we grew up, and the values which we had. Times were hard. I had a penny (that's 1d!) a day to buy an apple from the greengrocer on the way home from school, as this would have to do until my mother came home from work. Montefiore House was basic: no special clothing for games; no school trips (except a bus ride to the Geoffrey Museum in Shoreditch); no library; no parties – we had few, simple presents for birthdays; no electronically-delivered entertainment – a trip to the Saturday morning pictures for 6d was a real treat. But we generated a wonderful sense of values and work ethic which laid the foundations for our futures. We also acquired a love of language and literature, and facility with words and numbers. We can all look back on our time at that very basic primary school, and no doubt the many others of its kind, with huge gratitude and affection. Despite the war years and the hardships in the immediate post-war period, they were happy times and we all managed to work through the difficulties as a community.

Becoming a teenager

Like Leila, I passed the 11-plus examination. It was a great surprise for me, as I thought I had performed badly. I was expected to pass. I was always one of the first to put up my hand when the teacher asked a question, and I did not find the homework a problem. But I was aware of the importance of the 11-plus, and this was somewhat unnerving.

I was lucky enough to get my first choice of Grammar School, which was 'Grocers', more properly known as Hackney Downs Grammar School, but still then called 'Grocers' because it had originally been founded by the Grocers' Company. The immediate concern was that I needed a uniform, gym kit and everything else. It was a problem. We lived from day-to-day financially, although Mum did stash some cash in a tin to pay for the insurance and other bills. Alf was a tailor, and work was very seasonal and poorly paid. He was laid off for weeks at a time about twice a year. It was far from stable, and at times we were in a bad way financially. We lived very basically, but the children always came first.

Mum tried the charities. I remember being taken to the Jewish Board of Guardians, and elsewhere. It was the RAF Benevolent Fund which came to the rescue and fitted me out with a blazer, trousers and shoes. The blazer was rough, and when Mum sewed on the school badge it made it obvious that we could not afford the puckha job. The shoes were awful, the soles were made of steel, at least so it seemed when I tried to walk in them. It must have been very hard on Mum and Alf to have to resort to charity to clothe me, so I did not complain one bit.

Even so, life was not easy. Mum took in 'outwork', finishing dresses by hand, belt loops, lapels, and the like. She was paid just a few pence a garment, and so often I went to bed with her sitting in the kitchen with sore fingers and red eyes, and a huge pile of work still to be done by the next day. It was slave labour, but she did it so willingly because it was for her children. Knowing she was doing this, and why, was a strong lesson for me for later life. It rubbed off into a strong work ethic, and a reluctance to rely on help from others – if something is worth having, and not only in the material sense, then you work for it.

Leila left school as soon as she could, aged 15. She had been at the Skinners Company School (of similar foundation to 'Grocers'), right at the top of Stamford Hill, but was more interested in boys and having fun than lessons. She went to work in an office for £2.10s.0d a week, supplemented by serving in a sweet shop on Saturdays. This brought more money into the household, but it was still tough.

Leila's marriage to Jimmy was always going to be problematic. In those days, even to go out with a non-Jew was a crime. I realise now how brave she was. I was shielded from the all-round distress, and kept a low profile, but recall how upset was Mum. I feel sure that she felt that she was letting down our Dad – that's silly of course, but emotions take over at such times. The Goldstein family disowned her. She went alone to see Booba and Ziada to tell them, which must have been a terrible experience, and she was hung out to dry. Still a teenager, Leila left the house alone to get married and did not come back. But a loving mother, being just that, could not be at odds with her daughter, and very soon after Leila returned from honeymoon, she and Mum were reconciled. I know that Leila would never see it like this, but her outstanding commitment and dedication to Mum's well-being in her later years more than compensated for any distress Mum felt during those times.

My *Bar Mitzvah* was inevitably a modest affair, and for me pretty traumatic. I had persevered with the classes, but didn't have a clue what it was all about. I was a pretty good singer in those days, but I could find no logic in the way I was supposed to sing my portion. But I got through it of a fashion, and have the photograph to prove it. I still have the *kappel* (skullcap) and prayer book given by the *schul*. As for the celebration, Mum made Vienna sausages and chips for (I think) 23 people, all crowded into our tiny Council flat living room. What a Mum!

Meanwhile, I dearly wanted to have a bicycle, if only to avoid the two-mile walk to and from school. I first bought a secondhand one for £2.10s.0d in Club Row in the Brick Lane area of the East End, but the model I really wanted was a Raleigh 27, with 4-speed Benelux. I could not afford the price of £23.5s.2d, so I sold the old one in the same place I had bought it, and took out a 'Gradual Payments' account with Paskells in Stoke Newington High Street. The payments were 6/1d per week, and I still have the payments record book to prove I didn't default once. How proud I was to have paid for it myself. It is an experience and an attitude that has not left me all these years. And Ronnie's patience in teaching me to ride a two-wheeler had been rewarded.

I was shy and reserved as a teenager, and often found myself alone; fortunately I enjoyed my own company, and my bike was very important to me. On many a Sunday morning, I used to ride all the way to Southend, some 35 miles away, buy a small bottle of Pepsi Cola, and ride all the way back again, getting home in time for lunch. On other days I would ride to Epping Forest, walk for miles through the woodlands without seeing anyone and then ride home. It was a challenge and an escape, but I got to know myself well.

I can't recall what lead me to join the cubs, but I am so very pleased I did. The troop met in Montefiore House, so it was not too much trouble to go along. Later, the scouts helped me to grow in confidence and other respects. I recall some wonderful camps in Oxfordshire and at Gilwell Park in Chingford – wood-based fires, billycans, bivouacs, and mud! I learned a great deal but had to leave because *Bar Mitzvah* classes were on the same evening.

Reflections 3

These were very formative years for me. The basics of my education were well and truly laid at Montefiore House and then (as I describe in the next section) at Hackney Downs School. More than anything, I was encouraged by people who empathised with me, and I was in an environment which cared. I enjoyed school because it was challenging and competitive. Those who tried, worked hard, and achieved were encouraged even more. There were very few behavioural problems – OK, I 'got the cane' once at primary school for flicking a paper pellet, but that was the worst that I experienced. We were largely of similar background and family aspiration; we knew that school was important and had to be taken seriously. Perhaps there was a thought that we owed it to our parents to succeed; they had little, and sacrificed much for their children. What they had they had worked hard for, and that included the likes of me.

Hackney Downs School

A modest start

Just going to HDS, formerly the Grocers' Company School, was a huge privilege, and had an incredibly profound effect on my life. From beginning to end, it was an experience which I could live again and again; one I wish on all young people seeking to find out about themselves and to self-improve.

Every entrant had been first assessed by an interview with the Headmaster in his study. As an immature boy, lacking in confidence, my experience was painful. It meant I started off in the lowest of the three grades, Form 1C. I did well in the end-of-year examinations, earning promotion to 2B. Only the A-stream was deemed bright enough to study Latin, so I took German as the second language, and I was glad I did. At the end of the second year I was promoted to the top stream, 3A. I was pleased with myself, and managed to hold my own. HDS was like that: effective in gently bringing out motivation and hard work to achieve success.

My confidence had grown sufficiently for me to go on one of the annual overseas summer trips, that time to the Austrian Tyrol. Fortunately, it was possible to pay for this trip by instalments. The trip helped my confidence and maturity. It also allowed me to mix with more senior pupils, which was quite an eye-opener; their habits shocked me, and I don't just mean smoking. We stayed in the tiny hamlet of Rinn, above Innsbruck, and made friends with a couple of boys from local farms; but contact abruptly ended when they found out many of us were Jewish and showed their feelings with a big spit onto the ground.

Grammar school values

It is difficult to articulate what, let alone how, Hackney Downs School taught me beyond the curriculum. But I use such terms as loyalty, leadership, hard work, camaraderie, humility, discipline and respect. Indeed, it was a place of huge respect, for the school, the teachers and one another. It instilled in me important values that I hold so dear today. I met some marvellous human beings there, and was always conscious of the school's history and standing. I was immensely proud just to be there. Most of my Stamford Hill friends had not made it through the 11-plus, and were hugely disadvantaged as a result. That has stayed with me throughout my career; how privileged I was, simply because I was able to pass a test at the very young age of 11 years.

Discipline was excellent but not Draconian. We all knew, instinctively, the boundaries of acceptable behaviour, and abided by them. One or two masters were somewhat eccentric, and received some banter, but most were admired, even those who sometimes lost their tempers. The Deputy Head, Joe Brearley, who was also a teacher of English, enjoyed huge love and affection from everyone, but was infamous for entering a classroom of noisy boys and throwing the wooden-backed board-rubber – or even a bunch of keys – horizontally across the room to make a dent in the opposite wall. But he was, like many other masters at HDS, a real inspiration. He taught and encouraged none other than Stephen Berkoff and Harold Pinter, but he motivated many more of us. Indeed, the combination of the various English teachers I had gave me a love of the written word. I am by no means a literature freak – I had to drop English literature to study sciences from age 14 – but I do place high value on good written English, and like to think that I have high standards, even if I am sometimes boringly pedantic.

Athletics

HDS had a great ability, as mentioned before, to bring out the best in us, even in areas in which we did not excel. The dramatic example is athletics. There was no selection to the school based on athletic ability, yet for nearly the whole time I was there, HDS was outstandingly successful at the North London Grammar Schools Athletics Championships, winning most if not all the trophies available. This has to be attributed to the commitment and drive instilled by Leslie Mitchell, the senior Physical Education master. He inspired everyone. Even those who found it difficult to get into a trot had to run round the Downs – a mile or so for those not taking the short-cut via the putting green. I myself always tried hard, but did not shine, until I was timed at 10.6 seconds for the 100 yards, wearing plimsolls on grass at the school fields. That's very slow by today's standards, but at around that time the senior AAA GB Championship was won in 10.0 seconds, so I was quite chuffed. Barrie Sherman, who was older than me but whom I had caught up by the process of 'acceleration' (more of which later) was in the school athletics team and suggested I should train with him. I thus found myself in the company of the boy who was one of the finest athletes the school ever had – Brian Horeman. Brian was hugely encouraging, and took me under his wing, together with a contemporary, Leslie Steingold. I got to know Brian's parents, Marie and John, and they too were fantastic role models. Brian was an only child and clearly the light of their lives. They were astonishingly generous, and made everyone feel valued.

I worked very hard at being a good athlete, but despite Brian's tutelage, and hours of strenuous training on the Downs, and the running tracks in Victoria and Finsbury Parks, I never quite made the grade. I managed to get a place in the school team, achieved half-colours, and represented North London Grammar Schools against the South, feats of which I am immensely proud. But champion I was never to be.

It was a terrible blow when Brian was killed while at the University of Southampton; he crashed into a wrought iron gate when he hit the kerb riding down a hill on his bicycle. He was at least a year older than me, and left HDS to take an economics degree while I was still in the sixth form. His dear parents were distraught to a degree that still breaks my heart. The funeral, involving the hearse, draped in the school colours of blue irises and yellow daffodils, passing the school gates, was heart-wrenching.

Author winning the NLGSAA regional meeting (120 yards hurdles) at Eton Manor, 1957.

I kept in good contact with Marie and John after Brian's death. They took me into their hearts, and I became very fond of them indeed. Marie was a second mother. I deeply mourned their passing some years later. I learned a lot from them; they had a fantastic work ethic. I recall John regularly coming off working a shift in the Fire Service, having a bath (no showers then!), grabbing a meal, and rushing out to one or other of his secondary jobs. He had huge energy, as had Marie. She was wonderful cook who could rustle up a sumptuous meal in minutes, and was a seamstress of amazing ability and versatility, even making all Brian's clothes. But they also taught me the importance of love, and the value of humour in overcoming conflict.

The challenge of getting into higher education

In the fourth year at HDS we had to complete a form about career intentions. Not having a clue what I wanted to do when I left school, I leant across the gangway to Paul Crossick, and asked what he had put down. 'Industrial Chemist', he said. On the spur of the moment, I did the same. Believe it or not, that is the reason why I decided to study chemistry in higher education.

But staying on at school beyond age 16 was not an easy notion. Alf expected me to work and pay my way. Mum wanted me to stay on at school; she had so little formal education herself, but she knew its value as a route to a better life. The deal was I would get a Saturday job and thus contribute to the family income.

After a few Saturdays of trying I got a job in the True-Form shoe shop at Dalston Junction. I enjoyed working there greatly, and came to be quite close to the manager, Jim Bagguley. As he progressed up the True Form ladder, so I went with him: Kentish Town, King's Cross, Camden Town, and finally Hammersmith. He was very good to me, and I learned a lot about people from that experience. I worked for him in several summer and Christmas holiday periods. The pay was originally 17/6d for the Saturday, from which I paid over 3/- in National Insurance, but Jim made sure I always received at least five bob in commission. I very much regret losing touch with him; he was generous, encouraging, a good role model, and a fine human being.

I also worked in the shirt and men's underwear department of the famous Houndsditch Warehouse from 10.00 am to 2.00 pm every Sunday for £2 a day. It was hard work, but I enjoyed the challenge and the very fact that I was gaining independence mattered a lot.

I also needed somewhere to study. I had my own bedroom, but the Council flat was a noisy place. We could hear all the doors closing, all the toilets flushing and every bucket of coal going onto the fires in adjacent flats. It was not fair to Mum and Alf that I was trying to study, and David was a noisy child. So most days I went straight from school to the Reference Library in Stoke Newington, as did many others of my background, until closing at 9.00 pm. I built up good friendships amongst the group of us, including with Mary, a librarian, my first serious girlfriend (actually, the first of any kind), until she met Freddy. My mother was thankful the relationship failed, as Mary was not only a Christian but a staunch Catholic. But the point of this story is not to underestimate the problems of good study space for students from some backgrounds.

The school introduced a system of 'acceleration', in which those expected to do well spent just one term in the fifth form, taking O-levels in November and passing into the Lower Sixth the following January. A-levels were taken five terms later, so that the boys would be just 17 when they (hopefully) passed these examinations. They could thus take Oxford and Cambridge entry papers a year later, and still be aged 18 on progressing to University. The rumour was that this scheme increased the numbers in the sixth form, and thereby enhanced the Head's salary. When the names were announced of those selected for 'acceleration' and I was not amongst them, I was very upset. However, the next day I learned that someone had spoken up for me (I suspect it was Mr Dunning, who taught me German), and I would after all join the favoured group. I was delighted: it did much for my confidence.

I enjoyed the Science Sixth Form immensely. Most of the other pupils in the science group were planning to be doctors, pharmacists or dentists – highly paid professions, encouraged by their parents. My mother really wanted me to be a doctor too, but I didn't think I was good enough; when we went, years later, to the Albert Hall for my PhD to be conferred, I felt I had met her wish, albeit in a rather different manner. My Higher Doctorate, the DSc, some years later, was bewildering for her.

My A-level results were not good. In those days there were no grades, but I was told I was awarded 46% for Chemistry, 46% for Pure Mathematics, 42%

for Physics, and 43% for Applied Mathematics, hardly a great performance, and insufficient to get me into London University. I decided to stay on for the third year in the Sixth and improve my results, dropping Applied Mathematics so as to concentrate on just three subjects.

I had already arranged to go hitch-hiking with another boy, Brian Levy. He was in the Sixth Arts, and had always been in the A-stream, so I did not know him well. I was pretty unsure of myself, but under Brian's guidance we joined the Youth Hostel Association, got passports, and rucksacks (on which we sewed Union Jacks), money belts, maps…and off we went. I had just £20, as much as I could scrape together for the four weeks' planned trip, to include the ferry crossing, hostel fees, food and all other expenses. It was a wonderful experience, and we travelled through Belgium, Holland, Germany, Austria, and Italy right down to Venice, into France and Switzerland, then back home via Paris. It was rough at times, but we had amazing incidents; sleeping on the beach, in a gondola, on a train in a siding; eating just a bit of fruit and some bread for a few days. I met fellow hitch-hikers from across Europe, including a young German student from West Berlin, Lothar Eichhoff, who was very helpful in locating my father's grave.[3]

I did do better at A-levels next time round, with all three marks in the 60s. Perhaps I could have done better still, but I spent much energy on athletics training, and having been made House Captain I put in a great deal of time encouraging the younger forms in basketball, swimming, and, of course, athletics. I also took part in the school play for the first time, playing Lucius Septimius in George Bernard Shaw's *Caesar and Cleopatra*.

My main concern was where I would study chemistry. I was immature and scared to leave the safety of London. The very idea of living away from home with lots of clever 'posh' people was daunting, so I restricted myself to Colleges of London University. Imperial College, King's College, and University College had special entrance examinations, at which I was unsuccessful. For Queen Mary College I had an interview, which I would rather forget. So, after passing A-levels twice, and still just 18 years old, I had no university place to which to go.

I went to seek the advice of the head teacher, Vernon Barkway Pye. He was a stuffy man who was nowhere near as well liked as his predecessor,

---

3 See http://www.bbc.co.uk/ww2peopleswar/stories/57/a8407857.shtml

Mr T. O. Balk ('Toby'), someone much admired by pupils and parents alike. He consulted the University of London Year Book, and suggested I tried Bedford College. I was surprised that I had not come up with this option myself, but soon found out why: Bedford College (which no longer exists) was a women-only college!

I was working in the shoe shop, and thought that was where I would end up. It was Leslie Lawrence, the husband of my Aunt Jean, the youngest of the Goldstein children and inspiration behind this book, who suggested Northern Polytechnic in Holloway Road. Leslie had been a student there immediately after the war, one of many ex-servicemen to take special two-year compressed degree courses for ex- sevicemen. As he was at that time Head of Chemistry at East Ham Technical College, he knew the Head of Department, Dr William Gerrard, so arranged an interview. The 'interview' consisted of Leslie and Dr Gerrard gossiping for half an hour, the only question directed to me being about whether I wanted to take biology or geology as the first year option?

So – it was Northern Polytechnic for me.

The demise of Hackney Downs School

HDS was, without doubt, a fantastic school at least throughout the post-war period and up until the late 1960s. During my period there it was populated to a very large extent by second generation Eastern European Jewish immigrant boys, who had a huge work ethic and drive for self-improvement. They had the backing (sometimes more than that!) of their parents, many of whom, like mine, had little formal education of their own, but knew that education was the way for a better life for their children. The school produced an outstanding array of academics, doctors, lawyers, businessmen et al from that period, very many of them of Jewish origin.

But somehow it all went so badly wrong that Hackney Downs became infamous as the first school to be taken into the management of an 'Education Association' – a 'hit squad'. There was intense media attention, for all the wrong reasons. HDS was finally destroyed by what its last Head Teacher described as 'the vitriolic politics of Hackney'. Much has been written about the demise of this once wonderful and successful school, and readers are referred to the 'Further Reading' at the end of this book, because it is impossible succinctly to summarise the events of the time. Suffice to say that the death of HDS is a terrible tragedy; where the focus on education, the needs of the local children and the importance of structured and disciplined teaching all became of secondary importance to power struggles, excessive political correctness, extremist views and dogma. And the enormously successful multi-cultural and multi-faith approach for which the school was renowned, which 'Toby' Balk had created, and from which those of my generation benefited almost beyond belief, was destroyed.

I grieve for what HDS was and what it could still be. I can but hope that the new school which has recently been constructed on the site, Mossbourne Academy, can achieve something approaching the quality of opportunity of its distinguished predecessor. It will be a hard task.

Reflections 4

As I have said throughout this section, the impact on me of Hackney Downs School was profound and deep. I owe HDS, the whole phenomenon, so, so much. I know times have moved on, but how I wish I could recreate such schools and their influence across the land. We would surely not have the racial and sectarian tensions which are now so prevalent in our society; the violence, anti-social behaviour, underachievement and disaffection. Knowing what a good school such as Hackney Downs can do for working-class children has been a driver for my passion to provide higher education for those denied the opportunities which I experienced and enjoyed. My life has been so enriched, my career so enabled, my character so enhanced by Hackney Downs School; I have tried to compensate for the fact that others have not had such fantastic enabling experiences. And the fact that I had to struggle to make Hackney Downs work for me, financially, socially, and finding somewhere to study, has made me value my experience even more.

Northern Polytechnic London

The early polytechnic movement

And so I entered the polytechnic world. Little did I realise how profound an effect this would have on my personal development, values, and sense of purpose.

Although I now had an LEA maintenance grant, I agreed to hand it over for my keep, all £169 a year of it. I kept both the Saturday and Sunday jobs, and worked at Christmas-time and during the summer; as I would be living at home, I had enough money to survive.

Northern Polytechnic was one of a clutch of institutions in London known by that term well before the creation of the polytechnics nationally in 1969-1970. They began as 'Mechanics Institutes' in Victorian times to enable local populations to acquire trade skills. By the 1960s, they had evolved into significant providers of vocational further and higher education. Northern Polytechnic, so named presumably because it was the most northerly in the capital, was founded in 1896. By the time I went there, in 1957, it offered a wide range of University of London degrees in science (remarkably, since the 1920s); their status was between those of internal degrees provided by the genuine colleges of London University (Imperial, Queen Mary et al) and the External London programmes which were available at academic institutions throughout the Commonwealth. The London polytechnics were 'Institutions with Recognised Teachers of the University'. I learned later, when I gained that status in May 1967, that this meant that the 'teachers' were deemed by the university to be capable of supervising research students, a very early example of the anomaly, which demeans British higher education: research ability being used as a mark of ability to teach.

These institutions fulfilled an extremely important role of providing courses at a range of levels and modes of study, with ladders and bridges between them, and set professional and more academic courses side by side. They were more concerned with aptitude and commitment that with formal entry qualifications. It was seminal work, which laid the foundations for the later development of polytechnics at the national level.

Undergraduate days

So it was that I arrived at Northern Polytechnic, with considerable trepidation, in September 1957. Messages chalked crudely on a blackboard in the entrance lobby told me to where to go – there were about 50 or 60 chattering people in a stepped lecture theatre. We were sent to other rooms according to the course; I was on BSc (Special) Chemistry, denoting that it was not a General (ie two-subject) degree. There were about 15 students in my group from all over the country. About half had been 'chucked out' (their words) of colleges in London University at the end of their first year. It was said that Imperial College deliberately pruned out a third of the first year every summer. I have to confess that this disgraceful approach has coloured my attitude towards Imperial College ever since.

I soon got to know the other students. There were a couple who were older than the rest – taking mature students was part and parcel of the polytechnic style. I made particular friends with Alan Leftwick, who later was my Best Man, and Frank Bathie. Frank worked at the Laboratory of the Government Chemist, which had sponsored him as its first 'sandwich' student, alternating periods of study in the polytechnic with actual working experience. It was a pioneering concept then, and of huge benefit. I could see Frank's far superior laboratory skills, and he was so much more aware of the subject than me. I realised that there was no substitute for actually doing experimental science. I became an avid enthusiast of the sandwich principle in my later professional life.

In our first year, we studied chemistry, physics, mathematics and either biology or geology. For the latter option we had to attain roughly A-level standard in the year, and for most of us the subject was entirely new. Tuition was from 9.00 am to 5.00 pm every day, except Mondays when we returned for a session from 6.00-9.00 pm. How different that was from today's 10-15 hours a week even for science students. The teaching was entirely lectures, plus the extensive laboratory work; no tutorials, problem/discussion groups or seminars, except a weekly whole-group problem class in our final year. The large amount of laboratory work was essential, as there were two two-day examinations to pass. No continuous assessment or coursework – all unseen examinations.

The library was very poor (in every sense), with no quiet study spaces; Stoke Newington Reference Library continued to be my home every evening and throughout the holidays. Equipment was very basic, and old. The building looked in its final stages of life, as if it had not been maintained since the official opening in the mid-nineteenth century. There were no residential facilities and no help for students from out of town to find accommodation, indeed, no 'Student Services' at all. The Students' Union was one room, with just enough space to play bridge at lunchtime, and a single office; no sabbatical posts, no permanent staff, little money. I joined the Basketball Club – I loved the game, having played at HDS, even though, at 5'6" I was not good at it. We just about managed to drum up a team, and squeezed some money to get some coaching at the evening classes run at a local school, otherwise paying our own expenses. The only time we won a game was when we disguised our Coach as a student. I bought a set of black vests at a local cheap shop, and got Marie Horeman to sew on the numbers with white tape. What a contrast to the owned facilities and professional kit worn by our competitors from the London colleges.

The teaching staff at Northern Poly were of varied quality, but some were outstanding. Mike Lappert went on to be a Professor at Sussex University, gained an international reputation, and was elected to an FRS. Dr Finar – known forever by that formal name – was brilliant; he had written the only organic chemistry text books designed for the University of London BSc course, and they were bibles amongst generations of London students of all the institutions. Norbert Singer was excellent, making physical chemistry actually interesting and relevant! Coming from a similar ethnic background and being only a few years' older, he was to become my role model, mentor, friend, and confidant. Malcolm Fraser was a remarkable teacher and leader; he was a major influence on my career. The Head of Department, William Gerrard, was from the old school, but it was clearly his vision and drive that had made chemistry at Northern as good as many university departments, and a jewel in the London polytechnics' crown.

Jointly teaching different groups together created opportunities with reasonable economy. I was taught with students studying for the Graduateship examination of what was then the Royal Institute of Chemistry, and others taking the London General (joint Honours) degree, full-time and part-time students all together. Some forty years later, the traditional universities began experimenting with such arrangements, albeit more structured in modular formats. But this had been commonplace in the modern higher education world for years.

Just as I was due to start my final year, I went to the wedding of my cousin Leon, the oldest of three sons of my mother's brother, Ben. It was there that I met Janet. She lived opposite Leon in Walthamstow, and the two families were very close. Indeed, our mothers knew each other as mine was a regular visitor to Ben and his wife, Nelly. Janet and I began courting straight after that, and later became engaged. That was another blow for Mum, as I was now also about to marry out of the religion. But by then the world had moved on, and she did after all know Janet's family. So although it was still hard for her, and I know she was very disappointed, Mum did not stand in my way. The two of them formed as strong a mother-and-daughter-in-law relationship as ever could be.

Northern Polytechnic was a great success for me. I doubt I could have survived in a big University. I worked hard, and found the pace and style to my liking. I was good at passing examinations, and I understood the theory pretty well, but my experimental skills were awful. How I passed the two two-day practical examinations at the University of London laboratories, I will never know, and nor will those who tried to teach me the skills.

I was very uncertain what I would do on graduation. I did not see how I could ever be a proper, experimental chemist. I had applied for only one job, that of a Patent Examiner, which requires a high level of technical and scientific understanding, but is office- rather than laboratory-based. It seemed ideal for me. I went for the interview, but felt a hostile atmosphere. I don't know why, and I am not at all paranoid about such things, but I naturally thought of anti-semitism; I was uncomfortable throughout the interview and was not surprised that I was unsuccessful.

So, very unsure of what I would do, I continued to work in the shoe shop after finals throughout the summer of 1960, and was contemplating that being my career. It seemed like 1957 all over again, when I had some decent A-level results and did not know what to do with them. Now I was expecting a decent degree and I was three years older.

A few days before results were due I received a letter from Dr Gerrard, the Head of the Department. He asked me to see him 'with the view of doing research'. I was staggered. He could not know how bad I was in the laboratory!

But with few other options, I went to see him. The proposition was this: the department had recently bought a new piece of equipment, an infra-red spectrometer. They wanted someone to find out what it could do for the research that was being undertaken in his group. He had with him Eric Mooney, his bright-eyed boy, and Eric was reassuring; Gerrard clearly did not know much about spectroscopy!

I had nothing to lose, so became a salaried Research Assistant, on about £1,400 a year, for which I would do six hours a week 'demonstrating' to undergraduate students in the laboratories. I found the latter proposal truly ironic, but it was agreed that I would work in the physical chemistry labs, which would be much more suitable to me.

The day after my meeting with Dr Gerrard I went to Senate House in Malet Street and scanned the boards on which hundreds of London degree results were hand-written. Where was my number? I can't find it. There it is… wow! I had gained First Class Honours! I was elated, as this was quite a rarity in those days, especially for people from the polytechnics; grade inflation is a fairly recent phenomenon. I realised that Dr Gerrard already knew, as he was on the Board which had met a few days before. I now knew what I was going to do, at least for the next three years.

Postgraduate research

If I was nervous when I began my first degree course, I was petrified to turn up as a postgraduate in September 1960. True, I knew how the place worked, but my status and relationships were to be very different indeed. As an employee, I had to clock in. I became 'Mike' rather than 'Mr Goldstein'. I had a new set of people to get to know, and all seemed far better chemists than me.

I was allocated to Eric Mooney. He seemed to be in charge of the whole of Dr Gerrard's research team, but he was still working for his own PhD. He had come from industry – ICI Plastics Division in Welwyn Garden City – and was so capable and prolific that he was expecting to complete his Doctorate in one year. He was a huge help to me, and became my mentor and friend.

My work began as planned: examining the infra-red spectra of compounds synthesised by the various researchers in Gerrard's group; trying to make some sense of them; seeking patterns so as to be able to deduce something about their structure; helping to identify unknown materials from the various chemical reactions the researchers were investigating. It was very interesting and pioneering, and a huge learning curve for us all. I took great pleasure in explaining to other researchers what this new technique was and how it might be of benefit to them. That was the first indication that I might enjoy teaching.

My 'demonstrating' was very rewarding. It is a truism that one does not really begin to understand something until one teaches it, and I found that out for myself. I wanted to change the students' experiments, to bring them up-to-date and make them more interesting, but the person in charge was a senior man, Dr C. G. Smith, who was very fixed in his ways, and Victorian in appearance, style and science. But he commanded great respect amongst his colleagues, and I did not wish to upset him; nor had I the temerity to question what went on in his laboratory.

Eric Mooney was progressive, very ambitious, and set on cutting out his own role in the hierarchy. He introduced infra-red spectroscopy into the undergraduate laboratory curriculum, giving me even more opportunity to engage with students, which I enjoyed greatly.

I also ventured into the 'mixing and stirring' aspect of chemistry, trying to synthesise some target compounds in which I became interested. The laboratory in which did this was an area at one end of a teaching lab. That arrangement would never be allowed these days, and quite rightly too. The dangers were substantial, and during my time there were several small explosions and fires, which could have been serious. Safety standards were far lower than now. We only wore safety spectacles when performing particularly and known hazardous operations; that all changed several years later when there was a very bad accident in which a research student lost an eye, and all of us then present became the strongest advocates of mandatory wearing of safety glasses at all times.

Manual safety was also at a low level in the 1960s. Many of the substances with which I worked, without gloves of any kind, are now considered to be lethal and some are now even banned; para-benzidine is a known, serious carcinogen, but I used it with minimal precautions for some time. Indeed, I handled (literally!) aromatic and aliphatic amines, and chlorinated hydrocarbons, with abandon. In the spectroscopy lab, I worked in a confined and unventilated space with open Petrie dishes of dichloromethane and chloroform, both now banned for general use as they are believed to be carcinogenic; I even rinsed my hands with them before going home.

Notwithstanding how primitive were the facilities, Northern Polytechnic established a reputation for research as well as for teaching. I never once regretted doing my PhD there, and indeed I have always been proud to tell people I did. It was research which clearly distinguished the science departments at Northern from the others; and distinguished the London polytechnics from the rest of the non-university sector. That is something which has been lost, as a result of the more liberal attitudes to what constitutes higher education in the twenty-first century, and in my view is far more the cause of lowering of standards than so-called 'dumbing down' – more of which later.

Eric Mooney built up the spectroscopy facilities. He was aided by someone he knew from his ICI days, Harry Willis, a true guru of the field. He was immensely helpful to me, not only during my PhD work but also beyond. He came in Monday evenings for three hours to discuss and advise on the research work in progress. I thus became aware of the huge importance of linking higher education with the commercial world; having the added dimension of someone who worked in industry was of significant benefit to my understanding and scientific development. It is a value which I promoted for many years thereafter.

It was through Harry Willis that I was worked a few days a week over some months with David Adams at The Frythe Laboratories of ICI, the company's 'blue skies' research establishment in lovely woodland near Welwyn Garden City. David had built an amazing infra-red spectrometer which covered the wavelength range which no commercial instrument could do, part of the electromagnetic spectrum which I needed to explore for my work. I made the trip to the Frythe regularly, by motor scooter in all weathers, during late 1962 and early 1963. When ICI closed The Frythe, because corporate blue skies research had become unaffordable, David Adams went to the University of Leicester. I learned a huge amount from him, and our collaboration continued for many years after I gained my Doctorate and became a researcher in my own right.

I was also fortunate in being able to use some cutting edge equipment at the National Physical Laboratory in Teddington, Middlesex, constructed by Harry Gebbie: an instrument based on an entirely new and innovative concept – a Fourier Transform Spectrometer for far infra-red spectroscopy. This was an enormous privilege, and was to be extremely formative to my future research career. The particularly novel feature of the technique was the fact that complex calculations (Fourier transformation) were needed to obtain intelligible data, necessitating the use of computers. In the early 1960s, computers were very primitive, occupying vast rooms and performing simple routines very slowly. It was hard work getting the data; the instrument was contained in a huge steel tank under very high vacuum, and was temperamental; the computing involved long spools of five-hole tape, which had to be edited by hand and often gave meaningless output. A day's work could result in nothing of any use. 'Back to the drawing board' became a regular 'back to the spectrometer' many, many times.

It was in May 1962, when I was about half-way through my PhD work, that Janet and I married. We had to pay for the wedding and do all the arranging ourselves. The ceremony was in Walthamstow Registry Office and was necessarily modest. We hired the Conservative Club rooms at the top of Walthamstow High Street, engaged a small band and so on. We invited all our siblings and their families, and all our aunts and uncles. No one came from my father's side of the family – I did not expect any of them would, but we did the right thing and invited them along with the rest. I have to confess that if they had all turned up we would not have been able to pay the bill! As it was, I had to borrow £10 from my Best Man, Alan Leftwick, to pay the band. As soon as we were back from honeymoon I sold a few items to a pawnbroker so that the cheque with which I had paid the hotel bill would not 'bounce'. The wedding day coincided with the Cup Final, with one of the two big local teams playing, Tottenham Hotspur against Burnley (which Spurs won 3-1), so most people disappeared after the wedding lunch. We had a week's honeymoon in Bournemouth, travelling by train and splashing out with a taxi at the other end.

Shortly after I returned to continue my research, Dr Gerrard made a rare appearance in my lab. He asked me: 'Would you like to join the staff?' by which he meant be a lecturer in his department. I was stunned, as the prospect had not occurred to me. But I knew that another fellow student, Ron Rees, had joined the staff the year before he was due to complete his Doctorate; he was struggling as the task of developing and undertaking his teaching put back his gaining the PhD by about two years. So I rather cheekily replied to Dr Gerrard that: 'I would prefer first to complete my PhD'. Astonishingly, he accepted that response. I know I made the right decision: I did not want to be diverted from my research, and I was not even sure that I wanted to be a lecturer anyway. In fact, it was only then that I realised that I did not have a clue what I was going to do when (and if) I gained my Doctorate. I was too busy with the work, and enjoying it.

I worked very hard for my PhD throughout, staying on several evenings a week, taking minimal holidays, and also going in some Saturdays. It was remarkable that a place like Northern Polytechnic had a Saturday chemistry research school, with 10-20 people working away in the labs. Many were part-time research students, a real test of endurance and commitment.

Towards the end of my final PhD year in 1963, a report was published which was to have a truly profound impact on the whole world of higher education – the Government committee of enquiry, chaired by Lord Robbins, then Chairman of the *Financial Times. Higher Education in the Learning Society*, usually known as the 'Robbins Report' proposed a massive increase in higher education provision: 'higher education should be available to all those who can benefit from it' was a dramatic shift from the then highly selective, élitist system which then existed. The report argued that higher education was a critical element in development of modern economies, and was of huge social importance.

This heralded a programme of expansion of provision across the country, including at Northern Polytechnic. It meant that new positions of lecturer were created, and one such post came up just as I was completing my Doctorate. The job was advertised and I applied. But the timing was not soon enough for the start of term, so I was taken on a temporary basis, without prejudice, of course, to the eventual outcome of the selection process. I had been doing the job for about a month when the interviews were held, which helped my case enormously. I was over the moon when I got the job for real.

In the meanwhile, I wrote up my thesis and submitted it to the University. I took just four weeks to do it, a huge effort, and much quicker than the norm. The *viva voce* examination was very exacting – I realised how naïve and immature I was in the subject of infra-red spectroscopy. My External Examiner, Professor Ian Beattie of Southampton University, gave me some advice, which I took – get a real understanding of the principles – to my great benefit. I thus became 'Dr Goldstein', a title which I still use professionally.

Reflections 5

Why was chemistry at Northern Polytechnic so successful even though it was poorly financed and set in a broadly further education institution? I have no doubt that it was due to the individuals whom I have mentioned, viz William Gerrard, Malcolm Fraser, Norbert Singer and Eric Mooney. People who had ability, but especially drive, imagination and vision. I have since reflected on the current controversy of further education colleges offering degree courses under the validation of Universities, and whether the standards can possibly be the same as in Universities; in 2006, about 11% of higher education in England was delivered in further education colleges. During the time of the Council for National Academic Awards (CNAA), to which I shall refer later, very stringent conditions were set down for non-University institutions (polytechnics et al) to offer degree programmes; I am pretty sure that very few if any of those FE colleges now running degrees would meet these criteria. Yet it worked very well for me, and for countless others who went through Northern Polytechnic, because high quality people created higher education worlds within, and despite, the further education culture around them. They had to fight hard for every bit of money they needed; for equipment which was essential to meet the needs of their students; for staff of the right commitment and quality; for the very infrastructure which enabled research to be undertaken, and most of all for the flexibility to create real opportunities for those denied the traditional offerings of Universities. It is of great credit to the leaders of those institutions that they supported these pioneers in the way and extent that they did.

It is also pertinent to reflect on my own position in relation to the obsession of the Blair and Brown Governments with getting Oxford and Cambridge to take more students from working class backgrounds. I shall reflect further on this later, but suffice to say at this stage that I strongly believe this policy is misguided. As a first-generation higher education student, I trembled at the thought of even going to any University, let alone Oxbridge. While some of my contemporaries did manage the transition, it is arrogant and patronising for the likes of those from privileged or professional backgrounds to assume that Oxbridge is good for everyone. That environment was definitely not for me – and still is an anathema now. The environment provided by Northern Polytechnic was just right, the only thing missing was the same level of resources that the universities of the day enjoyed.

Setting Academic Values

A lonely step into the dark

It was October 1963. I had just been appointed lecturer in inorganic chemistry at Northern Polytechnic. There was no induction, and no written guidance of what was to be done. As for syllabuses (as they were then called), the University of London handbook simply stated 'aspects of inorganic, organic and physical chemistry' for a whole degree course! The only guide was to get hold of past examination papers. I had just ten minutes chat, standing next to the seated person who was then responsible for inorganic chemistry, Malcolm Fraser. I stood because there was no spare chair. Indeed, there was no space for me at all in the sole room for all chemistry staff; no separate desks, just chairs along a bench the length of the room. I did have a space in the spectroscopy lab, which suited me, because it meant I could easily mix my research with preparation and marking, although I tended to do that at home.

I was left largely to work things out myself. My first teaching was on Monday evenings, 8.00-9.00pm, to part-time day-release degree students. They had lectures all morning, practical work from 2.00-8.00pm, and then my lecture. The reason for this routine was to ensure they stayed until 9.00pm and did not slope off by cutting short their lab work. But it suited me, because I could organise my day more easily. I had some other lectures during the week, and a good deal of laboratory work to organise and supervise, but I still had time, especially by working into the evenings and taking work home, to develop research from my Doctorate.

Big changes domestically

When Janet and I married in May 1962 we rented a flat in Leytonstone. At four guineas a week it was not cheap, but it was in a decent area and newly refurbished. It was tiny: one bed-sitting room and minute kitchen with room only for small table and two chairs, and a 'Baby Belling' tabletop 'oven'. The toilet and bathroom were shared with other tenants. At the end of the two-year lease we found another flat in Crouch End, near to Finsbury Park station. This was a larger, split-level attic flat; the landlords lived in the house. It was freezing in winter, and unbearably hot in the summer. Shortly after we had moved on, the house featured on the front page of national newspapers – our flat had become an IRA bomb factory!

We needed to get on to the property ladder soon. House prices were increasing faster than we were saving. We could afford £4,000, requiring a £400 deposit. We found a new development being built in an Essex village called Stansted Mountfitchet. We bought a bright red Mini in place of the Vespa motorscooter, later replaced by a larger car. Driving to London and back every day was a chore, but we made light of it. But one day, on the way to work, we had a serious accident and were lucky to get away with very minor injuries, especially as Janet was several weeks pregnant; we decided to try to move back to London. That took some months, because of the controversial plans to develop Stansted as London's third airport. In the meanwhile, in June 1968, Richard was born.

It was not until early 1970, with Richard about eighteen months old, that we moved to Highams Park, into a house requiring a lot of work. We had little money for the renovation, so everything was done piecemeal on a shoestring, significantly aided by Leila's husband, Jimmy, who was a DIY whiz. We had a ten-year plan, but before that period was up, I was to move on.

Major changes in the environment

A year into my appointment, in 1964, Dr Gerrard retired. Malcolm Fraser was appointed as his successor, a hugely popular choice. He was the youngest Head of Chemistry in the country at the time, aged 33 [I was just one year older when I later gained the Headship at Sheffield Polytechnic]. There was an immediate change in pace. Malcolm was innovative and ambitious, and set about substantial development of the Department.

One immediate task was to plan the new Polytechnic extensions, a 14-storey tower block build on the Holloway Road frontage, with chemistry getting the top five floors. It was a fantastic project, which captured the imagination of all concerned. The spectroscopy labs moved to a new, larger location in the old building; the department was already too large for the tower. But the new location was a complete renovation to our design, and was a facility of which to be pretty proud.

The development of the institution was given a major boost when, in 1965, Anthony Crosland, then Secretary of State for Education in the Wilson government, delivered a famous speech at Woolwich Polytechnic (a sister institution to Northern) in which he announced the creation of a new sector of higher education, the (new) polytechnics. They were to have 'parity of esteem' with the university sector, but focus on applied subjects: science, technology and the needs of business; be close to employers; offer a range of modes of study – full-time, part-time, block release; and develop ladders and bridges between vocational, professional and academic study. The new sector was to be created by the merger of the larger and more advanced further education and regional colleges across the country. There was to be investment in buildings and equipment, and creation of a national degree-awarding body for non-university institutions, the Council for National Academic Awards (CNAA). This was truly a seminal moment, and it was evident that higher education in the United Kingdom would never be the same. We were excited by the prospects which the Crosland speech implied, although there were some fears about the unknown.

Malcolm Fraser, supported by Norbert Singer, by then his right-hand man, inspired the rest of us to meet the big challenges. Not everyone welcomed the introduction of the CNAA. We had been running London University degrees for years, and they had a known, international standing; there was a serious danger that CNAA degrees would never receive the same status and currency – 'parity of esteem' seemed implausible if not impossible. But freedom from the strictures of the University's requirements, and the opportunity to create something for ourselves, was compelling. Our CNAA chemistry course was designed for sponsored students from British Petroleum (BP), but in the event they provided only a handful of students. Nonetheless, it had the support of an industrial advisory committee, which ensured the course was based on what chemists actually do, rather than a list of topics handed down through the generations and which someone once felt chemists should know. The new degree was excitingly different: a sandwich structure; tutorials and problem classes; continuous assessment of laboratory work rather than artificial and design-constrained examinations; projects, and a complete re-think of the content and context. For the first time, emphasis could be given to developing communication and thinking skills, safety, experimental design, problem-solving, and breaking down the barriers between the traditional sections of chemistry which the former degree had emphasised. The London degree was soon forgotten.

Creation of the 'New Polytechnics' required merger to form more comprehensive and more substantial institutions. It was decreed that Northern would merge with North Western Polytechnic, which was scattered in a range of makeshift buildings around north London. This notion was very unpopular with the Northern staff – North Western was far less well developed, and was really a further education college of commerce; it had no postgraduate work, and no research culture, and moreover, it was full of the loony left! The merger was fraught with difficulties and strife. I recall the academic trade union, then the Association of Teachers in Technical Institutions (ATTI) trying to hijack a general staff meeting called by the Principal of Northern, Dr James Leicester, causing a very embarrassing scene. Few of the science staff were union members, but after this event many of us joined up and saw off the trouble-makers, at least from the Northern side.

It got worse. Dr Leicester retired and the Inner London Education Authority appointed Dr Terence Miller as 'Director' of the new Polytechnic of North London in 1971. He had been Principal of University College Rhodesia, and was immediately subject to intense and vitriolic attack as a collaborator with the Rhodesian Prime Minister, Ian Smith. Under Ian Smith's leadership, the Rhodesian government had already severed its links with the British Crown by an illegal Unilateral Declaration of Independence (UDI), and had left the Commonwealth. Ian Smith had been branded a racist, and the extreme left, who seemed to come out of the woodwork, charged Terence Miller with being of the same ilk. It was a terrible time, but the merger went ahead, albeit the last in the country to be formalised. Even at the formal inauguration ceremony, there was disruption when the President of the Students' Union forced his way onto the stage, ranting obscenities, just as the Secretary of State was about to present an address, only to be manhandled away by the Director himself!

Establishing position and influence

The battle to create the new Polytechnic of North London went on for a couple of years at least, ending with the departure of Terence Miller, a major enquiry, and reputational damage that took years to overcome. But it was awful, with mindless opposition to almost everything Terence Miller tried to do. Even getting the various departments to form Faculties was met with fierce objection and for no articulated reason. By that time I was involved in some of the organisational work, and was asked to convene a new Faculty of Science and Technology. I thus became an ex officio member of the new Academic Board. I was shocked at what happened at its first meeting. The constitution was something like 50% students, 30% elected staff, and just 20% ex officio members (Heads et al). Given that the student body was dominated by left-wing activists, (possibly members of the Revolutionary Communist Party, a Trotskyist splinter group), and the elected staff were all staunch trades unionists behaving like professional revolutionaries, there was little rhyme or reason about anything that the Board decided. Before the first item on the inaugural agenda, the Director ruled from the chair that there should be no smoking during the meeting, whereupon cigarettes and lighters were immediately brought into action. The first agenda item was a vote of no confidence in the Director, which was actually debated with shocking venom; in the chaos, I don't think the motion was ever put to the vote, but no doubt it would have been passed had it been. And it got worse. There were student occupations and the Director's office ransacked; a group of senior staff struggled to regain a semblance of control. After I had left, in 1984, there was the dreadful affair of Patrick Harrington, a National Front student activist who, rightly, demanded to be taught, but some staff violently refused to teach him, and no other students would sit in the same room; there were sit-ins, demonstrations, violent clashes, and much bad odour.

But the academic work continued regardless. We innovated in course design, the curriculum and in assessment. A cross-science modular structure broke new ground; new integrated, problem-oriented topics; multiple choice and open book assessments; group projects; completely new and novel approaches to laboratory work; the use of television to demonstrate laboratory techniques. It was one of the most creative periods of my professional career. I recall the visit of the CNAA Panel to consider the faculty degree scheme, chaired by someone who was held in awe by us all – Maurice Foss, Chair of the CNAA Chemistry Board and Dean of the Faculty of Applied Science at Lanchester Polytechnic in Coventry. He was later to be promoted to Deputy Director at Lanchester. I observed him that day as brilliantly astute and clever in teasing out the issues. Little did I realise that I was later to succeed him in both his CNAA role and Deputy Directorship at Coventry.

My research was going well, and I attracted a regular supply of research students, aided by the financial support which Malcolm Fraser was so adept in securing. Before he left, Eric Mooney had increased the equipment base for spectroscopy beyond recognition. We were one of the first academic institutions to have a commercial nuclear magnetic resonance spectrometer, a very primitive device by today's standards. It was very temperamental and having a permanent magnet was susceptible to any movement of large metallic objects. One of my students, Chris Mullins, needed to make some very precise measurements, so had to work during the night after the London Underground, which passed beneath the building, had closed down. We were also the second research group in the United Kingdom (David Adams at Leicester was the very first) to acquire a commercial Fourier Transform Spectrometer for far infra-red spectroscopy (FTIR), a development of the work of Harry Gebbie at the National Physical Laboratory, which I have described. The FTIR was my baby, and I spent every minute I could developing techniques and pioneering its applications. Over the next few years I became well known for this work. Some of my early results featured in an historical account of the subject.

I was fortunate to build an excellent research team of wonderful people. I am still in touch with three of them: Bill Unsworth, a creative serial entrepreneur who made his fortune in the dotcom world; Monica Seeley, whom I did not think could make the jump from MPhil to PhD but who proved me wrong by gaining her Doctorate some years later, now running her own a high-powered IT training consultancy; and Paul Davies, my only successful part-time research student, who later started up a company at the end of an old warehouse, which he grew and sold on so as to be able to be first in a classic car rally from London to Sydney, before developing a new successful business in England and Asia. I am immensely proud of them all.

Norbert Singer left to become Head of the Department of Life Sciences at the Polytechnic of Central London, which moved me up the Departmental pecking order. I also became more active and influential in the institution generally, especially in the new Faculty. When Malcolm Fraser left in 1972, to become Professor of Chemical Education at the University of East Anglia, everyone assumed I would get his job as Head of Department. I certainly was up for it, but was stunned by the interview Chairman's opening, disparaging remark: 'I see you have been concerned only with teaching'. I was almost speechless; the use of the word 'only' was an insult to the importance of the prime function of the institution, but the assertion was untrue regardless. I was producing more high quality research publications and supervising PhDs than almost anyone else, and I was heavily involved in development and leadership, not only in the Department but in the new Faculty. I confess not to recall any more of the interview, it was a done deal, and I was not valued.

Moving on

The person appointed to be the new Head of Chemistry was Dr Phillip Owston, an eminent crystallographer who had researched the crystal structure of ice, and had an Icelandic island named after him. By a curious coincidence, he had been at the Frythe Laboratories, where I worked with David Adams, as I have mentioned. He was a big contrast to Malcolm Fraser. He sat in his office and was invisible; he did no teaching or research. And while he was supportive of me, we never hit it off. For the first time I felt undervalued, and began to look elsewhere.

I applied, somewhat half-heartedly for lectureships in Universities, but didn't get a look-in, I guess due to my pedigree. And in any case, it really was a Headship I wanted. Three such posts came up at around the same time: Paisley College in Glasgow (a Scottish 'Central Institution,' on a par with English Polytechnics), Kingston Polytechnic in Surrey, and Sheffield Polytechnic. The Sheffield interview came up first, I was offered the job, and I accepted on the spot. I made the long rail journey home, arriving well into the evening. I put my head round the door, and said: 'I've got it!' I just had time to catch Janet from falling in a faint! A few moments later she asked: 'Where are we going?' I got out a map, as she had no idea where Sheffield was.

Reflections 6

I am immensely proud of my polytechnic background. I learned the trade at Northern; the knowledge, skills and especially the values of being a teacher-researcher in higher education. The link between teaching and research was so obvious; I could see its benefit even if I could not describe the mechanism. In my later career I fought to retain that link, but the powerful Oxbridge lobby persuaded governments to concentrate research funding to the detriment of the majority, and hugely damaging to higher education nationally, as I shall elaborate later.

I also learned how to be innovative and creative in the definition of the curriculum and in its delivery. All too often academics replicate their own experiences when they begin teaching, and I have even seen recently appointed staff teach from their own undergraduate notes. I was guided away from this stultifying and incestuous trend by my role models at Northern, Malcolm Fraser and Norbert Singer as they demonstrated refreshingly new thinking in content and teaching.

And polytechnic values were of huge importance to me. I found resonance with students from working-class backgrounds, and those who had been shunned by universities or were seeking an alternative route. Polytechnic students were the salt of the earth, many subject to social and economic disadvantage, striving to improve themselves; they deserved all the support we could give them. The synergy between motivated students and motivated staff created a wonderful atmosphere.

At the same time I realised that not everyone in the system was committed to these values. There were the trouble-makers, the political extremists, the anarchists. I realised I had to recognise such disruptive elements if I was to make progress in educational management; the early 1970s at Northern Polytechnic gave me a good grounding.

A New Life in Sheffield

Settling in

Leaving Northern Polytechnic was very difficult as I had been there man and boy, sixteen years in total. I loved the place and was fond of many of the people, a number of whom I had grown up with or even appointed. I was also going into a big unknown; I had undertaken a reasonable amount of research on Sheffield as a City (a couple of people in the department actually came from there), and on its polytechnic, but nevertheless I knew it was going to be a culture shock for all three of us.

After a couple of weekend house-hunting trips we found a dream house on Lodge Moor, 1000ft above sea level, adjacent to the Hallamshire Golf Course and almost overlooking the Rivelin valley, the road that leads to Snake

Pass. We would spend many hours walking on the moors there, exploring the delights of the Peaks, enjoying the fresh air and open spaces we were denied as children, and coping with the snow...

My appointment as Head of the Department of Chemistry and Biology was from 1 January 1974. I turned up at around 8.00 am on the starting date, only to find the place completely dark and locked up as 1 January was now a Bank Holiday! So I returned the next day and went up to the Department. I walked along the corridors, peering into the empty laboratories. I thought 'I am in charge of this', and my legs began to wobble.

On my desk there was just a single sheet of paper, left by my predecessor Alan Crawshaw, containing a short list of who was attending to current issues. It reminded me of the advice my Uncle Ron had given me when he heard that I was going to Sheffield: 'So it's a management job?' he asked. I hadn't thought of it in those terms but concurred. 'Well, this is what you do. You get in each morning before everyone else, make a list of all the jobs that need doing, write down the names of the people who are going to do them for you, and go home!' It was an amusing approach, but I remember it to this day because it has a ring of sense about it, although I confess never to have been good at delegation.

Over the next few days I spent time speaking to staff individually. There were some key players. Bill Geary had been the internal candidate for the Headship, so I realised there might be issues to deal with, and there were. Cyril Walker was the founding father of the Department and knew all there was to know about it. His opening remark to me was: 'I don't do research', but he recognised and supported its importance. He was a tremendous help, taking on all the chores and tasks that no one else wanted, deliberately freeing me up to concentrate on the development work. Roger Bawcutt was in charge of the Biology section, which was about half the size of the chemistry part and lacked a degree programme; he was suspicious of my intentions towards biology. Arnie Dwyer was the Chief Technician – he had a frightening power base, but would fix things for me that the academic staff would not touch.

The biggest concern expressed was the lack of support for research. This was most evident when I met David Allen. He was holding a shoe-box, which he said was his research lab! Even worse he had no dedicated space or locker, but kept his equipment and speciality chemicals in the box, taking them around until he found a spare space somewhere. This was absurd, but a reflection of the low value placed on research in many polytechnics at the time. First decision, made in week one: convert the undergraduate project lab, used for just six weeks a year(!) into a devoted research lab. The cost of this change was zero, the benefits to the researchers huge, and the impact in terms of policy and future direction was immense.

The Monday after I started was to be the second intake of a part-time MSc course in Instrumental Analytical Chemistry, but there were only 4 or 5 known enrolments, well below the minimum of 12 students set by the Regional Staff Inspector; anything less required special dispensation, and it was inconceivable that this would be forthcoming. As it happened, the Principal, Dr George Tolley, asked to see me on my second day; this was the ideal time to ask for his advice. I was amazed at his knowledge about this one small course amongst the hundreds in the Polytechnic. Indeed, he knew more about the course than was in my files. From this very first experience I held George Tolley in the highest esteem and respect. He was a model to which I could only aspire.

Making a mark in Sheffield

There were clear gaps in the Department's portfolio which were crying out to be filled; for instance, a part-time degree in chemistry, joint Honours across the science departments, and especially undergraduate and postgraduate degree work in biology (and physics in another department). Student recruitment was not easy; biology had potential to grow, while chemistry was only just holding its own.

But there were several reasons for optimism. New staff offices were being provided; additional staff posts were likely; my appointment was a clear signal for growth in research. We were part of a major national programme developing computer-assisted learning as a new technique in higher education; this was pioneering work, before the ubiquitous nature of computers.

Three years after starting at Sheffield, I was appointed to succeed David Hills, Head of Metallurgy, as Dean of the Faculty of Science. This was a three-year additional role on top of being Head of Department. I held this position from 1979 until I left Sheffield in 1983, as I had my first period of office renewed. It was very hard work, but I threw myself into it. It meant I was at the heart of much of the central decision-making of the institution, as ex officio member of all the major policy bodies below the level of Board of Governors. The rivalry between Chemistry and Metallurgy was sharpened by my appointment, and I frequently had strong clashes with David Hills. On one occasion I recall he became highly emotional and exploded, crashing his fist on the table so violently that I feared he had broken both. But we were also good friends and professional colleagues. We privately shared concerns and sought each other's advice. I learned a lot from David, particularly the importance of being able to disagree with colleagues without personal animosity developing.

I was determined to continue with some teaching and research, as difficult and as rare as that was for a Head, let alone a Dean. I decided to take a part-time HNC class, which was in the evening, making it a bit easier to ensure the regular commitment; to teach a short course with the final year Honours students related to my research, to help inspire them to higher study; and to take first-year students so as to influence their development as thinking chemists. It was very tough going, and I did not put in the effort as consistently as I should, but I was pleased to be leading from the front, and like to think I did a good job.

Research was somewhat easier in the circumstances. I was very fortunate to have two excellent and very able collaborators in Norman Bell, a superb synthetic chemist, and Ian Nowell, an outstanding X-ray crystallographer. We complemented each other in terms of expertise, and jointly supervised a number of excellent research students successfully to PhDs. It set a very good example for the rest of the Department.

At the same time, Sheffield was getting into our blood. Richard, coming up for six years old when we moved to Sheffield, settled in well. We lived on a main bus route, just a couple of stops down from the terminus at the foothills of the Pennines, where the snow fell heavily every year and was on the ground for three months or more. One year it was so bad that we were snowed in for a couple of days – the only time I missed going into work during nine years in Sheffield. Local people were incredibly friendly, and we made long-term friends. Most striking was their loyalty to Sheffield. They were fiercely proud of their City, read the local newspaper, listened to local radio, supported local sports teams, and so on. The City earned the title 'People's Republic of

South Yorkshire', coupled with the politically left-wing City Council Leader, one David Blunkett, later to be Home Secretary in Tony Blair's 'New Labour' government. But more formally, the City's strap-line: 'City on the Move' was fully justified.

Council for National Academic Awards

The CNAA was established in 1965 to provide quality assurance and validation of degree courses outside the university sector. It enabled polytechnics and colleges to offer degree programmes of assured quality without having to enter into tutelage with universities. Its essential task was to ensure the qualifications, and the courses of study leading to them, were comparable to those in UK universities. This could have resulted in a 'sameness', whereas the intention of setting up the new polytechnic sector was to make provision more related to the needs of business, while achieving parity of esteem. But it is to the enormous credit of those leading the development of CNAA that this did not happen. On the contrary, CNAA became an agency for innovation in programme design, curricula, assessment, and programme philosophy. CNAA operated until polytechnics were granted the powers to award their own degrees in 1992, but its influence and impact have been lasting.

At one of my first meetings of the Sheffield Polytechnic Academic Board, I was nominated for membership of the CNAA Chemistry Board, and I was duly appointed from the academic year 1975-1976. I found it a fascinating arena, one comprising experienced people from polytechnic chemistry departments, traditional universities, and industry. It was a potent mix, and I was privileged to join them. Over the next couple of years, I made the most of my membership of the Board, making contributions, being available for visits to institutions, participating in working groups, and so on. I made a good impression and impact with the Chairman, Sid Cotson (who had succeeded Maurice Foss), Deputy Director at Leicester Polytechnic, and I chaired some sessions at validation visits. I also became involved in validations of schemes beyond chemistry, across broad science areas, and indeed across whole institutions; such schemes were founded in the polytechnic sector and were ground-breaking, if complex to validate and deliver. It was therefore no surprise that I was invited to succeed Sid Cotson as Chairman of the Board from 1978-1979. This meant I became ex officio a member of other Boards and Committees, and hence more involved in CNAA policy. I visited virtually all polytechnics and major colleges and interacted with their staff at all levels. I thus acquired huge knowledge and insight into chemical education across the whole of the United Kingdom. It was an enormous privilege, and one which was so important to me in my professional development.

One particular encounter illustrates the power of the CNAA methodology and its bearing on my career. It concerned a submission from Coventry (Lanchester) Polytechnic for the normal quinquennial renewal of approval. The Chemistry Board found the proposals lacking. The course had not developed sufficiently, and the level of research and scholarly activity was unacceptably low, which showed in dated curricula and the general approach to the course. The Board renewed approval for just one year, when it would require a resubmission demonstrating improvement. If that resubmission did not address the Board's concerns, validation would be withdrawn. This was a very serious matter, as in the ultimate it would have led to the closure (or at least decimation) of the department, serious implications for students, major reputational damage, and loss of jobs and careers. But the Board was adamant, progress had not been made. It gave notice to the Polytechnic. A couple of weeks later the CNAA Secretariat received a letter from the Polytechnic Director demanding a personal meeting with me. I acceded to this 'request', but asked that I be joined by two other experienced members of the Board: David Booth, Head of Chemistry at Newcastle Polytechnic, and Ian Green, a senior scientist at the GEC Hirst Research Centre in Wembley. We met with a team from the Polytechnic: Geoffrey Holroyde, Director; Maurice Foss, by then Deputy Director; Brian Ray, Dean of the Faculty of Applied Sciences; and John Oubridge, Head of Department. We listened carefully to them, and explained fully the reasons for our position. We were sympathetic but firm. The upshot was acceptance by the polytechnic of the Board's stance – I had immense pleasure from that – and agreement that we would meet with the staff concerned with the course, to explain what the failings were and what needed to be done to overcome them to the Board's satisfaction. That meeting took place at the polytechnic in early September 1981. I deliberately made it low key, just the three of us plus the secretary; the only record would be a file note to say who went. The visit achieved all that we had hoped; the polytechnic responded, and in due course confidence in the chemists and the institution was restored. It was CNAA at its best, maintaining high standards, and showing resolve to make hard decisions, but being supportive and helpful to responsive institutions.

A year after that critical CNAA visit to Coventry (Lanchester) Polytechnic, I found myself interviewed there for the post of Deputy Director, replacing Maurice Foss. I am sure that the approach I adopted with their chemistry degree was of critical importance in landing that job.

Teacher education

In 1985 it was apparent that the production of qualified teachers was exceeding demand. The Government decided to reduce the training of teachers by a massive 30%. The impact on teacher training institutions was drastic, with three options given: close, diversify, or merge with a neighbouring university or polytechnic. In Sheffield, the City College of Education was one of the largest in the region, and not unnaturally its Principal wanted it to stay independent. In the event it was agreed that it should merge with the Polytechnic to form Sheffield City Polytechnic; the Principal took advantage of the very generous 'Crombie' redundancy package and George Tolley was announced as Principal – anything else would have been madness.

Within the institution new Departments were to be created from the College staff, focussing on degrees in school subjects which did not previously feature in the Polytechnic: history, geography and physical education along with others. Where there were like departments in both the College and the Polytechnic, there would be simple mergers, such as in mathematics. The College had a Biology Department of about 8-9 academic staff, and a Chemistry department of 2 1/2(!) academic staff; the decision was to split my department into separate Chemistry and Biological Sciences Departments, and combine each with the respective staff from the College. The two new posts of Head of Department were advertised internally, and I had to apply for what I considered to be my job because there was a so-called department of ridiculously small size in the College. The contrast was huge. The College had less than ten students studying chemistry in the Certificate of Education, not even a degree; no research; one technician; two labs. By contrast I had hundreds of students, six courses from HNC to MSc, loads of PhD students, around 20 academic staff, a dozen or more technicians, and about 15 labs. At the personal level, the Head at the College (Sam Selvey) had no postgraduate qualifications; and no experience of CNAA, the Royal Institute of Chemistry, the course approvals process, and so on. I did not prepare for the interview at all. But as I walked from my office to the interview room, I began to realise the enormity of what it would mean if I did not get the job; I suddenly felt very nervous. The interview was a disaster; I was not thinking straight. I left pretty distraught, and passed Sam Selvey as he was on his way in – he was relaxed and smiling. I felt worse. But he said I should not worry as he did not want the job and would tell them so! What a relief. The fact was he had to apply to get the generous 'Crombie' pay-off. So I got the job, more due to Sam not wanting it than from my own performance.

The merger allowed further progress to be made in the field of science education. I inherited a young lecturer, Keith Shaw. His interests were in school chemistry and in pedagogy, and I knew he would struggle in the general teaching work of the Department. The Cert Ed, by then with just two students, was phasing out. I already had two staff who were making their names in the world of chemical education – Des Rutherford, who later went to lead on staff development at the University of Birmingham, and Stuart Trickey, who progressed (after I had left Sheffield) to a like role in the new Sheffield City Polytechnic. They had undertaken some interesting research into aspects of chemical education, and had run some important national conferences; they had broken a lot of new ground, and I could see potential in joining them with Keith Shaw to form a centre of excellence in chemical education in my new Department. We had just started a part-time Postgraduate Diploma course in Chemical Education aimed at serving school teachers, and the merger enabled us to extend this to science education and to the MSc level. I had already developed the structure of the department to make Analytical Chemistry the largest group – this was the unique specialty of the department for which it was most widely known; now I added the Chemical Education section – innovative and distinctive.

Royal Society of Chemistry

The professional body for chemists, then the Royal Institute of Chemistry (RIC), was important to us. Gaining accreditation of our degree courses by the RIC was an additional quality check, and necessary for our graduates to get full professional membership. I first got myself elected to the RIC North-East Regional Committee, and within the year found myself as its Secretary and Treasurer. It was not a long-lasting role, as the RIC was to merger with the Chemical Society, to form the Royal Society of Chemistry (RSC) and the regional structure was to end. But I had the taste for the organisation, and was able to make further inroads. I served extensively on RSC Boards and Committees, including the Education Division Council (becoming its President), Divisional Affairs Board, Education Appeal Advisory Committee, Examinations and Institutions Committee, Education Publications Committee, Qualifications and Examinations Board (becoming Chairman), Council of the Society itself, and various working parties and the like. I met some great people through this work, brilliant chemists, outstanding industrialists, and excellent leaders of the profession.

Other professional work while at Sheffield

In 1981, I was elected to be Chairman of the Committee of Heads of Polytechnic Chemistry Departments – a self-help group, supported by, but independent of the RSC. To be elected by one's peers to lead them, was indeed a great accolade.

My role as chairman of the CNAA Chemistry Board led to several invitations to be External Examiner. This enabled me to have other markers of quality and to see how other institutions went about their academic work. I examined at Cambridgeshire College of Arts and Technology (now Anglia Ruskin University), Plymouth Polytechnic, Robert Gordon Institute in Aberdeen, and The National Institute of Higher Education (NIHE) Dublin (now Dublin City University); at one time I had to travel from Aberdeen to Dublin, and then to Plymouth all within a few days.

My CNAA role also led me to be invited to do similar work for the National Council for Educational Awards (NCEA) in Ireland, helping with validation at NIHE Dublin, Cork Regional Technical College, and elsewhere. The contrast with CNAA was interesting – NCEA was less formal, and often worked back-to-front; I remember at one institution meeting second-year students on a course not yet validated!

In 1981 I was privileged to be a member of a CNAA group that went to Hong Kong to advise the government on the suitability of Hong Kong

Department of Chemistry, Sheffield City Polytechnic; last day as Head of Department, 29 April 1983.

Polytechnic to offer degree courses. We were also asked to consider whether two private institutions, Baptist College and Lignan College were suitable for gaining State funding for higher education. The first visit, for two weeks in January 1981, was fascinating. I had never been there before, and was enthralled by the atmosphere and culture. It was important for us not to impose UK norms and expectations, while making judgements against international standards, so we spent a while understanding the context. We went back at the end of 1981, successfully to complete the work.

Around that time I also participated in a study tour of the USA, organised by the Central Bureau for Educational Exchanges in London. It involved an initial briefing for two days in Washington DC, on national structures and policies; a few days in Columbus Ohio, mainly visiting the State institutions and learning from the National Centre for Research in Vocational Education; and 4-5 days studying a range of institutions in Long Island and New York. I learned a great deal about the American approach to vocational education, and the types of State and Federal intervention in these areas. I also learned a lot about the tensions which arise between educational and social need on the one hand, and commercial and business imperatives on the other. Little did I know how these facets were to drift across the Atlantic in not too many years.

Our Sheffield experience

Sheffield was good to and for us. I matured there professionally: as an educator, a manager, a researcher; and I developed a national profile. I owe so many people at Sheffield Polytechnic a great deal: George Tolley, David Hills, Cyril Walker, Norman Bell and Ian Nowell whom I have mentioned; Doug Thacker the Deputy Principal; Brian Turner and David Mowthorpe in the Department; and Sharon Sedgwick (later, Etches), my secretary, who was incredibly loyal and supportive through thick and thin.

Janet went back to work, first on a part-time term-time basis, and then full-time, working in the Polytechnic (nothing to do with me; she landed these jobs entirely on her own and with no one knowing to whom she was married), finally in the Publicity and Publications Department and being responsible amongst other things for the annual Awards Ceremonies. Richard really did grow up in Sheffield, being there from age 6 to 15. In truth, he did not want to leave, and still regards Sheffield as the superior place and Sheffield United as a far better football team than Coventry City. He progressed smoothly from Primary to Secondary School, but I recall him coming home one day saying that a teacher had told them that there was no point in working hard as they wouldn't get jobs anyway. How damaging that was. It was true that the Sheffield economy was in deep trouble; it was a torrid time for the City, which struggled to reinvent itself. But that silly teacher's remark was so demotivating and damaging.

But it was time for me to move to a more senior role. My research and knowledge were getting dated, and I was too heavily involved in other things to remain a serious academic. I was totally committed to the polytechnic sector, passionately believing in its role and purpose, so never considered anything outside those institutions, and thus began looking for senior polytechnic posts. I applied for any Assistant Director position going: Bristol, Leicester, and even my alma mater, North London, but to no avail. When a post of Assistant Principal became vacant at Sheffield City Polytechnic everyone thought I would get it, but for the second time at Sheffield as an internal candidate I performed badly on interview. I was very deflated by not getting the job, and took a while to recover my confidence.

My tenth such application was for the post which would arise when Maurice Foss retired from being Deputy Director of Coventry (Lanchester) Polytechnic. I was confident, as I had earned the respect of the Director, Geoffrey Holroyde, for the way I had handled the validation issue about a year before. But I did not fall into the trap of being complacent. I researched as much as I could, and spoke to people in the know. I carefully crafted my CV and letter of application, and rehearsed answers to all the questions I thought I could possibly be asked. The selection process was gruelling, but I had prepared well and felt from the outset that I could get the job if I kept my head. I was elated when I did.

Reflections 7

Moving to Sheffield was a fantastic career move. I grew up there. It was a polytechnic through and through, more so than Northern because of its closer identity with the locality. George Tolley was a remarkable man who let those with drive and ability flourish.

There were so many things which I have carried forward from my Sheffield experience into my subsequent career: establishing effective partnerships with local schools and colleges; serving the needs of local employers; developing flexible curricula to meet changes in society; building a qualifications network of ladders and bridges; providing opportunities for those from disadvantaged backgrounds; redefining courses to meet students' needs rather than hewing to a traditional curriculum without other reason; the importance of teacher education for those teaching in higher education; the imperative of teaching higher education in a research-informed environment; learning from others on a national scale by sharing practice and standards; and recognising that education is not only a public good but must be run on proper business lines.

But perhaps the most fundamental lesson learned was that organisations can only be successful if they have a clear sense of purpose and mission, and hold true to their values.

Coventry Polytechnic

Arrival

Leaving Sheffield for Coventry was deeply emotional. I cried when I left my Secretary, Sharon. I had grown up in that place, professionally, and Sharon epitomised all that was wonderful about Sheffield.

Once again, I was commuting weekends for a couple of months, as there had been no time to sell the house before having to start in Coventry on 1 May 1983 (my 44th birthday). I stayed in Priory Hall, the student hall of residence on campus, insisting on paying the full rate for visiting staff. I soon realised what a dreadful place it then was. It was 1960s 'system' built as three linked buildings, two of which were tower blocks. They had been adapted to meet new fire regulations but were out-of-date and based on communal toilet and shower facilities, no kitchens, and dreadful décor – actually no décor. I thought I had escaped tenement living when I left home to get married. I resolved to do something serious about this; it was my first resolution, but was never completely achieved after twenty-one years in post!

But starting the job was much more enjoyable. Maurice Foss had left everything in order. He was a man with an exceptional eye for detail. I knew he was a difficult act to follow, and I soon found how influential he had really been. I spent many early and late hours working through the files, sorting things for my own use and priorities, understanding the background. What was lacking was a sense of the effectiveness of the Board of Governors, and relationships with the Local Education Authority; I very soon found out.

The legacy

During my first week in post, I was summonsed to see the Director of Education. I took this as courtesy, to be wished well for the future. But in a few minutes with him and his Deputy, I was told in no uncertain terms that it was they who really ran the Polytechnic. I was shocked and disappointed, but soon saw this manifest in all around me. But first, some of the history.

When the Polytechnic was created in 1970, it was formed by merging three institutions: Lanchester College of Technology, named after Frederick Lanchester, the inventor and motor car entrepreneur (to have called this 'Coventry College of Technology' would have caused great confusion with the existing Coventry Technical College); Coventry School of Art and Design, on an adjacent site to the Lanchester; and Rugby College of Engineering Technology. The town of Rugby being in Warwickshire, and Coventry by then being in the West Midlands Metropolitan Borough, governance was through a Joint Education Committee between the Warwickshire and Coventry LEAs. The two Authorities were at opposite extremes of the political spectrum, so the new institution, called Lanchester Polytechnic as a neutral name, was often the political football. During the late 1970s, the demand for engineering education diminished rapidly (exacerbated in Rugby due to the demise of the English Electric Company; in Coventry, due to the downturn in car manufacture). The decision was made to consolidate the Polytechnic on the Coventry site and change the name to reflect this while maintaining the historic link; hence Coventry (Lanchester) Polytechnic was designated.

But even though the institution now came under one LEA, there were huge problems. The provision of new buildings for the staff and students transferred from Rugby was wholly inadequate. The unions resisted full integration. Even when I arrived in 1983 there were still two physics departments (albeit with different names); separate departments of mechanical and production engineering; and likewise of electrical and systems engineering, each with its own accommodation, laboratories, workshops, technicians and courses, even though they shared the same buildings and corridors. Given that student recruitment in these areas was tough, the diseconomies and academic isolation were stunning.

However, when it came to corporate governance and authority, things were even worse. By 1975, Geoffrey Holroyde was appointed Director, the third in the short existence of the Polytechnic. He inherited a horrific situation. The Board of Governors was over 50-strong; Academic Board was over 60. There was a plethora of committees which acted as if they ran the institution, a so-called 'Non-Academic Board', and an elected Finance Committee reporting to the Board of Governors. The unions were all-powerful. There was huge distrust between the Polytechnic and the City Council, made worse by protracted negotiations over the future location of the Teacher Training College, which was promised to the Polytechnic but finally was merged with the University of Warwick.

By the time I arrived, some of this had been dealt with, but not all by any means. I was horrified at the control which the trades unions wielded and the way the City Council seemed to encourage them to make managing the Polytechnic difficult. The grip the Council had was totally inappropriate. To take some personnel examples: the title, grading and salary of every post in the institution had to be approved by the personnel department of the LEA; approval to fill every single vacancy, even the advertising copy was approved by the same process, and by the relevant trade union(!), and any disagreement which the trades unions had with the Director could be taken up with Council officers without involving the Polytechnic management. Academic planning was even more unacceptable. The Board of Governors had an 'Academic Programmes Committee', which, because of the dominance that the City Council had over the Board, was in effect external control over the curriculum. This was on top of the Byzantine system of national and regional controls, which required even modest updating of curricula to be approved by a Regional Staff Inspector and a Regional Advisory Council. Apart from the stultification and suppression of development and ideas which this caused, the waste in terms of cost of such controls was appalling.

Another example of antagonism between the Polytechnic and the Council was the name of the institution. 'Coventry (Lanchester) Polytechnic' was not a helpful name as the brackets added confusion, and new generations of students had not even heard of the name 'Lanchester'. But the City Council refused to sanction any change. Eventually, after lots of effort, it agreed to drop the brackets, so we became 'Coventry Lanchester Polytechnic', still generating confusion with Manchester Polytechnic, Lancaster University, and the Polytechnic of Central Lancashire. It took Geoffrey Holroyde a further year finally to persuade the City Council to agree to 'Coventry Polytechnic'. What a waste of time, effort and money.

The nature of the Polytechnic Board of Governors was at the heart of the problem. It was then around 36 people, roughly one-third City Councillors, one-third elected staff and students, and one-third people from business and the professions. On the face of it, that was a tenable mix, but in practice it was awful: the elected staff were trade union activists of left-wing and disruptive inclination; the students were even more to the left; several of the City Councillors were trades unionists who had left the ailing motor industry and blamed the bosses for the economic downturn in Coventry; the business people soon realised that their role was perfunctory, and there was huge collusion between the other constituencies, which had agreed positions on the agenda issues. Fortunately sufficient stalwarts from business stuck at it.

The Council held reserve powers such that often Board decisions were irrelevant. I recall being told at one Governors' meeting: 'You can decide what you like; we will overturn it across the road'. I had one shocking experience at my second meeting of the Board. I need first explain that polytechnics were funded through a national 'pool' of funds from all LEAs, so that Coventry Polytechnic was not a direct charge to the local rate-payers. The previous year the catering and residence accounts had made a significant loss, which was made good from the rest of the Polytechnic's budget. It was not a deficit which had any bearing whatsoever on the City Council. However, at this autumn term meeting of the Board, the management accounts for the year to date showed a deficit. This was expected because the financial year commenced in April, and the period in question covered the summer period when there were no students in residence but the City Council contracts employing the catering and residence staff gave them full pay throughout the summer; inevitably, every year at this time there was a deficit. Every thinking member of the Board knew the situation would rectify itself as the year progressed. But when I presented the accounts (Geoffrey Holroyde, the Director, was on sick leave) I was fiercely challenged by one Councillor, who bellowed threateningly: 'We baled you out last year [not true!], so don't think we are going to do it again!' And when I gave the explanation for the position he challenged even more strongly: 'Will you put your job on the line that you won't overspend again?!' I declined to respond.

The problem was the City Council itself. The average age of Coventry's Councillors seemed twenty years more than in Sheffield; they hated 'bosses,' and it seemed to be mutual. But more especially they proclaimed that although Coventry was going through a difficult time it would all come right soon. I was astonished. A year before I arrived, the Standard Works had shut, putting 7000 people on the dole; the entire district of Canley, which had been built to house the factory floor workers during the post-war boom of Coventry, was devastated. Complete families would never work again. Unemployment in Coventry exceeded 20%. The City was on its knees, and I did not think that many on the City Council had a clue what to do about it.

Making impact

It was clear that the Governors and the City Council had made control of student numbers an art form. They were rightly concerned that facilities were adequate for the numbers enrolled, and that students had sufficient personal attention. But the consequence was actually a deterioration of quality as much of the provision lacked adequate scale for economic operation. Furthermore, there was little room for development, and basic estates maintenance was seriously neglected. There was an urgent need to grow, and fortunately new government policy was on my side; creation of the National Advisory Body for Higher Education (NAB), replacing the national 'pooling' arrangements, provided the mechanism I needed.

I began negotiations with NAB for more funded student numbers. I built up a thorough understanding of what was needed, focussed on the criteria and made the arguments. We were very successful on all counts. NAB also introduced several competitive initiatives for new developments, and I led on those too, securing almost 100% success rates. NAB then introduced a competitive research funding stream, very modest by university standards: just £7M for the sector compared with the (smaller) university sector's £700M a year. Again, I led the bidding process, and we were one of the most successful institutions.

The requirement of Government that students from outside the EU should be charged full cost fees provided a source of unregulated income, and increased income was desperately needed. So we began actively to recruit from across the world, something which few polytechnics had done, but we had only limited residential accommodation. The private student housing market was good in Coventry, due to the economic down-turn, but the quality was often poor. An opportunity arose which was to have a particular significance in the future, about which more later. A City Council tower block, known then as John Fox House, in one of the most deprived areas of north-east Coventry, was only about one-third occupied; most of the tenants were in rent arrears, and there was substantial internal vandalism. There had also been a recent murder. Over a frantic summer period, the tenants were re-housed, and the property completely refurbished for student use as 'Caradoc Hall.' Serious security issues were thoroughly addressed. Many people thought we were mad even to contemplate locating students there, but such was our need that we made it work.

A key way in which we increased UK student numbers without needing more space was to franchise local FE Colleges to offer our certificate and diploma courses, and in a few cases the first year(s) of degree programmes, so that successful students would then progress to the Polytechnic. We developed this very significantly, with over 1500 students at 'Partner Colleges' across the Midlands. Many of the students would otherwise not have participated in higher education, for instance women returning to education after child-care, people who had lost their jobs and wanted to redirect their careers, those whom the school system had failed and were in low-paid or unsatisfying jobs, and so on; and a high proportion were from minority ethnic communities. The Colleges were excellent in supporting such people, and helping them make the transition to the Polytechnic.

I led the development of several other initiatives for adult returners over that period: 'Return to Learn'; 'New Opportunities for Women (NOW)' and 'Wider Opportunities for Women (WOW)'; the 'Associate Student Scheme', which enabled people to take short taster courses at low cost and accumulate credits towards recognised qualifications; and 'The Higher Education Lead-in Programme (HELP)'. A new policy was developed for part-time education, giving incentives to departments to create new such courses and actively recruit part-time students.

All this was to stand me in good stead when Geoffrey Holroyde retired. I had become aware very soon after starting that my appointment as his Deputy was part of his succession plan. Early on, Geoffrey invited Janet and me to spend a day with him and his wife, Elizabeth, on his long boat which he sailed on the Severn-Trent waterways. There was no doubt that the ruler was being run over me.

Taking over

In summer 1986, Geoffrey Holroyde announced his decision to retire the following year. I knew the competition would be fierce, because Coventry had an excellent reputation, and there were some very good Assistant/Deputy Directors around. I also knew that more would be expected of me as an internal candidate than of those from outside.

The interview was in two stages. I made it to the second stage, which was held in January 1987. There was a dinner with the Panel the night before the formal interviews. The winter weather began to close in during the afternoon, and the snow began to fall. Three candidates had not made it to the dinner because of the weather – one was coming from Glasgow, one from Teesside, and one from Sunderland. It meant there was just myself and two other candidates present, with about a dozen 'interviewers'. We were thus under closer scrutiny, but could each make our pitch in detail. The missing candidates made the interviews the following morning, but they were clearly jaded by not arriving until the early hours. Whether that would have mattered we shall never know, but the wonderful outcome was that I was offered the job.

The next six months were difficult. There was so much to do – organisational restructuring, new policies, personnel changes. But I was sensitive to Geoffrey Holroyde's position; after all, some of the changes I felt were necessary were contrary to his own views. He was still the Director, and I did not wish to undermine his authority or offend him in any way. I owed him a great deal – after all he had appointed me as his Deputy and supported my replacing him. At the same time, I wanted to get going and to modernise. One matter on which we did agree was that we sorely needed a corporate identity. As a result we engaged a nationally renowned company, consulted, and came to the final selection. I feared we would fall out over the choice. As Geoffrey was leaving I felt strongly that the decision should be mine alone, or at least not his. However, we agreed on the design, and even had to force through our choice against majority views!

There were two other critical matters to address. The first was to appoint a new Deputy Director to replace me; the second was the over-riding one of how to respond to the Government White Paper, *Higher Education: Meeting the Challenge* published on 1 April 1987, which was to have the most profound implications for the Polytechnic and thousands of lives.

Appointment of my successor was an extraordinary business. I had not yet taken up my post as Director, so it was undertaken by the Governors/City Council with only informal involvement from me. There was one applicant who generated controversy from his style and Rod Stewart appearance (he had discarded his earring for the day!), as well as his evident socialist views. But he said all the right things in a most charming and convincing way and it was difficult to argue on the day that he was not the best candidate. The City Councillors on the panel pressed for his appointment – I suspected there had been some prior political collusion – and that was it. From his first day in post, Mike Fitzgerald proved to be quite a handful.

Release from the LEA

The essence of *Higher Education: Meeting the Challenge*, that led to the Education Reform Act (ERA) 1988 was that polytechnics and major HE colleges were to be released from LEA controls. They would be incorporated as individual legal entities and come under a new national body 'The Polytechnics and Colleges Funding Council (PCFC)', alongside a 'Universities Funding Council (UFC)' in place of the existing 'University Grants Committee'. All the legal responsibilities of the new 'Higher Education Corporations' would be vested in totally reconstituted Boards of Governors – vesting day being 1 April 1989. Assets held by the LEAs at midnight on 31 March 1989 'for the purposes of' their HEIs would transfer to the Corporations on the next day. The whole labyrinth of course approvals (HMI, Regional Staff Inspectors et al) would be dumped. It was a development by Margaret Thatcher's government which was bold, profound, radical and hugely political.

Across the country, the news was greeted with jubilation in institutions and varying levels of disdain in local government. Geoffrey Holroyde was prominently quoted in the *Coventry Evening Telegraph* as saying this was: 'the most marvellous thing that had happened to the Polytechnic'. That went down with local politicians, staunchly left-wing and anti-Thatcher in the extreme, like the proverbial lead balloon. The announcement was close in time to the annual meeting of the Committee of Directors of Polytechnics (CDP), which coincidentally was being held in Coventry that year. At the conference dinner, the Lord Mayor, Winnie Lakin, tore into Geoffrey in her after-dinner speech; it was as if he had personally attacked all that the City Council had done to establish and develop the Polytechnic. I sat opposite the man who had just been appointed to chair CNAA, someone who was later to make outstanding contributions to education, especially higher education – Ron (later Sir Ron and then Lord) Dearing. He was deeply shocked at the venom of the opposition to the Government's proposals, and sympathised with us. Every time I met him over later years, he still recalled that dreadful occasion.

There was a huge amount to do to bring about the transformation required. The Department of Education and Science (as it then was) issued advice, and CDP co-ordinated the national actions, responses to consultation, advisory notes and the like. We set up a 'Formation Committee' to oversee the process. I was incredibly fortunate in engaging some great people: Patrick Lister, then chair of the Board of Governors, formerly Managing Director of Coventry Climax Fork Trucks, who was a tremendous strength to me over the entire transformation period and beyond; Len Grice, Director of Personnel at GEC, an outstanding human being with a passion for people development and a guru in the industrial relations world; Geoffrey Whalen, Managing Director of Peugeot, an East-End of London boy 'done good', who lived through the dreadful traumas of the trades unions' sabotage of the motor industry; Geoffrey Hughes, General Counsel of GKN, a man with great powers of analysis of legal and other complex issues; and Mike Collett, President of the Coventry Chamber of Commerce, and Policy Servicing Manger at Equity and Law, who had invaluable understanding of finance and audit. To try to bind in the City Council, we added the Chair of the Council's Education Committee, Cllr Harry Richards. We were supported superbly by Cyrrhian Macrae, whom Geoffrey Holroyde had appointed a year or so previously as his PA to replace Jill Macaire (tragically killed in a car accident) and who was to grow into a senior manager and make an outstanding contribution to the institution.

Staff were understandably concerned that this was some sort of 'privatisation' and that jobs would be on the line. There was vehement opposition from the trades unions, fuelled by hatred of the Thatcher government. We created and implemented a comprehensive communications strategy, which was very effective, to the extent that it continued right through until I retired.

The dominant academic staff union at the time was the National Association of Teachers in Further and Higher Education (NATFHE). But at Coventry there was also another – The Association of Polytechnic Teachers (APT) which it was pragmatic for us to recognise. We took the sensible and progressive view that there would be a joint consultative and negotiating committee, avoiding unnecessary engagement with the various staff groups separately. NATFHE refused to join any group involving APT, because APT was not affiliated to the TUC. I advised NATFHE that unless it agreed to joint arrangements, NATFHE would not be recognised by the Polytechnic Board of Governors, the new employer. The result was the first strike of academic staff in the sector. In the first week of incorporation, on 6 April 1989, there was a demonstration right outside my office window. I listened to loud-hailers ranting about how I would sack staff, act like a nineteenth century mill-owner, and all that kind of nonsense. Amongst this pathetic group was Dave Nellist, then the local MP, but later expelled from the Labour Party for being a member of Militant. I was amused but also hurt, as I and colleagues had put body and soul into giving staff every possible assurance about the positive future ahead. I hope those who were then slagging me off might now reflect on how ridiculously wrong they were.

We hit the national headlines for several weeks especially when we docked the pay of staff that went on strike – it astonished me to think that they would not expect us to do that. In what other sector would employees expect to be paid for striking?! The dispute was referred to the national level. The Polytechnic was represented by Roger Ward, Chief Executive of the Polytechnics and Colleges Employers Forum (PCEF), more of which later; while the union was represented by the General Secretary of NATFHE, David Triesman, later to become Lord Triesman of Tottenham, who has kindly provided the Foreword to this book. It did not take long for the matter to be resolved; NATFHE would co-operate with APT henceforth. I learned a lot from that experience, mainly that striking is a stupid way to seek to resolve employment disputes, and that it is crucial to stick to your guns when you know you are right.

We had more disputes – 'action short of a strike' (especially refusal to mark assessments) and actual withdrawal of labour, all to the detriment of students. We became quite expert at dealing with such situations, including the legal issues of withdrawing pay for 'partial performance of duties'. I was even sued by a few staff for pay deduction, but this was easily dealt with, much to the annoyance of NATFHE. Over the next ten to twelve years we experienced some stupid and mindless local union intransigence, some quite vicious and directed at me personally. Andy Skinner, Director of Personnel, was a great strength in these situations, as was Cyrrhian Macrae dealing with the communications issues. When I became significantly involved in national pay and conditions negotiations, I therefore became a target for union action, as I shall describe later.

I needed to enhance the management capability in preparation for incorporation, as there was the world of difference between operating City Council rules and procedures, and taking full responsibility as an independent organisation. I had some excellent people who were very competent and whom I judged would ably take on bigger roles, if they were given encouragement and development time. Geoffrey Holroyde had recently appointed a young Scot, Graham Law, who was perfectly capable to grow into a Director of Finance. Personnel and employee relations were vital to get right and warranted national advertising; I was fortunate to find Andy Skinner, who was a tremendous help and support during some extremely difficult and testing times. I was keen to develop a proper marketing and communications function, and identified Cyrrhian Macrae, then my PA, as having huge potential to fulfil that role in the future as this was evidently her forté. The Academic Registry and Student Services could wait for a while. There were, however, issues around the provision of computing services, and also industrial liaison, and I had to 'part company' with the people then heading up those services. This was the first time in my career that I had to do this, but I knew that it was the right thing to do in the interests of the institution; it required some real heart-searching, especially when the final session with one of the incumbents literally ended in tears.

Mike Fitzgerald was a handful. He was creative but not good at role delineation and management. Governors agreed to establish a second Deputy Director post, and I was exceptionally fortunate in appointing David Fussey. He was a polymath, having read engineering and been an organ scholar at Cambridge. He proved to be incredibly able and a great benefit to the institution and beyond. Tragically, David, who became Vice-Chancellor of the University of Greenwich in succession to my former mentor from Northern Polytechnic days, Norbert Singer, died of cancer in May 2000, aged just 56 years.

In the run-up to incorporation, we carried out a detailed financial analysis. It threw up some astonishing facts. For example, we were paying the City Council hundreds of thousands of pounds a year as contributions to the costs of running the City Council. We also found that our basic cleaning bill for 1989-1990 would be over £1M; closer scrutiny showed some astonishing Spanish practices. There were three cleaning workforces, one for main campus buildings, one for the Halls of Residence, and one for the fifty or so houses we had around the City. Shortages in one area could not be dealt with by moving staff even for the day; there were rigid lines of demarcation; overtime was institutionalised; the rates of pay, which were well above the market rate, were different; two groups were on 'attendance bonuses' designed to reduce sickness absence – except the absence rate was still over 20%, and the bonuses were paid in any event! This situation was intolerable and unsustainable. We had to start again, making all the cleaners redundant, and re-employing them on new, modern contracts. It was not an easy decision, but it had to be done. Virtually the whole cost of the redundancies, some £300,000, came from

PCFC under a 'restructuring fund'. Many of the staff would receive larger sums of money than they had ever had in their lives. They accepted the deal. But there was a backlash amongst some staff in the Polytechnic. I had a number of difficult meetings with a group of them, but they lobbied Governors. At a special meeting of the Personnel Committee, two Governors, Angela Griffiths and Meg Stacey, were determined to get me to back down, and I suspected they were encouraged by my own Deputy, Mike Fitzgerald. It was a very difficult meeting, and I had decided to consider resigning from the Polytechnic if I lost, but in the end my plan was agreed by 3 votes to 2.

There were several major problems with the process of incorporation caused by the obstructive and defensive behaviour of the LEA. I tried in vain to explain that the Polytechnic would remain true to its mission and values, and that it was in everyone's interests for it to take responsibility for its own actions. There was intense local, and some national media coverage, and I took every public opportunity to explain the Polytechnic's case. But the political hurt was deep. The implications of the City Council's attitude were extremely problematic; a few examples will suffice.

Unusually for Polytechnics, the City Council had required us to build up a £1M reserve. I was horrified when, shortly after the ERA was published, I was told the Council would claw back our reserve. It would also take the £600,000 operating surplus we were returning that year. This was daylight robbery. The money was not theirs but had been provided via the national 'pool' for the Polytechnic. What the City Council was intending could be deemed *ultra vires* [4] but in any case was morally indefensible. It took many hours of meetings and letters, over several months, plus threats of legal action, to get them to come to reason.

We clearly needed to establish our own financial management, but the Council charged us some £350,000 a year for administrative computing, and would not forego this income lightly. After several months of prevarication and fruitless discussions, which seemed designed to run out of time for development of our own systems, we were forced to accept a three-year post-incorporation deal, costing nearly £1M.

---

4 In corporate law, *ultra vires* describes acts attempted by a corporation that are beyond the scope of powers granted by the corporation's Charter or in a clause in its Memorandum of Association; in the laws authorizing its formation, or similar founding documents. Acts attempted by a corporation that are beyond the scope of its charter are void or voidable.

A similar situation arose regarding transfer of personnel records. The Council performed our payroll and pensions' functions. We had tremendous trouble getting information from the staff in the Council, which continued for well over a year after separation from the LEA. Months after incorporation Council staff still thought they had power over our vacancy-filling and advertising procedures.

The final example relates to the transfer of land, buildings, and contents.

Under the ERA if the asset was 'held for the purposes of' the Polytechnic at midnight on 31 March 1989, it would automatically transfer to the Higher Education Corporation on 1 April 1989. It mattered not how or for what the asset had been originally purchased. The Council took strong exception to this part of the ERA. I was told that it would not allow the hall of residence, Caradoc Hall, to transfer and that we had to vacate it by 31 March 1989. They were not at all interested in arguments from our lawyers or the 150+ students in residence. How the students were to be re-housed mid-term was our problem. It was outrageous and absurd. Fortunately, I thought, the ERA also set up an Education Assets Board (EAB) to deal with the transfer of assets and any disputes, so we were confident that all would be well. Not so. I received a call informing me that the EAB was about to close the deal with the City Council on our assets transfer and we had a few hours to comment – without us even seeing the transfer documents! I could not believe my ears. By the time I went to bed that night I had instructed our lawyers to issue notice of Judicial Review on the EAB. It took weeks of further heated exchanges with the Council and EAB before the matter was resolved.

Of course, in the meanwhile there were big changes nationally. The advent of the PCFC transformed the way we were funded; the employers' association, PCEF, began its reform programme. Governance was totally changed, with fundamentally new Instrument and Articles, greater authority to 'the Principal' and pragmatic definition of the dividing line between the roles of the Principal (Director) and Governing Body, which was constituted in a way that was far better suited for the purpose. All this was hugely modernising and enabling. The new arrangements allowed institutions to be managed, with proper safeguards and balances so that powers were not over-concentrated or unaccountable.

There were also routine and 'normal' development matters to attend to.

Mike Fitzgerald, my Deputy, was making his impact felt, and not always with acclaim. He was much liked by many, but others regarded him with suspicion or worse. But he brought new ideas and a 'different' style. We modularised the entire range of degree courses across the institution, which was far more significant and controversial than it sounds, and made further strides in developing the network of FE College partnerships. In March 1988 we became one of the first institutions to be accredited by CNAA for taught programmes, taking greater responsibility for validation; I was particularly pleased with this as I had developed the processes, written the submission, and guided the accreditation process myself – alongside everything else.

We addressed some significant structural issues, particularly reducing the number of academic departments (from 26 when I first arrived to 19 eventually before I introduced the School structure in 1992) so as to be more efficient and enable modern interdisciplinary academic developments. These were usually strongly opposed by academic staff and their unions. The merger of Mechanical Engineering and Manufacturing Systems for example was particularly fiercely fought, to the extent that even though I had persuaded the Academic Board of its virtue (and technically that should have been the end of it) the Board of Governors set up an appeal mechanism. The case for merger was overwhelming – two departments, both in financial difficulties with insufficient enrolments, duplicating laboratories, workshops and technical and administrative staff; squabbling over ownership of future developments; not meeting the changing needs of the industry. It was a huge waste of time to get to the right result, but thankfully the Governors did.

During 1987 the opportunity arose to bid for housing the only School of Occupational Therapy (OT) in the West Midlands. It was the first time such a provision in the NHS had been offered for tender. Coventry had been the first English Polytechnic to incorporate a School of Physiotherapy back in the 1970s, and I always felt that linking professional practice to academic study was our forté. We did our homework, and won the contract. There were difficulties with the professional body, which wanted to determine whom we appointed as the Head of the School, but we overcame them.

On Friday 13 November 1987, the usual delivery of bread to Priory Hall of Residence took place at around 5.00 am. However, the driver forgot he was driving a higher van than usual, and as it entered the deliv-

Princess Royal at opening of the School of Occupational Therapy, Coventry Polytechnic, 1987.

ery yard under the tower block, the van collided with the overhang, or rather the main gas pipe fixed to the underpass. The nine-inch pipe fractured, and gas poured out, right under the Hall. I was called at home around 6.00 am and was at the scene about 20 minutes later. It took ages to locate the correct main valve to turn off and then un-jam it… Frighteningly, sounding the internal fire alarms had little effect. As is common in student halls, inebriated students setting off fire alarms is all too common; the solution for Priory Hall residents was to stuff newspaper into the fire bells. Students were still emerging late in the morning. It was amazing there was no explosion – I was in fear of a Ronan Point disaster all day. It was an awful experience for all concerned, a true 'Friday 13th'. We replaced the manual bells by an electronic system as a matter of urgency – a few hundred thousand pounds well spent.

Just over a week later, in the early hours of 21 November 1987, there was a major flood in the computer science building, caused by a tap being left on, which wiped out two floors of equipment and teaching facilities. But even worse was to come. Almost exactly two years after these events, in mid-November 1989, a structural engineer, who was working with our Department of Civil Engineering and Building, asked to see me as a matter of urgency. He asserted that a major building, then known as D-Block, was in serious danger of collapse. I challenged him and conferred with our own estates staff and academic experts. The implications were horrific. This was a major building, housing the science departments, and home to around 2000 students. I did nothing else that day but agonise. I left for home around 10.30 pm, exhausted and drained, but with a clear programme of action for the next day. We brought in the 'dangerous buildings' people from the City Council, and shared our fears. By the end of the morning we had been persuaded not to rush into things because there were such major implications all round, and to take a more considered approach was sensible. Suffice it to say that we did have to vacate the building for a major structural investigation and strengthening, but this was for just one month, and we were able properly to plan the whole programme so as to minimise disruption to student work.

I certainly learned not to take my eye off estates maintenance after these events! When PCFC instigated a special funding programme to help with refurbishment and modernisation, Coventry Polytechnic was extremely successful, gaining amongst the highest levels of funding in the country. We had done our homework well, and were now able to put right some of the appalling examples of neglect of public buildings.

'Coventry Polytechnic takes off!'

The day we became free of City Council control was a day for celebration, but also one for giving reassurances to staff, students, local businesses and the community at large. We adopted the slogan 'Coventry Polytechnic Takes Off!' This was our first ever concerted public relations campaign, ably created and led by Cyrrhian Macrae, and involving a range of events, merchandising, advertisements on all the main approach roads in Coventry, a trailer placard driven around town, media articles and interviews. We held our first institution-wide Open Day, to reassure members of the local public that we were still serving local and sub-regional needs.

Nationally, grants were phasing out and student loans introduced. CNAA was allowing greater autonomy. I was particularly proud that we were in the first crop of polytechnics to achieve accreditation for the award of research degrees, as I had personally developed the procedures and quality systems, and written the submission. We were also doing well in the HMI quality assessment stakes, being ranked third in the country in the 1991 rankings, boosting enrolments above the 10,000 mark for the first time.

At last Ministers were talking about polytechnics and universities with the same breath, although there were continuing inequities, not least in research funding, which I shall describe later. But the final step was soon to come. Publication in May 1991 of a bold White Paper by the John Major government: *Higher Education: a New Framework* heralded a further dramatic and profound change to the higher education scene. Polytechnics were to join the university sector and be allowed to use the word 'University' in their titles; CNAA was to be abolished; the UFC and the PCFC were to merge to form the Higher Education Funding Council for England (HEFCE). The binary line was to be no more!

Reflections 8

It wasn't until I came to Coventry that I realised how stultifying was the control of the Local Education Authorities. We were treated as a school, with very little understanding by the elected members (and even some of the officers) of what we were really about. Our responsibilities and purposes went far wider than meeting the needs of local citizens. We had to follow rules and procedures designed for entirely different purposes, and be subservient to officials who rarely had sufficient ambition for us, or understanding of the enormous potential we could achieve. It was hugely frustrating and disabling.

Disengaging from the City Council gave us the opportunity to think for ourselves, build a more relevant infrastructure, and become a truly creative and innovative organisation. It released energy and imagination, enabling us to create something special, whilst allowing us to set our own vision, and bring about ambitious aims and objectives. It was a new dawn for the institution.

I was hugely privileged to have been part of this transformation, and I have carried these lessons into other areas in my later career.

Coventry University

Birth

Three years after launch of the Polytechnic as independent from the City Council we swung into action again. The theme was similar – to give reassurance to local people that we were not going to be diverted from our purpose, that our mission and aims were to be unchanged, and that the new status was a natural progression, not a new direction. But we also needed to be clear that this was a significant and valuable development for all our stakeholders. So, on vesting day, 15 June 1992, we embarked upon a campaign: 'A change in name but not in style'. We had lots of media coverage, including a special insert in the *Coventry Evening Telegraph*. We gave the campaign substance by launching new initiatives – thirty new courses, partnerships with colleges, 'educational compacts' with local schools, Europeanisation of curricula, and wider international work. We also gave prominence to the fact that we were now awarding Coventry University degrees. And that itself relates another symbolic aspect: we simply changed 'Coventry Polytechnic' to 'Coventry University'. We did not adopt the pompous 'University of Coventry', which also meant we made only the one-word change to our corporate identity, thus saving many hundreds of thousands of pounds.

There was much to do to back up this transformation. Academically, our CNAA pedigree was a sound basis; writing our own set of academic regulations was tedious, but not as difficult as if we were starting from scratch. But I was unhappy with the academic structure of the institution. The type of academic programmes and research which would be more important in the future, were those which were interdisciplinary and gave academic spine to applied and professional subjects. I had many discussions with employers from all sectors about what they saw as important in the future. The common themes were breadth, interdisciplinarity and ability to work in teams which focussed on real issues and contemporary problems, not on narrow subjects. I needed to break down the barriers which had plagued higher education, where even chemists and biologists talk different languages and find it hard to collaborate. And we needed to be more cost-effective. Having 19 separate Departments, linked into Faculties led by Deans was one layer of management too many. Early on I had brought Departments together to form

'Coventry Business School', and had just done the same in forming 'The Coventry School of Art and Design'; now was the time to move to a uniform School structure. It was not easy, as some existing Heads were downgraded. But I carried sufficient good will and trust that it went through with less hassle than I thought I might have. It was a radical approach, and I was somewhat amused when, about ten years later, several traditional universities decided to restructure in a like way. Not for the first time we had taken the lead.

Growth and maturity

We began to increase student numbers on exit from the LEA in 1989. By 1992-1993, our first year as Coventry University, there were over 14,000 students in the University – a near doubling since I took over in 1987-1988 – a 20% growth in one year (2,000 more students). That same year, part-time student numbers reached 3,500, about a quarter of our total. This included over 1,000 students studying 'minimodules'; these were short courses at low cost to encourage mature students back into learning and leading on to longer, degree-level work subsequently.

Continued growth was an imperative to generate more income to invest in the neglected infrastructure and in new developments. But it was also a matter of principle and belief. The whole ethos of the institution, and a profound commitment of my own, was to provide higher educational opportunities to as many people who could benefit, especially those who, for whatever reason, did not enjoy the privilege of good school education, or who were otherwise disadvantaged and failed by the system. I believed in this role and purpose passionately, and was driven to improving the quality of the lives of as many people as we reasonably could. A further reason for growth was to support the development of Coventry. The University was in the heart of the City, and had a fantastic potential to improve its economic, cultural and intellectual life; a flourishing university would be of immense benefit to the lives of everyone.

It was therefore critical that the University grew space, with high quality fit-for-purpose accommodation. At the heart of our plans was a commitment to develop in our existing neighbourhood. And rather than borrow, we preferred to pay our way, creating a 'New Building Fund' into which we put £1M a year – not much given the task, but very symbolic nonetheless. It was

Cutting the tape on 'Coventry University' Vesting Day, 15 June 1992.

also highly controversial, and I came in from strong and offensive criticism from many quarters for 'spending money hard earned by staff on buildings rather than on staff salaries'. But it became accepted as the sensible policy in the end.

Over the next few years we were very fortunate in having the opportunities to fulfil these aims. We purchased a redundant electronics factory (GEC) just a couple of hundred metres from the campus, in which to relocate estates, security, careers, counselling, and the student residence office, as well as providing a nursery and fitness centre; this released space on the main campus for teaching. A modest extension of an existing building provided a cafeteria, a decent restaurant and much needed lecture theatres. But the biggest project so far at the time was to buy the local DSS building, originally a factory for motor cycles, then wartime armaments, then a Morris car engine plant, in fact a huge property of great history. We spent two years totally gutting and rebuilding it, with two floors added to the top. It became the home of 'Coventry Business School' with state-of-the-art facilities. It was a huge boost, and set the standard for the rest of the institution. The total project cost, paid for out of our own cash, was around £13M, then regarded as a huge expense, but worth every penny for the benefits to thousands of students ever since.

Another landmark in our first year as Coventry University was to build a student village. Canterbury Street, a short walk from the main campus, was the red light and drugs district of Coventry. At the centre of it all was a derelict factory, originally the Singer bicycle works, later Hills Precision Engineering, but now boarded-up buildings surrounded by barbed wire and debris. I was heavily criticised for even considering building student residences in what was considered to be a highly dangerous and risky area; no students would live there, I was told. I found this offensive. We had the opportunity to improve the environment of a deprived area. And we did. 'Singer Hall' was soon a tremendous success – 622 beds in groups of suites which exemplified the best in the country in student living. And I was particularly proud that we purpose-designed 100 of the rooms for students with disabilities. We retained the old Singer house as a student centre – a fine example of how the University preserved some of Coventry's heritage buildings. What was particularly remarkable at the time was that it was entirely funded from £9.3M of private investment, raised through the Business Expansion Scheme.

Over the next few years we purchased and developed a vast industrial wasteland on the edge of the campus for the Technology Park; the Odeon cinema in the midst of our buildings for a performing arts and media centre; the Gulson Road Hospital site, immediately adjacent to the Business School, as the location of the new library and further expansion of academic buildings in the future; the YMCA and the YWCA buildings, each within walking distance of the University, for student residences; the Coventry Working

Men's Club in the centre of the campus, and the 'Edge' nightclub as Students' Union venues. The last-mentioned was a disaster. At the time, nightclub provision in Coventry was very poor, and this was a negative for marketing the University, so we decided to create our own. However, it lost large sums of money because we allowed the Students' Union to run it and competition soon emerged. It has recently been demolished and is now a temporary car park! By 2000-2001, we had spent more than £40M on new buildings, over 90% of the money being generated by growth. Two of these schemes are of such significance that they warrant further mention.

At the turn of the twentieth century, the British motor car industry emerged in Coventry. On what was then the edge of the City Centre, several small companies set up works, and over time, a complex of 30 acres developed and changed: Armstrong Siddely Motors became Armstrong-Whitworth, the Bristol Aircraft Company and then Rolls-Royce Aerospace. When Rolls-Royce moved to modern premises at nearby Ansty, the Parkside site became a ghost town of dereliction. Norman Bellamy, recently appointed Pro-Vice-Chancellor, conceived the idea that we might purchase this land for a science park. It had long been an ambition of mine to develop such a facility in Coventry, but I felt it was too early in our development to contemplate such a project just then. Norman was very persuasive, and he was right; it was an ideal location, the opportunity of a lifetime. But it was a huge gamble, with massive risks; remediation costs alone could run into many millions. Demolition and infrastructure costs for the 30 acre pile of bricks and heavy duty concrete were formidable. The Board of Governors was unimpressed by the arguments, and even less by the putative business plan. But I saw huge potential in encouraging students to stay in Coventry, starting up their own businesses especially in new technology sectors – the employment of the future. About 10 acres would be for housing, thus helping the viability of the project. We chose 'Technology Park' to distinguish it from Warwick Science Park and give it an applied orientation. All these touches helped, but the Board commissioned consultants to give an independent view and carry out a detailed business plan and risk evaluation. The results highlighted the risks. But with further argument, conveyed with some deep passion and nerve at a Board of Governors' meeting I will never forget, I managed to get the go-ahead. There were many obstacles, especially securing the £5M European

Regional Development Fund grant, working with the City Council, dealing with the machinations of the Government Office for the West Midlands and the national agency English Partnerships. But Norman Bellamy worked tirelessly, over several years. By 1998 the University's first building, the TechnoCentre, housing incubator units for start-up businesses and a state-of-the-art conference centre, was officially opened. The £3M Enterprise Centre, for grow-out businesses, came next, in 2000. There was some controversy. At the edge of the complex was a structure which local mythology claimed was the site of manufacture of the first motor car in Britain, 'the Swift', but which I wanted to pull down. I was quoted as saying it was hideous (true!) and not worth saving (an error on my part). But I misjudged the power of the local newspaper editor. I was leaned on by the City Council, and I relented. Anyway, Coventry University Technology Park has been very successful and is a well-known landmark and facility, although it is not yet fully built out. I confess to being concerned that those now in charge have lost their way; the University is using the land as an extension of the University rather than to develop new businesses and new economy, and some of the tenants (e.g. a local firm of solicitors) go nowhere near to meeting the criteria set by the UK Science Parks Association for a facility of such designation.

The second major building development to highlight, was the creation of a completely new library. The existing one was designed for about one-third of the student population we now had. It was not purpose designed, was an awful study environment, and would cost a fortune to get up-graded for IT. It was not a realistic option to modernise it: we needed to start afresh. Two years were spent in defining the need – surveys of students and staff, literature searching, and visits to identify best practice (including a USA study tour); and a major project to evaluate potential locations. We finally decided on the site of Gulson Road Hospital, contiguous with the University campus and on which I had my eye for some years. The hospital site was known to have a limited life and was right for us. It was another period of long drawn-out negotiations. We wanted to build an iconic, landmark building which was 'future proof' as far as changing methods were concerned, and it needed to be as economical as possible to run. The outcome was a fantastic facility with some outstanding and ground-breaking features – a deep building that uses the minimum of electric lighting, naturally ventilated, adjustable 'everything', computer workstations integrated with books and periodicals, professional help on tap, advice on IT alongside traditional library advice. It is truly a stunning facility, not just the building but as a working library. When it was officially opened by HRH The Princess Royal in September 2001, she began her unrehearsed opening address with: 'I like libraries!' I am immensely proud of that development, and enormously grateful to many people who worked fantastically hard to bring it about, in particular Norman Bellamy, the Librarian Pat Noon, and the Director of Estates, Bill Woolhead and his team.

Academic developments

Growth is not simply about taking more students into existing courses. We needed to develop new areas for the future. So innovation in course content and objectives was a key feature of our plans. Some examples where we led the field nationally include Disaster Management, Equine Studies, Business Enterprise, Motorsport Engineering, Acupuncture, and Technical Authoring; and we were the first university in the country to gain delegated authority from City & Guilds to award their Senior Awards. But there were also incredible innovations in emphasis and 'packaging' of learning opportunities across all areas of the University. This was enabled by modularisation to a common format across the whole institution, so that it was possible for students to have available a very wide range of programmes according to their interests and strengths. How much better this was than in my day. I wanted to study chemistry, and that was it – much of a muchness across the country with little variation. In Coventry we developed degrees in Applied Chemistry, Environmental Chemistry, Pharmaceutical Chemistry, Chemistry with Business, Chemistry combined with a number of other subjects such as Biology, Physics, Mathematics, Statistics, and Computing, and Chemistry combined with languages for example, French, German and Spanish. Later were added Forensic Chemistry, and with the option of study or work experience abroad added to all of these variants.

We also grew by acquisition. Performing Arts (music composition, small scale theatre and dance) came under the aegis of the University from 1994-1995, prior to which it was part of a range of activities run by the LEA. Its highest level work was a Higher National Diploma delivered in poor accommodation in a secondary school some four miles distant on the southerly edge of town. We developed a suite of degree programmes, and this whole area was given a huge boost when we transferred it to the rebuilt Odeon Cinema (but retaining its early twentieth century façade and domes), which we acquired, directly opposite the rest of the School of Art and Design. My only regret is that the area grew so much (responding to demand) that the space for public performances was much less that I wanted. It was a huge disappointment when I saw the final plans, but having delegated the task of putting the quart into the pint pot I did not over-rule my colleagues; perhaps I should have done so.

Another acquisition of great strategic value was nursing and midwifery. Providing the appropriate education and training for such employment areas is just the kind of job in which the polytechnics and their modern university successors excel, by combining professional formation with a sound educational core and applied skills development of the highest order. When the opportunity came to incorporate nursing (and midwifery) education into the University, we grabbed it. There was then a tendering process across the West Midlands, involving all the NHS schools of nursing and midwifery. It was pretty obvious which school would go with which university. In Coventry and Warwickshire it was us, because the University of Warwick, our neighbour, had no real experience in this field; it had its eyes on acquiring a medical school. So Coventry University was indeed the only bidder for the contract. But to my dismay our price was deemed too high. The fact that we had years of experience in pricing such activities and in determining costs (with physiotherapy and occupational therapy) seemed to count for nought. So the School was taken into the major hospital for a year (Walsgrave Hospital), its costs reduced (through redundancies), and a re-tender process instigated. Both the University of Warwick and the University of Central England (UCE) in Birmingham were pressed into bidding. It was a terrible experience. Getting the contract was a critical part of the University's strategic development plan. It would be a tragedy of huge proportions if we failed. This was of no real strategic value to Warwick, and UCE had enough with the contract for the whole of Birmingham and Solihull. Neither would have the same commitment and passion for the work and its importance to the sub-region as we would. I lost a good deal of sleep, but was overjoyed when we won the contract. The rest, as they say, is history.

Community

Traditionally, universities were in places, not part of them. Their fundamental purposes were to be centres of scholarship and research, with no local emphasis. My mission was different; a university could have an international reputation for its service and contribution to local communities; that was my vision of what a university could aspire to be.

And so we engaged substantially with local affairs – education policy and delivery; cultural organisations; physical development projects; social improvement schemes; voluntary and charitable organisations; the business communities; the health agenda; the media; opinion-formers of all kinds. The list is far too long to describe, and indeed the engagement became part of our normal daily routine and unrecognisable as anything but our core business. But this is such an important part of what I regard as a defining characteristic of my time as head of the institution, and something of which I regard as a valued legacy, that a few examples are warranted.

By the time I retired in 2004, nearly 30% of our full-time UK students came from Coventry and Warwickshire (up from 15% in ten years), with 62% coming from the Midlands. Around 5,500 of the 17,000 students studying on campus were part-time. In addition, our work with local colleges operating on a franchise or validation (accreditation) basis was running at well over 2,000. Within these overall numbers are some outstanding examples of how we had worked closely with schools, colleges and employers to provide relevant, purposeful opportunities, especially for those who had missed out in education in their past, or for whom university education always seemed out of reach. I describe this in more detail later in the section 'Widening Participation'.

I personally engaged with everything I could that was Coventry, and to do what I could to improve the quality of life of the local people. Examples include: putting real personal emphasis on relations with the LEA; being a Governor of Woodlands School Coventry and of Rugby College of Further Education; contributing to the LEA's 14-19 Strategic Forum for Education and Training; being a member of the Local Learning Partnership; being a Trustee of the Spencer's Industrial Arts Trust; developing Associate College status for all local FE Colleges; establishing a 'Compact' scheme with local schools; judging awards such as Young Enterprise, National Training Awards, Lord Stafford Awards, LLSC Training Excellence; playing a leading role in the Coventry & Warwickshire Training and Enterprise Council and its successor, the Local Learning and Skills Council (LLSC); chairing the group which formulated the first economic strategy for Coventry and Warwickshire; being heavily involved in The City Centre Company (Coventry) Ltd which was the first public/private sector partnership company nationally, responsible for management of the City Centre, and being appointed Vice-Chair of its successor, CVOne Ltd; being a founding member of Coventry, Solihull and Warwickshire Partnerships Ltd, another public/private partnership, this one being the focus of economic regeneration of the sub-region; and last but not least supporting the establishment of the City of Coventry Ambassadors, the 'great and the good' from the sub-region who would promote the name and the reputation of the City and its region world-wide. We also sponsored many organisations and events: the Business Awards; the Community Awards; various matches of Coventry City FC (I was very prominent in my full and genuine public support for the City's football club); Young Entrepreneurs of the Year; the 'Coventry is Making It' campaign; the 'Spirit of Coventry' campaign; the 'Image Working Group', which in 1998-1999 under Cyrrhian Macrae's leadership created and promoted the City's enduring slogan 'Coventry Inspires'; the local NSPCC Centenary appeal; the Macmillan's nursing appeal; and Coventry Common Purpose – another Coventry 'first' and in which I was prominent in supporting and sponsoring from the start – it was a huge disappointment that my successor as Vice-Chancellor ceased all connections and support for this excellent programme for developing community leadership.

The University also developed a range of high level public activities for local people. David Fussey started a 'Speaker's Corner' lecture series (free, and open to anyone who wished to come), jointly with the University of Warwick and Coventry Cathedral (although in truth we made the running), in which distinguished national figures spoke about contemporary issues of broad cultural, religious or ethical interest. We initiated a unique Ambassadors' Lecture series, in which invited Ambassadors or High Commissioners spoke about the contemporary social, political and cultural issues of their countries and the potential effects globally. This unique and high profile series, inexplicably now abandoned, was designed to contribute better understanding between different nations and cultures, something which I regard as an important function of universities.

We made much of University events such as the outstanding annual awards ceremonies in Coventry Cathedral. In 2000, we had naming ceremonies as we replaced the literal designation of the buildings by names of famous people who had particular links to Coventry, and with whom we wished to be associated, such as George Eliot, Ellen Terry, and Sir Frank Whittle. Other events included a celebration of the 150 years since the Coventry School of Design was established in 1843, the furthest back we could trace our heritage.

Two events initiated by others warrant special mention. The first was the occasion of the giving of the Royal Maundy gifts by HM The Queen on 13 April 1995 in Coventry Cathedral, right opposite the main University entrance. This was a wonderful event, for it seemed as if the whole City had turned out for the occasion. The University erected a huge marquee, and gave lunch to over 320 people – the Maundy money recipients and their supporters, as well as dozens who had helped behind the scenes. The uplift to the people of Coventry, as well as the huge credit which the University gained, was memorable beyond description. A similar occasion was the commemoration of the Home Front on 3 March 2000, again in Coventry Cathedral. This

H.M. Queen on occasion of the Maundy Money Centenary at Coventry Cathedral, 13 April 1995.

received huge national profile; Janet and I were deputed to host Tony and Cherie Blair, and the University again provided refreshments for hundreds of people, many of whom had special needs, and included all the main political leaders, namely David Trimble, Donald Dewar, William Hague, and Charles Kennedy.

I was extremely proud of all the University achieved in its community role. We were very much ahead of the field. In 2004, as it happens coinciding with my retirement, the City of Coventry Ambassadors decided to inaugurate a series of annual awards for the sub-region. I was incredibly honoured and flattered to be nominated and then win (by voting by the Ambassadors themselves) the first Godiva Award for 'Outstanding Personal Contribution to Coventry and Warwickshire'. I can't begin to describe how much this means to me, more than any other award I have ever received. It is a huge honour, and one which reflects so well on the incredible contribution which University staff and our supporters have made to our area over the years.

Widening participation

Polytechnics created opportunities for those who could benefit from higher education but who did not achieve through traditional routes of state ex-

Prime Minister Tony Blair and Cherie Blair, at the occasion of the Home Front Commemoration at Coventry Cathedral, 3 March 2000.

aminations. They successfully delivered alternative routes and mechanisms to support success. I had taught hundreds upon hundreds of students whose lives were thus transformed, just as mine had been. That is why I was determined to carry this work through into Coventry University; I wanted as many people as possible to benefit as I had done.

I was particularly concerned to raise the aspirations of those from deprived communities, or who were otherwise disadvantaged or failed by the system. Too many young people capable of benefiting from higher education come from backgrounds where the value given to education is negligibly low. Those very few who did aspire and entered university often had little if any family support, and were even embarrassed to tell their friends. And all too often, physical disability appeared to preclude participation in what for others was practical and accessible. Coventry University became a leader in achieving this 'widening participation'. To quote a few data from 2004-2005 full-time undergraduate entry:

Type	Percentage of type in UK	Percentage of type in Coventry University
Young entrants from lower social classes	28.2%	38.5%
Young entrants from neighbourhoods where HE participation is low	13.7%	19.6%
Mature undergraduate entrants with no previous HE qualification and from low participation neighbourhoods	16.2%	23.3%
Percentage of UK domiciled entrants from ethnic minority groups (2005/06)	16.1%	28.0%

We also made good progress in providing for students with disabilities. Data published in 2002, the most recent when I retired, showed that 2.5% of Coventry University's full-time UK undergraduates were in receipt of the disabled students' allowance, compared with a national average of 1.4%. This was not happenchance; we had made significant investment in academic buildings and residences to improve physical access, but also had provided pastoral and advocacy support at high level. Our first Disabilities Officer, appointed in 1993, was Mike Adams, a victim of the thalidomide tragedy who had a fantastic personality and quiet determination to overcome dreadful disabilities. He had been President of the Students' Union, and was a perfect role model. He later became a national figure, heading up the National Disabilities Team for higher education, which was based in the University, before moving to the Disabilities Rights Commission. He was hugely admired by us all.

Widening participation became increasingly part of national policy when the Labour Party swept to power in 1997. At the 1999 Labour Party conference, Tony Blair first announced the target that by 2010, 50% of people should have a higher education experience before the age of 30. This target has been widely quoted, and usually misquoted. It does not aim to have half of all school leavers going on to Honours degrees – I wish it were as ambitious as that, but that's not what it states. But it is nonetheless challenging (although it has since been 'watered down' in the light of media criticism, by using the phrase 'working towards 50%'), given that when it was formulated the actual proportion was around 42%. And it is not really just about volumes, but about improving the divergence of participation across the population at large. I gave a talk to a breakfast meeting of Coventry business leaders, in which I referred to HE participation in the south of the City being about ten times(!) that of the north: 'Why the difference?', I challenged. 'Can it be something in the water?' No, of course not, it is social injustice writ large.

In its White Paper published in 2003 *The Future of Higher Education*, the Government gave a powerful expression of its commitment to widening participation:

> Education must be a force for opportunity and social justice, not for the entrenchment of privilege. We must make certain that the opportunities that higher education brings are available to all those who have the potential to benefit from them, regardless of their background.

I was most encouraged by this statement. But opportunity is one thing; success is another. National data show a correlation between widening participation and poorer progression rates; not surprisingly, students from disadvantaged backgrounds are less likely to complete their studies. The introduction of up-front tuition fees, about which I shall have much to say later, exacerbated this trend. In fact, in the performance indicator which is used for non-completion, the proportion not proceeding to the second year of study, Coventry University performs quite well (11% locally compared with 12% nationally, despite the very different entry profile). But I was particularly pleased when specific funding was provided to back up the rhetoric. That year, Coventry University received an additional grant of £2.8M to support retention of students from non-traditional backgrounds. This sounds a huge amount, but is actually trivial in relation to need. Moreover, this was not new money. Paying for this initiative was achieved by reducing the general per capita student funding!

One aspect of the Government's widening participation policy which causes my blood to boil is its obsession with getting more students from state schools into so-called 'top' universities. In 2004-2005, Oxford's new undergraduates from state schools and colleges comprised just 53.4% of its total UK intake – compare that with Coventry's 96.4%, and the national average of 86.7% for the same year. Astonishingly, universities with low intakes from state schools have been given huge amounts of money to address 'the problem'. In my view, this is misguided, wasteful and obsessive. I recall a 'conversation' with Alan Johnson, then Minister for Higher Education, on 1 December 2003 when he visited to formally open a new building, the Bugatti Building, in which we had established the most advanced computer modelling facility for large objects such as concept and prototype motor vehicles. I had personally driven him to Coventry station for his trip back to London. As his train approached we touched on the issue of state schools. He said: 'But we have to get Oxbridge to take more students from working class backgrounds' (or words to that effect). I had no more than seconds so I didn't mince my words, replying forcefully: 'Sod Oxford and Cambridge! If you want to increase the number of such students in higher education, just do three simple things, all within your powers and not requiring legislation. Firstly, give working class students sufficient money so that finance is not a barrier; then give the institutions, like Coventry, that actually want to take them sufficient funds to do the job properly; and finally, extol the virtues of such universities and call them the "top" universities'. I stood between him and the train as it waited for passengers to get on and off, so he would listen, but had to let him go. He went off with wave…and a thought or two!

'Dumbing down' and 'Mickey Mouse' degrees

There are still many who consider that greater participation in higher education is a thoroughly bad thing. They argue that more means worse; that there are now already too many graduates on the market, many undertaking low level jobs, and that the standards being achieved by such graduates are rock bottom. These same critics go on to say that in order to meet the government's artificial target of 50% participation, some institutions have introduced low grade 'sexy' courses of little academic or intellectual merit. There is probably nothing in this world which makes me angrier when I hear or read such nonsense. These attitudes are born of ignorance, fear and sheer academic snobbery in the extreme.

First of all, it is hardly surprising that universities with the entry profile such as Coventry's should produce graduates of more modest achievement than those from better heeled institutions. A high proportion of them come from backgrounds where there is no tradition of higher education, with little family support, and little in the way of personal books, computing or study facilities. Nearly all have to undertake paid employment for 10 or even 20 hours a week, often at times which adversely affects their participation. But these students have tremendous personal qualities and life skills through their full experiences. They work hard against the odds, and deserve far more recognition. It is a travesty that many employers recruit from a selective group of traditional universities rather than take proper note of the new style of graduates from enlightened institutions.

As to the denigration of newer degree courses, as 'Mickey Mouse' degrees, that is where the ignorance and prejudice is even more evident. Have those who use such an insulting term ever taken the trouble to examine these courses with the open mind that is supposed to be the hallmark of an educated person? Why on earth should it be assumed that a study of Shakespeare or Chaucer is in some way 'superior' to a study of the social, cultural and economic impact of modern literature experienced through new media? What makes a degree in History an OK academic subject, but not one in

Psychology? Why is it that a degree in Ancient Greek is admired, but one in Surf Science (which covers some high level physics, design, sociology, oceanography, and business) is considered to be a joke? The modern universities have been fantastically creative in providing courses which students want, which are academically rigorous and intellectually challenging whilst being firmly anchored in the real world – providing employment-specific as well as transferable skills, knowledge and aptitudes for successful students to live full and worthwhile lives. They are to be applauded for this wonderful contribution to social and economic development, not criticised and ridiculed. Memories are short. When the polytechnics began courses in business studies and computing they were mocked and derided by Luddite institutions, all of which now proudly boast Business Schools and Computing programmes.

Research

For me, teaching and research go hand–in–hand in higher education. Teaching at Honours degree level and above needs to be well informed and carried out by those who are themselves developing their subjects. This is not to say that every teacher in higher education needs to be a world-class researcher; but students need to be taught in a research-led environment. The polytechnics struggled to have this philosophy recognised, with CNAA the firmest ally. They had no specific research funding for a long time, and only later in their short lives would a small amount of money be available (£7M pa, compared with £700M pa in the then university sector, which had fewer students).

Prior to the merger of the polytechnics and colleges sector with the universities in 1992, funding for the latter included a large element based on numbers of students (so-called 'SR' funding). This recognised the principle which I outlined above, that research supported teaching. But merger of the sectors would result in over half this sum being transferred to the polytechnics, as they had more than half the students of the combined sector. No one was surprised that the rules changed before this was allowed to occur; SR was abolished at a stroke! The new funding methodology was based on assessment of research quality. The 'Research Assessment Exercise' (RAE) was open to the polytechnics and colleges joining the new sector, as its first impact would be in 1992, the year of the ending of the binary line. Not surprisingly, after years of trivial funding compared with the huge sums paid into the universities, the polytechnics gained only a minor proportion of the funding. There was sufficient for the more motivated and better prepared polytechnics to begin the slow build up of research capacity and capability, and in the next RAEs, in 1996 and 2001, the modern universities (as they then were) did indeed demonstrate increasingly strong research performance. But that did not mean that they received more funding. The rules gradually changed to prevent this. The Government decided, on powerful lobby from the research heavy-hitters, to concentrate research funding on fewer and fewer institutions. The threshold for research funding was thus gradually raised and the rules perversely modified to keep the modern universities in their place.

To illustrate the Coventry University story, the diagram below shows the growth in research quality as measured by successive RAEs while I was at the University. Quality grades were then awarded on a scale 1 (some work of national importance) through to 5 (most work of international importance) for each of the 'units of assessment' (subject areas); from 1996, grade 3 was divided into 3a and 3b. It is evident that we significantly improved our gradings over these three RAEs:

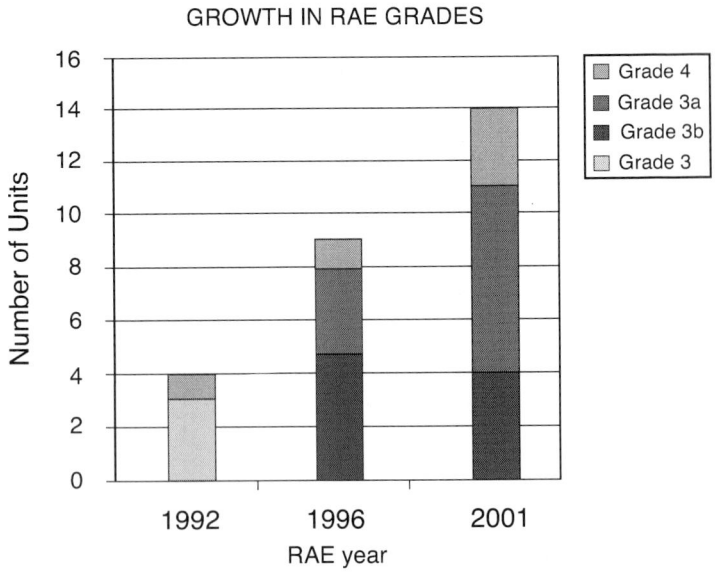

We also increased the numbers of staff deemed to be 'research active' in a parallel manner:

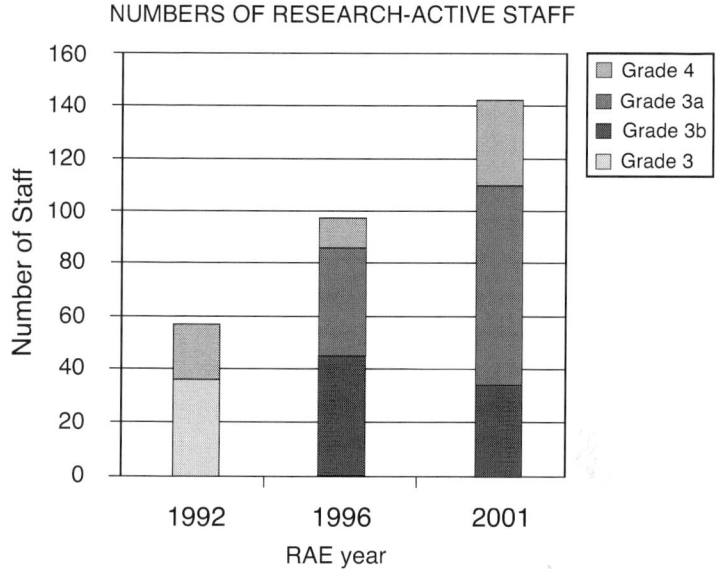

But our annual funding for research did not increase accordingly. The rules were changed at each RAE to ensure that developing universities did not get any of the funding which would otherwise go to the established players:

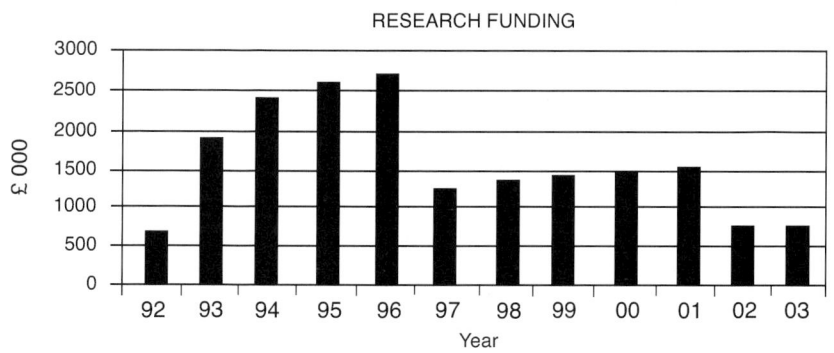

In other words, despite our substantial improvement in both quality and quantity of research over a period of twelve years, our funding at the end of this period was virtually the same (much less in real terms) as when we started. Clearly there is something fundamentally unfair and perverse with a system of funding that purports to reward success but does not.

Of course, a measure of concentration is necessary to maintain world-class research capability. But producing world-class research is not the only function of universities. The support of a research culture, so critical for high quality teaching, is just as important, and needs a reasonable amount of funding. Current government policy will, in my view, prove to be very damaging to UK higher education in the longer term.

There is one further aspect of UK research funding which, as a citizen and tax-payer, I find astonishing: the research funding distributed by HEFCE now totals over £1.46Bn a year, yet there is no requirement to demonstrate exactly how this money is spent, let alone any check on value for money. I can think of no other part of public funding which enjoys such lack of accountability.

League tables

University league tables came into the public consciousness during the mid-1990s, but not until the advent of official national data did league tables take on a measure of authenticity. *The Times Higher* was the first newspaper to publish such tables, but soon the *Guardian*, the *Independent*, and the *Financial Times* all joined in. All used data sets such as entry qualifications (A-level points), proportion of good Honours achieved, employment rates, expenditure per student on libraries and computing, and the like. Not surprisingly, the tables showed the traditional universities dominating the top half, with the modern universities almost entirely in the lower half. Some blurring of this boundary took place over time, but the very nature of the parameters used made any other pattern more than unlikely.

The reasons for this bifurcation are quite simple. The traditional universities have always been more selective than the former polytechnics by mission. Further, the former polytechnics were always far less well endowed in terms of campuses and facilities. So entry qualifications are higher in the traditional universities. This naturally results in a greater proportion of good Honours, and better employment rates. Moreover, the funding of traditional universities is much higher than in the modern universities, because of the disparity in research funding, which supports more academic posts per student, better libraries, in fact more and better facilities generally. So it is not surprising that they perform better in league tables, given the parameters used.

These league tables give very little weight to the student experience, support for learning, relevance of curricula, pastoral and personal development, equality of opportunities, widening of participation, and all the things on which the modern universities focus and excel. If only there were ways to quantify such aspects of higher education, and combine them with a notion of 'value added', the league tables might have my support, and be of real value to the world at large.

Profile

We had to work especially hard to achieve the reputation we deserved. This meant making sure we received as much good news and high profile in the public mind.

One way we achieved this was to produce an Annual Review. At the time, most traditional universities published a very boring 'Annual Report', in some cases little more than a list of research publications and grants. None published the kind of review which the private sector was developing to huge effect. We did, and the effect was ground-breaking. We produced it all in-house, and in the early years put on a launch presentation to a large number of stakeholders, thus actively disseminating our performance and progress. Over the years, our Corporate Affairs Unit published some stunning Reviews, and achieved several national awards and prizes, not only from the education sector (*Times Higher* and *Heist*) but also from professional organisations such as the British Association of Industrial Editors.

There are very many examples of how we achieved a better reputation with employers in the area, but I will mention just two, which also demonstrate broader contributions to the local economy and prestige.

In the early decades of the nineteenth century, Coventry's role as a centre for ribbon manufacture was threatened by cheaper imports flooding into the country. To counter this trend, a School of Design was established in 1843 to enhance the quality and design of ribbon products. Over the years, this evolved into the Coventry College of Art, one of the three institutions brought together in 1970 as the Lanchester Polytechnic. Ever since, design has been an important feature of the provision in Coventry. It has evolved dramatically in line with the evolution of the indigenous industry, and particularly as the UK motor industry established in Coventry. Transport design degrees were developed in close collaboration with employers, in just the same way as the training programmes of the original School were over 150 years ago, and are now truly outstanding and world-class. Graduates from these programmes occupy senior roles in all the major design houses in the industry, and have been responsible for design of cars (exteriors, interiors, and components) from virtually every major marque globally. The School won the prestigious World Automotive Design Competition for the 'Best Design School in the World' in 2004, beating Schools from China, Brazil, Japan, France, Korea, Italy, Spain, India, Sweden, the USA, Canada, as well as winning three of the seven individual categories. And in 2007 it was awarded a Queen's Anniversary Prize, the most prestigious higher education prize in the UK. I was privileged to attend the Buckingham Palace ceremony on 14 February 2008. I am immensely proud of this area.

My second example is the University's work with Jaguar Cars, perhaps the most prestigious ever Coventry company. When Ford became the owner of Jaguar, a new Managing Director was appointed, Nick Scheele, and he made a huge impact. He saw the value of Coventry University actively seeking close collaboration with industry, and willing and able to be responsive and flexible, without detriment to standards. Over the next few years we jointly produced some of the most innovative and high performing programmes I have ever known. We structured some programmes into three week blocks – a week of preparation, a week of intensive study in the University, and a week of report-writing for assessment. The modules were free-standing, allowing students to gain credits towards their awards over time, so if work commitments required they could simply defer commencement of their next module for the time being. Other programmes were delivered on Friday afternoon/evening and Saturdays. The curricula were devised using company data and case studies, delivered jointly but independently assessed, and reviewed in partnership. Jaguar augmented the facilities, sponsored the building in which the University-based study took place, and supported two Professorships, which recognised a principle I have espoused, that teaching at this level needs to be well informed. The company was keen that the experience was available more widely, including for its sister companies Land-Rover and Aston Martin, and also for companies in their supply chains. The impact was therefore very substantial indeed. In all, we provided for several hundred students a year from scores of engineering companies across the Midlands.

When polytechnics began to award their own degrees (as universities) in 1992, the larger higher education colleges needed to find a university to take the place of CNAA for validation. We took on the task for Worcester College, at its behest, and moreover worked closely with the College over a number of years, helping to improve its capacity and capability. In due course, the College received its own degree-awarding powers; the institution is now the University of Worcester, a richly deserved status. I was very pleased with the way we had supported the development of this institution, and flattered when it made me an Honorary Fellow. We also took on the validating role for Newman College Birmingham when the Principal, Brian Ray (who had been a Pro-Vice-Chancellor with me at Coventry) became disenchanted with its previously validating university (Birmingham). Together with the validation and franchising work in FE Colleges, this meant that in 1994-1995 there were over 7000 students studying for Coventry University awards based in other UK institutions, more than the total student population of some universities.

Employment relations

I became involved in national pay and conditions negotiations during the period 1989 to 1992, under the aegis of the Polytechnics and Colleges Employers' Forum (PCEF). This carried forward into the combined sector, as the Universities and Colleges Employers' Association (UCEA), and I was a member of the UCEA Board from 1994 to 2001. At various times I chaired the separate negotiating groups for manual, administrative and academic staff, which gave me huge experience but also had its downside in that Coventry became a target for selective action in times of disputes. The extreme case was in 1992, when there was a major dispute in the negotiations of the annual pay award for administrative staff; the main union, NALGO (since transformed into Unison), called a national strike in support of its claim. The strike action was applied selectively, and because I chaired the employers' side of the negotiations, Coventry University was one of the few institutions targeted. NALGO tried to close the University Library over a six week period, all in term-time (October and November). Around ten staff, out of a normal complement of over sixty, managed to keep a semblance of service going over this period. We had to limit hours of opening, and operate an honesty system for loans – we did lose some books, but not half as many as we feared. In the end, after a terrible experience for many of the staff involved, the union accepted the offer which had been on the table since July that year. I was and remain deeply appalled by the wanton way in which unions use the damage to third parties (in this case students) to further their ends.

It had been very clear for many years that the academic staff contract in the former polytechnics was hopelessly inappropriate for the new era. For one thing, it gave the right for 14 weeks a year paid leave, and many staff actually took all that time off. A modern competitive university could not possible run on such lines. And within the teaching weeks there was a specification of the maximum hours of teaching, with reduction of the hours taught for a variety of functions e.g. visiting students on placement, supervision of projects, and various administrative roles. It meant that the actual amount of teaching done could be very small indeed, but more to the point it allowed for all kinds of Spanish practices and actually incentivised inefficiency. There was no clear recognition of the need to keep up-to-date or engage in any research or scholarly activity, and no reference to intellectual property matters. Changing the contract became a major task for PCEF in its short existence. After national negotiations broke down, the management and union sides agreed to set up a joint working group under the aegis of the Arbitration and Conciliation Advisory Service (ACAS), chaired by an experienced independent expert. Out of the blue, I was invited to chair the management side. It was several weeks of extraordinarily hard work, staying over in London for days at a time, and involving meetings into the late evening. I committed much energy to this task, drafting quite a bit of the new contract myself, and consulting fellow polytechnic Directors by telephone at all hours of the day and mainly over the weekends. I recall what seemed to be a whole weekend sitting on the stairs at home, talking to dozens of people by telephone, trying to get a consensus. In the end, the two sides presented their proposals to the independent chair. I was elated when he came down on the management side. We never looked back, and the contract, although not perfect, remained in force nationally from that day right until the time I retired, some twelve years later.

Not all my employment relations experience was as satisfactory. Taking disciplinary action against two Deans at different times were really tough experiences; but I was also myself the subject of a vexatious grievance, and a completely unwarranted charge of racial discrimination against me, which reached an Employment Tribunal (but never heard because of a technical failing in the case). There were also occasions when we had to enforce redundancies, and in one sequence had a major Employment Tribunal lasting several weeks, involving two staff who claimed to have been victimised because of their union roles. Complete nonsense, of course, as confirmed by the Tribunal, but necessitating a huge amount of work and stress, and considerable cost.

UCAS

I had been associated with the Polytechnics and Colleges Admissions System (PCAS) since 1983, shortly after joining Coventry Polytechnic. This came about when Keith Thompson, Director of North Staffordshire Polytechnic was appointed as chairman. We were significantly involved in the difficult merger of PCAS with the University Central Council for Admissions (UCCA) in 1995. Keith became Chairman, following a transition period with the former Vice-Chancellor of York University, Berrick Saul, in the chair, and I became the Deputy Chairman. I succeeded Keith in 1997, and served for four years.

This was a very formative experience for me, as it required much care and tact. The Board was largely a representative one, and conflicting interests for most issues had to be resolved. One such was the growing calls for a post-qualifications admissions system (something which, over ten years on, is still under discussion). But perhaps the most controversial matter I dealt with was the introduction of the UCAS tariff. At the time, the points system was simple: grade E at A-level counted one point; two for grade D and so on; grade A was allocated five points. It was neat, but deeply flawed, being based only on the alphabet and sequence of integers. Why should grade A be worth five times as much as grade E? No one had asked that question before, but in setting up a tariff the issue could not be avoided. The new proposals gave

240 points to grade A and 80 to grade E, a ratio of 3:1 rather than the 5:1 of the previous system. This was portrayed as 'dumbing down' and caused much strong argument. How I managed to get the UCAS Board (and thus the Minister) to agree to it I still don't know, but I did, and this is perhaps my lasting impact on UCAS.

The Chief Executive of UCAS, appointed as such after the transition period under Berrick Saul's Chairmanship, was Tony Higgins, who had been in the comparable role in PCAS before that. I grew close to Tony. He was immensely energetic and innovative, with huge drive and ambition. This sometimes gave rise to scrapes with those who preferred a more measured and low profile approach. I recall on one occasion I was almost pinned to the wall by a senior DfES official who told me to 'control Higgins', because Tony had just issued a press release which was taken by the Minister to imply criticism of the tuition fees policy, more of which later. A few years after I left UCAS I was immensely saddened to learn that Tony was very ill. I visited him in hospital and later met him for lunch; it was distressing to see him a shadow of his former self, barely able to walk or hold himself upright. He passed away shortly afterwards.

Tuition fees

During the late 1980s and through the 1990s, there was a significant growth in the higher education sector without a corresponding increase in funding from government grants. Funding per student thus halved over about a ten year period. The system was creaking, yet no Vice-Chancellor would admit that standards were actually falling, because the impact on recruitment and PR could be disastrous. The Russell Group of universities (so-called because their Vice-Chancellors meet in the Russell Hotel in London) – the most research-driven Universities – were lobbying for additional funding, and for the right to charge fees, to reverse the recent decline in per capita income. There were other policy issues needing to be addressed too, so the Government, with all-Party support, set up a 'National Committee of Inquiry into Higher Education, chaired by Sir Ron (later Lord) Dearing, to:

> …make recommendations on how the purpose, shape, structure, size, and funding of higher education, including support for students, should develop to meet the needs of the United Kingdom over the next twenty years.

The Committee published its report under the title *Higher Education in a Learning Society* in July 1997. It was a mammoth report, each copy weighing 2.2kg, extending to 2000 pages, and with 93 recommendations. The Committee had worked intensively for 14 months, holding 240 meetings and 380 public sessions. The recommendations relating to higher education funding and student finance are more than relevant here.

Dearing recognised the need significantly to increase funding of higher education institutions for teaching, and recommended that the bulk of the shortfall should be met by the students themselves. Students were, after all, direct beneficiaries of their higher education. Specifically, Dearing recommended that each undergraduate should contribute a flat fee of £1000 a year (to be index linked), payable on an income-contingent basis after graduation. He also recommended that maintenance grants, which were already being phased out, should be reintroduced, on a means-tested basis so as to help students from less well-off backgrounds.

It was a bold report, and the recommendations about student funding made the headlines. But the drama was more about the Government's response. On the very day the Dearing report was published, David Blunkett, the Secretary of State for Education in Tony Blair's new Labour Government announced that a £1000 fee would indeed be introduced, but it was to be means-tested and paid up-front on enrolment, while maintenance grants would be abolished. Why the Government decided not to follow the lead of Dearing is shrouded in mystery, and proved to be a tragic mistake. In due course, the new arrangements were set out in the Teaching and Higher Education Act of July 1998, for introduction from the 1998-1999 academic year.

The implications of the Government's decisions were profound and deeply disruptive. Up-front payment of fees meant that institutions had to collect fees on enrolment; this was a costly chore, but moreover resulted in terrible student hardship. Many students at universities such as Coventry University just did not have the money to put on the table, bearing in mind the other costs such as residential fees which needed to be met at the same time. We put in place arrangements for fees to be deferred in cases of hardship, or paid by instalments, but then had to ensure fee recovery during the year. This led to a huge amount of administration to track thousands of students and pressurise them into paying. The culture was an anathema to us – to 'force' students to pay for their education. Students' Unions from across the country organised campaigns to discourage institutions from recovering student debts. We had to instigate a series of actions and letters, escalating the pressure on students to pay. By the end of the first term we were forced to tell students that unless they paid their fees they would be denied access to facilities, and that later they would be excluded. But this is easier said than done. Universities don't take formal registers, and in modular structures students can attend teaching sessions (or not) quite freely; the optional arrangements mean that the concept of a cohort is not apparent. The very flexibility which we had purposefully developed for good educational reasons was now contriving to make it difficult for us to restrict access to those who had not paid their fees. I wrote letters to hundreds of students each year excluding them from their courses. I signed them personally, hoping that this would demonstrate the seriousness of their situations. We had students going through the whole year without paying fees but being prevented from attending end-of-year examinations, although the queue at the finance desk of students paying the day before their first examination caused serious problems.

It was a most distasteful thing to do, but we simply had to recover the money due to us, amounting each year to several millions of pounds. No organisation could regularly suffer bad debts of that magnitude. In practice, the consequence was that our funding did not improve to the extent that the new policy had assumed. But more than that, our relationships with students were badly affected, and our reputation was also damaged because the press found our action something to be sensationalised. There were student protests throughout the country, albeit nothing like those of the 1960s, including a half-hearted occupation of my own office, aided by a local City Councillor who was a member of the Socialist Party – Rob Windsor (a protégé of Dave Nellist, whom I have mentioned).

As Mike Fitzgerald had often said, students are not consumers of education: they are partners in its creation. Yet here we were treating them as customers who did not pay. The majority of our full-time students had to take on term-time jobs; an early survey showed that over 70% worked up to 20 hours a week, such was the socio-economic profile at Coventry. This clearly had an impact on their performance. A study at Oxford Brookes University showed that working during term-time reduced final Honours performance by as much as a whole classification.

I spent much energy and time arguing and explaining my objections to the Government's policy on tuition fees. I accepted, reluctantly but pragmatically, that students should make a financial contribution to their higher education. But I was totally and vehemently opposed to the manner in which the Blair Government had decided to implement this principle. The hardship it caused was immense, the damage immeasurable. But worse was to come. The greedy, research-driven Universities, with strong voices in the corridors of power derived from their privileged Oxbridge networks, were not satisfied. They wanted more money still, regardless of the impact. The principle of students paying fees had been established, so now the screw could be turned by having the amount increased. But for the first time, higher education was a political issue. It was no real surprise, therefore, that the Labour Party Manifesto for the 2001 General Election promised, explicitly and unequivocally, that fees would not be increased during the lifetime of that Parliament.

That promise was hollow. Throughout 2002 there was an on-going debate about higher education funding. Universities were said to be in financial crisis, one report exaggerated the shortfall to £1Bn; the flat-rate fee of £1000, rising only by annual inflation, was already under threat. At the same time the Government announced its target of 50% participation. The new Secretary of State, Charles Clarke, announced a review of funding and student support; this was delayed. It was clear that the Government was in difficulty with the Treasury! The political temperature was rising. Tony Blair and Charles Clarke were under increasing pressure. A White Paper *The Future of Higher Education* was published on 22 January 2003. Press reports suggested that changes to pacify the Labour back-benchers were introduced the night before, but even so it was received with very mixed views. Throughout 2003 there were campaigns and lobbying way beyond what anyone had ever witnessed before; the passion and furore were unprecedented in the world of higher education. I had taken an outspoken stance, vehemently opposed to the principle of variability of tuition fees. I found myself in the national spotlight, with interviews for BBC Radio 4, BBC Online, and Radio 5 Live. I made TV appearances on 'Politics Today', 'Panorama' and BBC2 'Newsnight'. The two most notable spots were to be a panellist in a mock-'University Challenge' programme, and a participant in the questioning of Tony Blair hosted by Jeremy Paxman. I was very pleased to have the opportunity to express my strong feelings, but more especially to put the case for students.

In the event, the Government was under huge pressure to make further concessions by the time the Higher Education Bill was published on 8 January 2004. Tuition fees were to be allowed to be raised by individual institutions to a maximum of £3,000 a year from 2005-2006. They would be 'capped' at that level (apart from annual inflation increases) until at least 2010, with an independent review in 2009. The main concessions were to abolish the upfront payment and reintroduce maintenance grants. An 'Office for Fair Access' (OFFA) would be created to ensure institutions invested a proportion of their increased income in providing scholarships and bursaries, as well as taking steps to widen participation. Nonetheless, there were still major misgivings by many MPs of all parties. Right up to the debate on the first reading in the House of Commons there were behind-the-scenes negotiations around the levels of grants, the details of the means-testing and such like. In the end the Government got its way. But the voting was exceptionally close – 316 votes to 311, thanks to votes of Scottish MPs – and Scotland would not even be affected! I was disappointed that the three Coventry MPs (all Labour) voted with the Government, despite one assuring me that he and one of the others would oppose.

I was forced to accept that student contribution to tuition costs were here to stay, and that the only way Universities could meet the demands upon them to good standard was to raise the level from the £1,000 limit. But I was totally opposed, and shall be to my dying days, to the principle of variable fees. The only justification for charging students anything is to enable Universities to do a better job by them. Tuition fees were thus income to spend on students (not research), and my students deserved as much spent on them as those from any other University. What was the moral justification for a system which enabled the better off to have more money spent on them? If anything, I needed more income than the average because I needed to remedy the disadvantage which my students had suffered before coming to Coventry.

But that was not the end of the story by a very long way. The Russell Group soon began an intensive campaign for the £3,000 cap to be lifted, with some suggesting that fees needed to rise to £10,000 or even £15,000 for more popular courses. I was appalled and deeply upset. What have we come to if we create a so-called market, pricing out from education those who already have social disadvantage?

I recall one of my dear mother's simple sayings: 'Money goes to money'. I now know what she meant. Well-endowed universities which attract well-off students become even better financed than those seeking to rectify gross social injustice. And the particular travesty and unfairness is that there is no evidence that the quality of the provision for undergraduate students has improved since the £3,000 tuition fees were introduced. Where has the additional income gone? A substantial proportion has been used to improve staff pay, especially academic staff pay. There is no doubt that pay in higher education fell behind during the 1980s and 90s; the introduction of tuition fees has allowed this situation to be addressed, but has it resulted in better and more effective teaching? After all, it is broadly the same workforce doing the same things as before. There has been no real change in practice, and performance management is barely understood. I hoped that the review of tuition fees which the Government decided to undertake in 2009 would be evidence-based, including a proper evaluation of what the additional income generated by fees since 1998-1999 has been used for. After all an average university with say 10,000 full-time United Kingdom and other European Union students would be receiving nearly £20 million a year extra for no additional work! No-one seemed to be asking the crucial question: what benefits had accrued to undergraduate students, and what was the true purpose of any lifting of the £3,000 cap? How wrong I was to hope that such questions would be asked, as I shall describe.

The decision to commission the 2009 fees review had all-party support. That was not surprising, since it was a way of passing on a political hot potato to whichever Party proved successful in the next General Election. As it transpired both Labour and the Conservatives were able to avoid declaring their hands until the Election was over. But the Liberal Democrats did not do so, for in their Election Manifesto they promised to remove all tuition fees. At the time, it was a reasonable ploy; they had little chance of being elected, so they could make attractive but hollow promises. It was, of course a profoundly stupid policy, as there was no way the clock could be turned back without bankrupting universities. But it became a flagship policy of the Party, and they promoted it particularly in constituencies with large student populations. The absurdity of abolishing fees seems to have been recognised in a formal pledge, which was still hugely optimistic, signed by over 1000 Liberal Democrat Parliamentary candidates, including all their MPs and, critically, the Party leader, Nick Clegg. The pledge stated: ' I pledge to vote against any increase in fees in the next Parliament and to pressure the Government to introduce a fairer alternative'.

Before the fees review began, Tony Blair resigned as Prime Minister after ten years in post, to be succeeded by Gordon Brown on 27 June 2007. His successor did not have a happy tenure as Prime Minister. There were some profound mis-judgements, public concerns about style and effectiveness resulting in huge downturns in opinion polls, a global financial crisis which had major effects on the national debt, and emerging long-term implications of unprecedented magnitude. Nonetheless, Gordon Brown resisted calls for a General Election for over two years, before he finally set the date of 6 May 2010.

In the event there was no outright majority in the 2010 General Election. The Conservatives achieved the largest number of seats, and, surprisingly perhaps, entered into a Coalition with the Liberal Democrats, with David Cameron as Prime Minister and Nick Clegg as his Deputy. The Conservatives were in favour of increasing fees, from both pragmatic and ideological perspectives, whereas the Liberal Democrats had declared their opposition in the terms of the pledge they had all signed, so there had to be recognition of this difference in the Coalition Agreement between the two Parties. This was achieved by agreement that the Liberal Democrats would be allowed to abstain in any vote to increase university fees.

In the meanwhile, the promised fees review, chaired by Lord Browne of Madingley, former Chief Executive of BP, was launched on 9 November 2009, some months before the 2010 General Election. However, it did not report until 12 October 2010, and by that time the full and dire extent of the financial situation which the Coalition had inherited from the Labour Government had become apparent. Huge cuts had to be made in all public services, and universities were seen to be fair game for some of the most Draconian. I have absolutely no doubt whatsoever that the outcome of the Browne review, which was supposed to have been independent, was in fact dominated by the determination of the Coalition Government to cut university funding to a level that no-one had ever envisioned. The only way universities could survive was by a drastic increase in tuition fees. In fact, the Browne review went as far as anyone could have predicted:

- The 'cap' on full-time undergraduate fees (by then, £3,290) would be completely removed so that universities could charge as much as they wished
- Up-front loans would be provided to help with fees and living costs, with means-tested grants provided for students from lower-income families
- Students would repay the loans after graduation at 9% on income over £21,000 (previously £15,000). Any debt not repaid after 30 years would be written off (previously 25 years).

The reaction to these proposals soon built up to a furore. The Government, realising it had to act quickly, announced its response to the Browne Review just three weeks later, on 3 November 2010. While they accepted most of the recommendations, they broke from the review's most controversial proposal by deciding there should be a cap on the maximum fee which could be charged, setting this at £9,000 a year. Even so, this was a huge increase on the existing cap of £3,290. Universities wishing to charge at this maximum level would have to contribute to a National Scholarship programme, and there would be sanctions for those not widening access to university entrance.In the month that followed, there were protests on a scale not seen for many a year. The worst was in London on 11 November, with a small number of the tens of thousands of protesters demonstrating violence not seen since the Poll Tax riots of March 1990. Nevertheless, on 9 December 2010, MPs approved the raising of the fee cap to £9,000 by 323 votes to 302. The split in the Coalition's ranks was obvious, with 21 Liberal Democrats and six Tory MPs voting against the Government, but the majority was more than the Blair Government achieved in 2004 when it raised fees to £3,000. The vote in the Lords was even clearer – a majority in favour by 283 to 215.

But that was not all. Nick Clegg came in for considerable personal attack for not keeping his tuition fee pledge. The broken pledge was generally considered to be one of the factors as to why the Liberal Democrats performed exceptionally badly in the 2011 local elections; the other being defeat in the National Referendum for an Alternative Voting System, which the Liberal Democrats, and Clegg in particular, had strongly supported.

In the weeks following the Parliament votes, the Coalition came under attack on various counts: the amount of research carried out by the Browne Review was derisory, certainly in comparison with the Dearing Report (just £68,000, largely on a single unpublished opinion survey of parents and students); financial calculations were deemed to be flawed; new modelling showed there would be disproportionately adverse financial effects on lower-income families; rather than create a market for higher education based on price, the majority of universities decided to charge the maximum of £9,000 a year for some or all courses, the effect of which put the Government's calculations of cost to the public purse seriously out of kilter; courses in the arts and humanities would get no or very little, if any public funding and many would cease to exist (they will be dependent entirely on student fees, despite Government pronouncements of the importance of these areas); various announcements by Ministers were shown to be untenable or seized upon by the media, and were quickly withdrawn, in one case by direct intervention of the Prime Minister.

The whole proposition therefore became a complete and utter mess, which was barely clarified by the subsequent White Paper published in June 2011.[5] And what really upsets me, now from the sidelines, is that throughout this catastrophic period, the opposition from the Vice-Chancellors has been pathetic, with most of the public pronouncements and comments actually in favour of the new order. True, universities are now between a rock and a hard place, because the reduction in Government grant has to be made up somehow. But where were the Vice-Chancellors when the funding policy was being formulated? Why has it been left to the trades unions, students and the socialist and anarchistic extremist groups to be the sole public voices of opposition? Those in the corridors of power, the higher education élite, once again were manipulating the policy makers to their own nasty advantage, with little regard for the plight of the rest, such as the majority of current and future students who do not have the influence they deserve. When tuition

---

[5] *Higher Education: Students at the heart of the System*, (HMSO), June 2011, (Cmnd 8122). See also http://discuss.bis.gov.uk/hereform/white-paper

fees were first introduced, and again when they were raised to £3,000 a year, we were able to squeeze some concessions and improvements in what was on offer, albeit modest ones. But this time round, with fees and student support issues ramped up beyond belief, the lack of dissent and contrary argument from the sector has been deeply disturbing. I would go so far as to say that the silence and inaction of the modern universities has been a betrayal of their heritage.

I suppose I am also frustrated at not being in there, being part of the action, as I was when fee issues were previously to the fore in 2004. But there is a bit of me which is also delighted that once again the Government and the élitist, selfish crew have not had their way entirely; ironically their attempts to enforce a fees market, with variable fees creating variability in the resourcing of provision for students, has again been thwarted by the extent of the cuts requiring most universities to go for the same, maximum, fee. That at least is one result which I heartily applaud. But the frustrated Government responded with a scheme to remove students who gain A-level grades AAB or better from the student number cap on individual universities, and to top-slice 20,000 from the remaining places nationally to be open for 'bids' from institutions charging fees of £7,500 or less. The Government's main intention is clearly to put pressure on the majority of institutions to reduce their fees, but its arguments are deeply flawed.[6] The consequences will be highly elitist by widening the resource gap between groups of universities even further. In particular, the overall impact will be to impoverish those institutions which cater for the most disadvantaged in our society. The policy demonstrates appalling ignorance and disregard for its adverse effects.

Reflections 9

I was at Coventry Polytechnic/University for a total of twenty-one years, seventeen as the institutional head. Disengagement from the City Council was the most profound and far-reaching development during that period, but I should not under-estimate the impact of the change in title to Coventry University and the merging of the binary divide.

---

6 Commons Select Committee for Business Innovation and Skills session 2010-12, *The future of higher education*. Supplementary written evidence submitted by Professor Nicholas Barr. See http://www.publications.parliament.uk/pa/cm201011/cmselect/cmbis/writev/885/m61.htm

I have often been asked if the change from Coventry Polytechnic to Coventry University was a good thing, and usually the question has been put with the implication that it has been retrograde. I was not one who was banging the table to get the change; I am a product of the polytechnic system, hugely proud of that and privileged to have been part of the polytechnic movement. I spent a good proportion of my career extolling the virtues of the polytechnics, and arguing their values above those of the traditional universities. But, as I hope I have described, the development of the institution since the polytechnic days – in size, scope, maturity and impact – has been phenomenal. I very much doubt much of this would have been possible as Coventry Polytechnic.

On a much broader front, I am equally adamant that the removal of the binary divide has been of immense benefit nationally. Polytechnics were often accused of 'apeing' universities, and since they themselves became universities they have been charged with losing their values and becoming poor imitations. But, in my view, the bringing together of the former polytechnic and the traditional university sectors into a unified(?) system has had an impact just as much on the latter as on the former. The new policy agenda for the whole higher education sector is very much that of the former polytechnics: wider access; strong partnerships with employers; greater credit for workbased learning; valuing higher level skills; serving socio-economic needs; regional responsibility; concern for teaching; curricula which respond to needs of students, a range of modes of study, and so on. The traditional universities have changed, and for the better, due to the impact of the post-1992 institutions.

And yet, I remain bitterly disappointed that in many other ways very little has changed. Indeed, the disparity has increased and threatens to escalate even further in the future. The research agenda is still the major driving force of the older parts of the sector; concentration of research funding accelerates unabated, with recent Government decisions to withdraw funding from the rising stars (and even when the RAE becomes the Research Excellence Framework this will continue to be the enduring characteristic); undergraduate tuition fee income is being used to supplement research and to pay interest on borrowing to construct more and more grandiose schemes of edifice for Vice-Chancellors, rather than to enhance the quality of the teaching and learning experience of students. Successive Governments continue to kow-tow to Oxbridge and the like. Very little inroads have been made into the socially and economically privileged profiles of student intakes in to the traditional institutions, despite exhortations and huge amounts of public money being thrown at them. Academic snobbery and elitism is as endemic as ever it was. Progressive universities are accused of being second rate, not making good use of public money, having high 'dropout' rates, 'dumbing down', lowering standards, focussing on 'bums on seats' rather than on being selective, and so on. And yet these institutions, of which I am proud to include Coventry University, are doing a fantastic job in providing genuine life-changing opportunities for those who would otherwise unjustly be denied such experiences, and doing so with outstanding success which is the envy of the rest of the world. I hope and pray that the new era of £9000 a year fees will not destroy for future generations the opportunities I was able to create for generations past; I have a deep sense of fear those opportunities will be soon be history.

Author, Investiture of CBE, 1997.

During my time at Coventry Polytechnic/University, I was hugely privileged in being able to meet Royalty, Ministers and leaders of political parties, international statesmen, heavy-hitting business people, leading athletes, and many other public figures. I have visited several foreign countries, and have been a guest at 10 Downing Street and Buckingham Palace. I have been able to pay a national role, and have some influence on the quality of life of the Coventry and Warwickshire sub-region. I have been associated with some outstanding organisations nationally and locally. But above all else, I have been fortunate to have been able to contribute to the development of tens of thousands of fellow human beings, very many of whom would, in former times, have been denied the opportunities which Coventry University provided.

My own educational development, from being a shy and uncertain undergraduate student at the modest and dilapidating Northern Polytechnic, right through to being Vice-Chancellor of Coventry University, demonstrates how higher education can transform lives. I have benefited enormously from my higher education, and this has been my motivation: to do all I can to enable as many people as possible to reap the rewards, achieve the quality of life, which I have been privileged to enjoy.

Further reading

Susy

Jacob, Rabbi Louis, *We have reason to believe*, (Vallentine Mitchell), 1957.
Black, Gerry, *JFS: The History of the Jews' Free School, London since 1732*, (Tymsder Publishing), 1998.
Excellence and Enjoyment can be downloaded from: http://www.standards.dfes.gov.uk/primary/publications/literacy/63553/
Faith in the System can be viewed online at http://www.dcsf.gov.uk/publications/faithinthesystem/pdfs/faithinthesystem.pdf
Fullan, Michael, *Leading in a Culture of Change*, (Jossey-Bass Inc. Publishers), 2001.
Hopkins, Belinda, *Just Schools: A Whole School Approach to Restorative Justice*, 2004. Available at: http://www.incentiveplus.co.uk
Korczak, Janusz, *Ghetto Diary*, (Yale University Press), 2003
The Bullock Report can be viewed online at http://www.dg.dial.pipex.com/documents/docs1/bullock.shtml
The Warnock Report can be viewed online at http://www.sen.ttrb.ac.uk/vierwar2.aspx?contentId=13852

Jean

Educational Psychology Service, *Every child matters,* 15 August 2005. See also www.everychilmatters.gov.uk/ete/psychology
Lawrence, Jean, Steed, David and Young, Pamela, *Disruptive children – disruptive schools?* (Croom Helm, Nichols Publishing) 1984.
Lawrence, Jean and Tucker, Margaret, *Norwood was a difficult school: a case study of educational change,* (Macmillan Education), 1988.

Learning Behaviour. The Report of the Practitioners' group on School Behaviour and Discipline chaired by Sir Alan Steer [Steer Report]. Department for Education and Skills, 2005.
National Union of Teachers, *HSE management standards for work-related stress.* NUT circular 072/H&S, 18 May 2005. NUT, Hamilton House, Mabledon Place, London WC1H 9BD
National Union of Teachers, *Teacher stress: NUT guidance on stress audits and risk assessments.* NUT circular 96/01(H&S), 20 May 2001. NUT, Hamilton House, Mabledon Place, London WC1H 9BD
Ofsted, *Managing challenging behaviour,* (HMSO), 2005. HMI document reference 2363; http://www.ofsted.gov.uk
UK Observatory for the Promotion of Non-Violence. See also www.ukobservatory.com

Michael

The eight stories written by Michael for the BBC WW2 website, 'The People's War', can be accessed at: http//www.bbbc.co.uk/ww2peopleswar/user/17/u2883517.shtml
The Future of Higher Education, DfES, London, (HMSO), 2003, (Cmnd 5735).
Higher Education: report of the Committee appointed by the Prime Minister under the Chairmanship of Lord Robbins, 1961-63, (HMSO), London, 1963, (Cmnd 2154).
Higher Education: Meeting the Challenge (HMSO), London, 1987, (Cmnd 114).
Higher Education – A New Framework (HMSO), London, 1991, (Cmnd 1541).
Higher Education in the Learning Society. The Report of the National Committee of Enquiry into Higher Education, chaired by Sir Ron (Lord) Dearing, (HMSO), July 1997.
Higher Education – A New Framework, (HMSO), London, 1991, (Cmnd 1541).

Higher Education: Students at the heart of the System, (HMSO), June 2011, (Cmnd 8122). See also http://discuss.bis.gov.uk/hereform/white-paper.
Jacka, Keith, Marks, John, and Cox, Caroline, *Rape of Reason: the Corruption of the Polytechnic of North London,* (Enfield Churchill Press Ltd), 1975.
Widening Participation in Higher Education, DfES, London, (HMSO), 2003.
Securing a Sustainable Future for Higher Education. An independent review of higher education funding and student finance. 12 October 2010, A Review Chaired by Lord Browne of Madeley. www.independent.gov.uk/browne-report.

Clio Publishing is a small independent company with a growing reputation for providing bespoke publishing answers for authors and researchers in the humanities. The speed, flexibility and cost-efficiency of print on demand digital technology combined with the marketing opportunities of the internet, direct mail, social networking, and 4G mobile communications now offer authors powerful new ways of exploiting their intellectual property and creative ideas.

If you are an author in the humanities that would like to take charge of your publishing destiny, please email the publisher, Dr Susan England at lalaclio@hotmail.co.uk

Alternatively, you can contact us on the Clio Publishing website at http://www.emage.biz/ or send a message to Clio Publishing Facebook.